Norway

WORLD BIBLIOGRAPHICAL SERIES

General Editors:
Robert L. Collison (Editor-in-chief)
Sheila R. Herstein
Louis J. Reith
Hans H. Wellisch

VOLUMES IN THE SERIES

VOLUME 67

Norway

Leland B. Sather
Compiler
Edited by Hans H. Wellisch

CLIO PRESS

OXFORD, ENGLAND · SANTA BARBARA, CALIFORNIA
DENVER, COLORADO

British Library Cataloguing in Publication Data

Sather, Leland B.
Norway.– (World bibliographical series; v. 67)
1. Norway – Bibliography
I. Title   II. Series
016.9481   Z2591

ISBN 1–85109–010–X

Clio Press Ltd.,
55 St. Thomas' Street,
Oxford OX1 1JG, England.

ABC-Clio Information Services,
Riviera Campus, 2040 Alameda Padre Serra,
Santa Barbara, Ca. 93103, USA.

Designed by Bernard Crossland
Typeset by Columns Design and Production Services, Reading, England
Printed and bound in Great Britain by
Billing and Sons Ltd., Worcester

THE WORLD BIBLIOGRAPHICAL SERIES

This series will eventually cover every country in the world, each in a separate volume comprising annotated entries on works dealing with its history, geography, economy and politics; and with its people, their culture, customs, religion and social organization. Attention will also be paid to current living conditions – housing, education, newspapers, clothing, etc. – that are all too often ignored in standard bibliographies; and to those particular aspects relevant to individual countries. Each volume seeks to achieve, by use of careful selectivity and critical assessment of the literature, an expression of the country and an appreciation of its nature and national aspirations, to guide the reader towards an understanding of its importance. The keynote of the series is to provide, in a uniform format, an interpretation of each country that will express its culture, its place in the world, and the qualities and background that make it unique.

SERIES EDITORS

Robert L. Collison (Editor-in-chief) is Professor Emeritus, Library and Information Studies, University of California, Los Angeles, and is currently the President of the Society of Indexers. Following the war, he served as Reference Librarian for the City of Westminster and later became Librarian to the BBC. During his fifty years as a professional librarian in England and the USA, he has written more than twenty works on bibliography, librarianship, indexing and related subjects.

Sheila R. Herstein is Reference Librarian and Library Instruction Coordinator at the City College of the City University of New York. She has extensive bibliographic experience and has described her innovations in the field of bibliographic instruction in 'Team teaching and bibliographic instruction', *The Bookmark*, Autumn 1979. In addition, Doctor Herstein co-authored a basic annotated bibliography in history for Funk & Wagnalls *New encyclopedia*, and for several years reviewed books for *Library Journal*.

Louis J. Reith is librarian with the Franciscan Institute, St. Bonaventure University, New York. He received his PhD from Stanford University, California, and later studied at Eberhard-Karls-Universität, Tübingen. In addition to his activities as a librarian, Dr. Reith is a specialist on 16th-century German history and the Reformation and has published many articles and papers in both German and English. He was also editor of the *American Society for Reformation Research Newsletter*.

Hans H. Wellisch is a Professor at the College of Library and Information Services, University of Maryland, and a member of the American Society of Indexers and the International Federation for Documentation. He is the author of numerous articles and several books on indexing and abstracting, and has also published *Indexing and abstracting: an international bibliography*. He also contributes frequently to *Journal of the American Society for Information Science, Library Quarterly*, and *The Indexer*.

To my parents
Thorvald Eric Sather
Isabel Marie Sather
for my roots

Contents

Contents

Contents

Contents

Contents

Introduction

Geography has endowed the countries of the world in many ways but few have been given features as distinctive as those of Norway. It is both long and narrow, being over a thousand miles in length from Kristiansand in the south to Kirkenes or Vardø in the north, it is slightly less than 270 miles wide at its widest point and only 4 miles across at its narrowest spot. The country's substantial length is exaggerated even more by long fjords reaching so deeply into the interior that the coastline extends to approximately 12,000 miles. The ruggedness of the country is demonstrated by the fact that only about 20 per cent of the land may be used for its timber resources and only about 3 per cent is suitable for agriculture.

Originally in Old Norse, Norway's name was *Nordvegr*, 'the Northern way,' and this meaning has been perpetuated in the later versions, *Norwegen* in German, *Norway* in English, and *Norge* in modern Norwegian. From the beginning, both Norwegians and foreigners, from ancient geographers, to King Alfred, to modern tourists have been fascinated by this land, pointed like an arrowhead towards the far north. It is often Norway's contrasts that have created the greatest amount of interest among outsiders, such as the high mountains that plunge to long fjords below, the image of coldness and darkness that is far different from the summer midnight sun and the climate of the North Cape coast that is much milder even in winter than one might expect because of the warming influence of the Gulf Stream. The land and environment have always forced its inhabitants to find at least a part of their living from the forests, the mineral resources, and especially from the sea. These conditions certainly fostered localism and perhaps some of the independence of spirit and ruggedness of character that were ascribed to the Norwegians by 19th-century Romantics.

Exact information on the migration of man to Norway is not

known with certainty, although it is believed to have taken place ca. 10,000-8000 BC; alternative arguments have been presented for man's movement into the country first from the south, east or north. Archaeological research undertaken during the last century has extended our knowledge of early Norwegian civilization considerably, but the first literary evidence for the existence of Scandinavia comes from the Greek Pytheas of Marseilles, from Ptolemy, and from Roman scholars with only an uncertain perception of the region. The first written Scandinavian records in the form of rune stones come from a later date but also leave much to be desired.

Our knowledge of Scandinavia in general and Norway in particular increases with the onset of the Viking Age in the late 700s, but is also limited in the sense that the records concentrate on the deeds of the Vikings outside Scandinavia rather than conditions within. Although useful, they are also biased in their emphasis on the violence and misdeeds of the Vikings and are therefore not always objective or analytical. Archaeological work and place-name research, for example, during the last century in such places as Normandy and the Danelaw, and more recently in Dublin, York, and Newfoundland have shed new light on the more mundane activities of the Vikings, such as trade and colonization.

The Norwegians participated as much as the Danes and the Swedes in these enterprises. Although the Swedes are often regarded as the chief agents of Viking expansion in the East, Norwegians were also involved. The Norwegian presence is much easier to detect in the Viking activities in Western Europe, including the British Isles, and is particularly distinctive in the North Atlantic. Norwegians were primarily responsible for the conquest and settlement of the Orkney and Shetland Islands and Iceland, and the descendants of these Viking pioneers and first-generation Norwegians settled Greenland and finally ventured to Vinland in the late 900s.

As several recent scholars have suggested, if one date may be said to signify the end of the Viking Age it would be King Harald Hardråda's death at Stamford Bridge in 1066. This mid-11th century king also represents another feature of Norway during this period, namely the efforts to create a single state from the small kingdoms and earldoms that had developed earlier. The first such attempts at unification had been made by Harald the Fairhaired in the late 800s and Olav Trygvasson a century later. The death of Olav Haraldsson on 29 July 1030 at Stiklestad indicates that opposition particularly from the jarls of Lade (Trøndelag) was often both determined and successful.

The introduction of Christianity during the Viking Age formed an important link between Norway and Western Europe, and was also a significant factor in the creation of a national monarchy. Olav Trygvasson and Olav Haraldsson had not found conversion to Christianity incompatible with their activities abroad and attempted to impose it as an agent of unification at home. Resistance was at first great and Olav Haraldsson became more effective as a rallying point for Norwegians after his death, when they were threatened by Danish rule, than he had been when he was alive. His canonization and enshrinement at Trondheim as St. Olav was a milestone for both the church and the state in the late 11th century. Cooperation between the two led to their common growth during the 11th and 12th centuries as their bureaucracies began to move downwards and outwards to reach an increasing proportion of the population and to break some of the tentacles of localism that had previously prevailed.

The Norgwegian state continued to extend its contacts with the other Scandinavian countries and with the rest of Europe. This often involved intermarriage between Norway's royal house and those of Denmark and Sweden. Although advantageous in some ways, these relationships also threatened the country's independence. In 1397 the Union of Kalmar combined the three crowns of Denmark, Sweden and Norway under Queen Margaret and her successors. Norway was particularly vulnerable in such an arrangement after cooperation between the church and the Crown turned to hostility, the Black Death had weakened all groups within society but particularly the nobility, and the Hanseatic League had established a vice like grip upon Norway's foreign trade.

Norwegians often look upon the period from the late 1300s until the early 1800s as the '400 years long night' when Norway did not really possess a history. That is obviously an exaggeration but Norway might well have been better off without sharing some of the political experiences of other states during this period.

An important religious change occurred during the 1530s when the Lutheran Reformation was accepted in Denmark by King Christian III and therefore imposed on Norway as well. It was initially resented but was ultimately accepted by both the church and the people. During the 17th century, there was also territorial change, for as compensation for Danish losses to Sweden, Norway lost the provinces of Jämtland and Härjedalen to Sweden.

Introduction

Since the Viking Age, Norway has been a vital part of European cultural life and has also developed its own unique styles. The sagas as a literary form are generally associated with Iceland because many of the stories were written there but they are, in fact, the product of a truly Scandinavian folklore and oftentimes the legends and heroes belong as much to Norway in particular as to any other individual Scandinavian state. Perhaps the single greatest collection of the sagas is the *Heimskringla*, the stories of Norway's early kings, which were written down by the Icelander Snorri Sturluson but reflect at least a common Norwegian-Icelandic literary tradition. A cultural phenomenon which is unique to Norway during the Middle Ages is the *stavkirke* (stave church), of which only a few have survived.

During the 18th century, a national revival began in Norway. The shipment of copper, iron, fish, and timber abroad as well as the invisible exports derived through the carrying trade of its merchant marine, made a significant contribution to the economic well-being of the Helstat, the union of Denmark and Norway. Due to the virtual extinction of the nobility in Norway as a result of the Black Death, a society had developed that was dominated by the great landowners and shipping magnates of Trondheim, Bergen, and Christiania, (renamed Oslo in 1924). These men were cosmopolitan in their business affairs and cultural tastes, influenced by the Enlightenment and by early Romanticism. Under their influence, there was a renewal of interest in Norway's glorious past of the Viking Age and support for a number of societies and published works that described Norway's history and geography and glorified Norway's peasants as the backbone of society.

This group was not inherently hostile to the government in Copenhagen which was, in fact, one of the most enlightened régimes in Europe at that time. The merchant princes were able to articulate their own needs and occasionally those of Norway, as in the 1790s when they argued for the establishment of a university in Norway. A far greater test of their loyalty and leadership skills occurred during the Napoleonic Wars, when Denmark-Norway's alliance with France led to damaging war with Great Britain and Sweden.

These events were an important prelude to those of 1814. Denmark maintained its alliance with Napoleon and as a result was forced to cede Norway to Sweden by the Treaty of Kiel of 14 January 1814. Although such a union had its supporters in Norway, a group committed to independence emerged to provide

xviii

the first native political leadership of the country in centuries. The group was willing to accept Prince Christian Frederick, the heir to Denmark's throne and Norway's regent at the time, as their king and therefore the prospect of a renewal of the Danish union, so long as the king's powers in Norway were limited by the concept of popular sovereignty and the separation of powers. With great nerve and resolve, the independence movement imposed this solution upon Christian Frederick and those favouring a union with Sweden through the *Grunnloven* (Constitution), which was accepted by the *Riksforsamling* (National Assembly) in the small town of Eidsvoll not far from Christiania on 17 May 1814.

However, such a settlement was not acceptable to either Sweden or the Great Powers. Karl Johan's Swedish troops invaded Norway in the late summer and the new government was soon faced with the spectre of defeat. The men who had been the architects of the attempted independence were, however, able to save much of what they had created. The agreement of 4 November 1814 established a dynastic union between Norway and Sweden, but acknowledged Norwegian self-government in domestic affairs and suffrage provisions, thus making it the most liberal state in Europe in this regard.

The 19th century was one of rapid population growth and of of gradual economic change. During the century the population rose from about 800,000 to over two million; it is now close to five million. The process of economic change was a slow and arduous one, but agricultural rationalization, the freeing of both domestic and foreign trade from earlier restrictions, and the gradual development of industry helped to promote economic development.

The 19th century was also notable for the popular folk movements that were organized to express the increasingly articulate demands of the common people. These included movements for popular education, temperance, women's rights, and the origins of the trade union movement. Of great importance was the religious movement founded by Hans Nielsen Hauge. He and his followers emphasized a greater sense of personal salvation and of lay participation than did the state church. The long-term result of Hauge's work was to spur reform within the church and to provide an alternative to it within the general structure of Lutheranism.

Politically, this was a time of domestic reform. Throughout the century ever greater numbers were allowed to vote so that universal male suffrage was granted in 1898 (and women received the vote in 1913.) Ministerial responsiblity of the king's Norwegian ministers as a constitutional principle was achieved in 1884 when it was feared that they might otherwise be too subservient to royal and foreign influences.

During the last years of the 19th century, Norwegians became particularly aggressive in their demands for an independent consular service to promote Norwegian economic interests more effectively. When the Swedish government refused to grant this request, the Norwegian *Storting* (Parliament) under the leadership of Christian Michelsen undertook a programme leading to independence. King Oscar II refused to accept the government's resignation over the issue on 27 May 1905 because he did not believe that another government could be formed. The Norwegian cabinet and the *Storting*, on 7 June 1905 declared that the king had ceased to exercise his functions and that Norway was independent. Two referendums during the same year demonstrated the almost unanimous support for independence under a constitutional monarchy. Europe's Great Powers supported Norway's actions, including the selection of the younger son of King Frederick VIII of Denmark as Norway's King Haakon VII (1905–57).

The last decades of the 19th century and the first of the 20th were, from a cultural standpoint, some of the most significant in Norway's history. It was a golden age for literature, due to the contributions of Henrik Isben, Bjørnstjerne Bjørnson and the young Knut Hamsun. Edvard Grieg was the most significant of a number of important composers, and the period witnessed the beginning of the artistic careers of Edvard Munch and Gustav Vigeland. Norwegians also made important contributions in other fields, most notably, Fridtjof Nansen and Roald Amundsen in Polar research and exploration.

An important feature of this period of Norwegian history, is the large-scale emigration which took place, particularly to the USA. From 1825, when the first shipload of Norwegians left Stavanger aboard the *Restaurationen* until 1914 approximately 800,000 Norwegians left their homeland for other countries. Most went to the United States but others emigrated to Canada, Australia, and elsewhere. In these places they were only a part of a much greater migration, but the Norwegians, as well as other Scandinavians, have left a discernible mark through the organizations and institutions they established abroad to stay in contact with each other and eventually to transmit their heritage to their descendants. This phenomenon has generated scholarly research, both in Norway and the United States and has produced stirring literary accounts, such as Ole Edvart Rølvaag's *Giants in the earth*.

Norway received independence in 1905 but not immunity from the problems and dangers experienced by 20th-century nations. She was able to maintain a precarious neutrality during the First World War but faced many difficulties in adjusting her economy to the restrictive conditions of the interwar period. One manifestation of these difficulties was the labour strife that occurred during the 1920s. Another response to these difficulties was the development from the 1890s onwards of social legislation, which increased rapidly during the 1930s.

Despite the success of Norway's policy of neutrality during the First World War and the country's remote location on the fringe of Europe, the realities of international politics were brought home to Norwegians in 1940 as Norway became a pawn of the Great Powers. Both Britain and Germany were interested in Norway's strategic location in the North Atlantic and the Norwegian port of Narvik was important for the transport of Swedish iron ore to Germany during the winter months, as it remained ice-free all year round.

The British and Germans sent naval forces to Norway in early April 1940 but the German invasion force arrived first on 9 April 1940. Certain that their neutrality would be respected, the government and King Haakon were completely surprised by the attack, and determined to resist. They were forced to flee northwards and westwards across Norway until they finally left Norway from Tromsø for London to form a government-in-exile on 7 June 1940.

For Norway the war was a difficult experience as its government was technically headed by the Norwegian, Vidkun Quisling. The 350,000 strong German occupation was an indication of the grudging respect German officials had for Norway's unusual geography and the firmness with which Norway's judges, churchmen, educators, and ordinary citizens offered passive resistance to German demands and oftentimes outright resistance. The day of liberation from German rule, 8 May 1945, and King Haakon's return to Norway on 7 June, five years to the day after his flight, must be reckoned among the most joyful and emotional in all of Norwegian history.

Since the war, the country has been able to chart a unique course. In the immediate post-war years there was a rigid emphasis on economic planning and austerity programmes to deal with Norway's losses during the war and to pay for the extension of the welfare state undertaken by Norway's Labour Party with the support of a substantial majority of voters. The discovery and exploitation of oil and natural gas deposits in the North Sea since the early 1970s has stimulated many segments of the Norwegian economy, eliminated the fear of recurrent fuel shortages, and promoted the economic growth of West Norway, particularly the Stavanger area. On the other hand, it has also led to constant battles against runaway inflation and staggering balance of payments deficits.

Norwegian foreign policy after the Second World War has been much different from that followed before the war. After considering a return to pre-war neutrality and a Nordic military alliance, the Norwegian government in 1949 decided on membership of the North Atlantic Treaty Organization (NATO). Norway is sometimes perceived as playing a limited role in this alliance because of the restrictions that have been placed on the peacetime use of Norwegian bases by her allies and her seemingly peripheral position in the North. However, Norway's oil resources and her proximity to the USSR, and particularly to the massive Arctic naval base at Murmansk, have increased her strategic importance considerably.

No single recent event reveals the different cross-sections and divisions in Norwegian society as clearly as the referendum held in 1972 in which a slim majority of Norway's electorate rejected membership of the European Economic Community (EEC). The election indicated the conflicting interests of different sectors of the economy and geographical regions of the country. It also revealed the different attitudes that had developed regarding the degree of contact Norway should maintain with the outside world and the cultural forces that might influence the country in the future.

Other issues and problems have developed too. The creation of the oil industry has been instrumental in the articulation of environmental concerns. The booming economy has attracted workers to Norway from other parts of Europe and the Third World for whom new services must be provided. The native Lapps have developed a greater self-awareness that has led to demands for recognition and preservation of their life-style and culture.

The single most obvious division that persists in Norway today is the matter of language. Although the country's population is small, it now possesses two official languages, Nynorsk (New Norwegian) and Bokmål (Book Language or Dano-Norwegian). The language controversy developed in the 19th century when reformers such as Ivar Aasen proposed the eradication of Danish influence on the language and the creation of a truly national language based on the rural dialects of West Norway. The debate on this issue during the 1800s was often acrimonious and tended to emphasize the already existing conflicts between East and West Norway and rural and urban districts.

A large majority of the population still prefer the Bokmål form which is used extensively in business and in publications, although a significant degree of compromise has developed between the two groups. The changes undergone by Bokmål during this century reflect the influence that Nynorsk has had. The latter has been legally equal to Bokmål since 1885 and regulations have been established to ensure its instruction in schools and its use in government documents and on the public broadcasting facilities for both radio and television. It is therefore unlikely that a single language acceptable to all will develop in the near future but that efforts toward accommodation and toleration will continue.

Norway today is a prosperous nation, with a much greater economic and strategic value than ever before, anxious about its ability to retain its own values and culture and proud of still being 'the Northern way.'

The bibliography

Some observations ought to be made about the preparation of this bibliography. Although coverage of the Vikings is extensive, I have restricted the number of entries on the sagas and Old Norse literature to those that pertain most directly to Norway. This has been done in part to keep the size of this volume within reasonable limits and also because of the thorough treatment already given to this subject by John J. Horton in the *Iceland* volume in this series. Readers ought also to note that the Norwegian alphabet includes three extra letters, æ, ø, and å that are usually placed after z. To facilitate the use of this bibliography by the English speaking public, I have, however, ordered entries with words containing these vowels as if they were ordinary letters of the English alphabet. I hope this will prove helpful to most readers and neither confusing nor offensive to those who know better.

Introduction

Acknowledgements

It is appropriate at this juncture to thank the many people who have contributed in some way to this work. My interest in such a project first began while a graduate student working under Professor H. A. Barton, now of Southern Illinois University at Carbondale. I was in Norway during the 1979–80 academic year on related projects supported by a sabbatical leave from Weber State College and grants from the American-Scandinavian Foundation. In addition, the Norway-American Association, and the United States Educational (Fulbright) Commission in Norway permitted me to extend the bibliographical work I had done earlier. Very special thanks are due to the Norwegian Information Service in the United States and its director, Consul John Bjørnebye, for the Norwegian Government Grant I received during the summer of 1985 that allowed me to complete the research for this project.

I would also like to thank Mr. Bendik Rugaas, Director of the Universitetsbiblioteket (University of Oslo Library) and his entire staff for their assistance during my research there. Special recognition should also be given to Mr. Louis Janus, Department of Norwegian, St. Olaf College; to Mr. Craige Hall and the staff of the Stewart Library, Weber State College, particularly to Mrs. Peggy Pierce; Drs. Eric Jacobson and James Minor of Weber's Academic Computing Services; and Mrs. Dorothy Draney and Ms. Susan Lowery, secretaries of the History Department. I appreciate the efforts of all of these people very much while also noting that any errors or omissions in this book are my responsibility alone.

I also wish to thank my three children, John, Katie, and Brittanie, for their patience and help during this project and more so than anyone else, my wife Wendy, for her indispensable interest, assistance, and support during the last two years.

The Country and Its People

General

1 **The Norwegian way of life.**
   Frede Castberg. Melbourne, Australia: Heinemann, 1954. 110p.
   bibliog. (Way of Life Series).
A brief overview of Norway prepared by one of its leading experts in
constitutional law. The author discusses such topics as national character, society,
economic and social controversies, and Norway's role in international relations.
One of Norway's leading economic historians, Wilhelm Keilhau, has written a
brief chapter, 'The importance of Norway's economic structure,' as an appendix
to the work.

2 **A family diary: everyday life in Norway.**
   Gundel Krauss Dahl. Oslo: Tanum, 1971. (Tokens of Norway).
This volume is based on a series of programmes presented in English on 'Radio
Norway'. It portrays the everyday activities of an 'average' Norwegian family
living near Oslo with one or two entries made per month to represent the type of
activities likely to be carried out at that time.

3 **Come along to Norway.**
   Arnold Hauerslev-Haverlee. Minneapolis, Minnesota: T. S.
   Denison, 1973. 209p. map.
This study begins with a brief summary of Norway's history and major cities,
followed by chapters on a variety of subjects such as skiing, Norwegian explorers,
government, industry, and education. Written for the general reader.

4 **The voice of Norway.**
Halvdan Koht, Sigmund Skard. New York: Columbia University
Press, 1940. 313p. Reprinted New York: AMS, 1967.
A collaborative work by two of Norway's greatest scholars of the 20th century.
The volume was intended to generate support for Norway in Britain and the
United States during the Second World War but it also provides a summary in
English of the authors' works and views. Koht wrote the first half of the book,
'Free men build their society,' which is a sweeping survey of Norwegian history
from the Viking Age to the 1930s. It emphasizes Norwegian respect for law and
freedom. In the second half, 'Life unfolds in literature,' Skard provides an
overview of Norwegian literature, with particular emphasis on the work of
Ludvig Holberg, Henrik Wergeland, Henrik Ibsen, and Bjørnstjerne Bjørnson.
An abridged edition was also published (London: Hutchinson, 1944).

5 **Norway.**
Ronald Popperwell. London: Ernest Benn, 1972. 335p. bibliog.
(Nations of the Modern World).
An introductory study which focuses on Norway's history, language, and
literature. Discussion of art, theatre, and other cultural aspects is not equally
detailed but is still useful for an understanding of the contemporary Norwegian
scene.

6 **The Norwegians: how they live and work.**
Arthur Spencer. Newton Abbot, England: David & Charles, 1974.
147p. maps. (How They Live and Work Series).
A survey of modern Norway for the general reader outlining briefly the
governmental system, industry, employment, social security programmes, transportation systems, and forms of recreation. Although some of the statistics and
monetary equivalents cited in the text are now in need of revision, this volume
still provides a useful overview of contemporary life.

7 **Modern Norway: a study in social democracy.**
William Warbey, A. M. F. Palmer, A. J. Champion, Anne
Whyte. London: George Allen & Unwin, [1950]. 180p. bibliog.
The Norwegian government, economy, foreign relations, and way of life is
described by Fabian Society members invited to visit Norway in 1948 by the
Norwegian Labour Party. The volume focuses on the positive aspects of
Norwegian life perhaps for this reason, but is nevertheless an interesting
examination of the country during the immediate post-war years.

8 **Norway: paradise retained.**
Robert Wright. *Wilson Quarterly*, vol. 8, no. 2 (1984), p. 114-41.
map. bibliog.
The geography, culture, and language of modern Norway are discussed. Terje I.
Leiren has contributed a bibliographical essay, 'Background books,' (p. 140-41)
with suggestions for further reading.

Norway as a part of Scandinavia

9 **Nordic democracy: ideas, issues, and institutions in politics, economy, education, social and cultural affairs of Denmark, Finland, Iceland, Norway, and Sweden.**
Edited by Erik Allardt, Nils Andrén, Erik J. Friis, Gylfi T. Gislason, Sten Sparre Nilson, Henry Valen, Frantz Wendt, Folmer Wisti, translated by Erik J. Friis. Copenhagen: Det danske selskab, 1981. 780p. bibliog.

A collection of thirty-one essays by leading Scandinavian scholars covering a wide range of subjects such as history, government, politics, law, economics, society, foreign relations, education, culture, and the mass media. The essays not only attempt to discuss a particular topic but also to relate it to the central theme of the book, namely, democracy in the very broad sense of economic democracy and social democracy as well as political democracy. This is the latest of several works on the subject. Earlier studies with a similar purpose include *Scandinavian democracy . . .* and *Scandinavia between East and West* (q.v.) Articles in this work may therefore be read not only for their intrinsic value but also as a continuation of and an interesting comparison with earlier treatments of this theme.

10 **Scandinavia past and present.**
Edited by Jørgen Bukdahl, Aage Heinberg. Odense, Denmark: Arnkrone, 1959. 3 vols. maps.

The first volume covers many aspects of modern life and culture, while the last two volumes present a detailed survey of Scandinavian history by some of its most distinguished scholars. Organization of the work is topical but it is generally subdivided into sections by country. The work contains a number of specialized articles which deal specifically with Norwegian history, and it is therefore particularly valuable for providing information which is not available in other English language studies.

11 **The Scandinavians.**
Donald S. Connery. New York: Simon & Schuster, 1966. 590p. map. bibliog.

The author begins with a general introduction to the region, refuting the three stereotypes attached by people unfamiliar with Scandinavia during the 1960s of sex, suicide, and socialism. Five subsequent chapters deal with each of the Nordic nations in turn. In a section on Norway, p. 177-277, Connery outlines some of the country's history, political developments, famous artists, writers, and politicians, the welfare state, and the basic characteristics of its people. The book is typical of the positive impressions that many Americans derived of Norway during the 1960s and is still useful for the observations it makes.

12 **Nordic views and voices.**
Edited by Patrik Engellau, Ulf Henning.   Gothenburg, Sweden: Nordic Council, 1984. 117p.

Twenty-three brief essays, often selected from previously published works, are grouped around the themes of the Nordic soul, the Nordic model, and Nordic futures. Although similar to other works dealing primarily with the welfare state, foreign policy, and politics, this study also places some emphasis on the cultural setting.

13 **Scandinavia between East and West.**
Edited by Henning Friis.   Ithaca, New York; New York: Cornell University Press, 1950. 388p. bibliog. (A Publication of the New School of Social Research).

A collection of eleven essays describing the development and nature of Norway, Sweden, and Denmark until the mid-20th century. General subjects covered include politics and government, economic and social policies, and foreign relations. Many of the articles are now somewhat dated but they continue to provide an interesting picture of the region, covering: its past, its dreams, and the basic concepts that have continued to affect the area.

14 **Scandinavian democracy: development of democratic thought and institutions in Denmark, Norway, and Sweden.**
Edited by Joseph Lauwerys.   Copenhagen: Danish Institute, Norwegian Office of Cultural Relations, Swedish Institute, in cooperation with the American–Scandinavian Foundation, 1958. 437p. bibliog.

A collection of twenty-two articles by prominent Scandinavians discussing various aspects of culture and politics, generally with the goal of showing how these subjects represent or have influenced the development of democracy in the Scandinavian countries. Although superseded by works such as *Nordic Democracy* (q.v.) these essays are interesting studies in the goals and views of Scandinavia at mid-century.

15 **Scandinavia.**
William R. Mead, Wendy Hall.   London: Thames & Hudson, 1972. 208p. maps. bibliog.

An attempt to produce a sense of the spirit and attitudes of Scandinavia. It contains a brief historical sketch and separate chapters on each country, followed by a discussion of the states as social laboratories, the art of design, Nordic integration, and the different forms of contact that have developed between Scandinavia and the rest of the world over several centuries. A brief 'Who's who' section at the end provides short biographical sketches of prominent Scandinavians mentioned in the text.

16   **The Nordic enigma.**
     Daedalus, vol. 113, no. 1 (1984), 214p.

Two issues of the journal were devoted to a discussion of contemporary
Scandinavia. They were published to commemorate the observance of 'Scandinavia Today' in the United States during 1982-1984 by the American-Scandinavian
Foundation and several participating organizations and firms. The first contains
articles by respected scholars on a variety of economic, social, cultural, and
political issues. Some previous background knowledge of present-day Scandinavia
is perhaps desirable but by no means necessary. This issue and that of the spring
of 1984 have been used in Scandinavian literature and cultural classes as an
introduction to the region.

17   **Nordic voices.**
     Daedalus, vol. 113, no. 2 (1984), 279p. bibliog.

This is the second consecutive issue of the journal devoted to Scandinavia, and
consists of eight articles by leading Scandinavian scholars. The essays in this issue
differ to some degree from the first by being more analytical than descriptive,
more critical and reflecting a greater sense of uncertainty about Scandinavia's
future.

18   **Scandinavia: Denmark, Norway, Sweden, Finland, and Iceland.**
     Edited by Doré Ogrizek, translated by Paddy O'Hanlon, H. Iredale
     Nelson.   New York: McGraw-Hill, 1952. 438p. map. (The World
     in Colour).

Includes short discussions of the art, literature, and history of Scandinavia and
descriptions of the individual countries. Mariel Brian's chapter on Norway, p.
155-252, provides brief sketches of Oslo, Bergen, and Trondheim as well as the
coastal regions all the way to Northern Norway. The author not only describes
Norway at mid-century but also includes anecdotal accounts of Norway's heroes
in the past.

19   **Scandinavian roundabout.**
     Agnes Rothery.   New York: Dodd, Mead, 1946. 256p.

This work is still a useful introduction to Norway and Sweden, particularly for the
young adult. It covers a range of subjects, including geography, explorers,
Norway's royalty, literature, Norwegian-Americans, and Norway's involvement in
the Second World War.

20   **Scandinavia.**
     Franklin D. Scott.   Cambridge, Massachusetts: Harvard University
     Press, 1975. 330p. maps. bibliog. (American Foreign Policy
     Library).

Originally published in 1950 as *The United States and Scandinavia*, this work was
revised and enlarged in 1975 by the dean of American social scientists specializing
in Scandinavia. An excellent introduction to late 20th century Scandinavia, the
volume covers its governments, economic structures, social welfare programmes,
and foreign policies until the early 1970s with a final chapter on the past and
present connections between Scandinavia and America.

21 **Scandinavia.**
John H. Wuorinen. Englewood Cliffs, New Jersey: Prentice-Hall, 1965. 146p. maps. bibliog. (Modern Nations in Historical Perspective).

A basic introduction to Scandinavia which provides a brief coverage of the region's climate, resources, people and history. There is a more detailed discussion of the region during the First and Second World Wars. About half of the book deals with the position of Scandinavia at the middle of the 20th century, covering its political parties, governments, post Second World War economic patterns, foreign policy developments, and efforts at cooperation, especially the Nordic Council. Although now in need of some revision, this is still a useful sketch of the region in which Norway receives her share of consideration.

Picture books

22 **Look at Norway!**
Arne Beskow, introduction by Pio Larsen. Oslo: Gyldendal Norsk Forlag, 1981. 144p.

A collection of colour photographs emphasizing scenes from nature and the rural areas of Norway. The captions which accompany the photographs are in both English and Norwegian.

23 **Scandinavia: a picture book to remember her by.**
Designed and produced by David Gibbon, Ted Smart. London: Crescent Books, 1978. 78p. (A Picture Book to Remember Her By Series).

Contains an extensive section of colour photographs from many parts of Norway in its different seasons.

24 **New Norway 5: an introduction to Norwegian industry on entering the 1980's.**
Gunnar Jerman, translated from the Norwegian by Rolf Gooderham. Oslo: Grøndahl & Søn, 1982. 144p.

A richly-illustrated volume of colour photographs produced by the Export Council of Norway, which covers virtually all aspects of life and nature. First published in 1970, editions have also appeared in French, German, Italian, and Arabic.

25 **Lapland: the world's wild places.**
Walter Marsden and the editors of Time-Life Books. Amsterdam:
Time-Life Books, 1976. 184p. map. bibliog.
A picture book covering the North Cape region of Finland, Sweden and Norway
which provides an informed description of nature through the narrative and many
colour photographs.

26 **Norway today: scenery and natural resources; people and history;**
literature, art and science; sports and outdoor life; economy; regional
descriptions; travelling and tourism.
Oslo: Dreyer Forlag, 1970. 9th rev. ed. 152p.
A general introduction to the country that combines brief summaries of a wide
range of subjects with pictures of Norwegian art, handicraft, and scenery.

27 **Norge sett fra luften.** (Norway from the air.)
Edited by Per Voksø. Oslo: Forlaget Det Beste, 1979. 384p.
A collection of aerial, colour photographs from all over Norway. Although the
text is in Norwegian, those unable to read Norwegian will also find the volume
useful as the selections are organized geographically by region and a table of
contents and a detailed index are included for the benefit of anyone wishing to do
some armchair sight-seeing.

28 **Norway: pictures and facts.**
Edited by Erling Welle-Strand. Oslo: Nortrabooks, 1973. 108p.
Contains 108 photographs of different aspects of Norwegian life and in the final
three pages, a brief outline of the country's climate, geography, and economy.

The Laplanders: Europe's last nomads.
See items no. 320.

News of Norway.
See item no. 883.

The Norseman.
See item no. 886.

Norway Information.
See item no. 889.

Life in Europe: Norway.
See item no. 923.

Travellers' Accounts

29 **Sport in Norway and where to find it together with a short account of the vegetable productions of the country to which is added a bit of the alpine flora of the Dovre Fjeld and of the Norwegian ferns, etc.**
M. R. Barnard. London: Chapman & Hall, 1864. 334p.

Two interesting tendencies of 19th-century travel literature are reflected in this volume, namely: a penchant for long titles and the desire to cover more than one topic in a single work. The author first briefly describes the *amter* (counties), and goes on to discuss the vairous animals and birds that could be hunted, salmon fishing, and the various flora forms.

30 **Northern paradise: the intelligent alien's guide to Norway.**
Philip Boardman. Olso: H. Aschehoug, 1963. 339p. bibliog.

Entertaining but also penetrating 'tongue-in-cheek' look at Norwegian life after the Second World War. The language controversy, the modern welfare state, the press, and Norwegian politics are but a few of the subjects Boardman discusses. He also provides sharp sketches of a variety of individuals, such as Bishop Eivind Berggrav and the writer Arnulf Øverland. For another entertaining look at Norway, see Boardman's *How to feel at home in Norway: some hints* (Oslo: H. Aschehoug, 1960. 247p.).

31 **Travels through Norway and Lapland during the years 1806, 1807, and 1808.**
Leopold von Buch, translated from the German by John Black, with notes and illustrations chiefly mineralogical, and some account of the author, by Robert Jameson. London: Henry Colburn, 1813. 460p. map.

An account of the travels in Norway of the noted German geologist, Leopold von Buch. The dates for his trip(s) which are recounted in this volume are not entirely established. His trip from Christiania (Oslo) to Trondheim and then to North Norway is dated 1807 but his account of Christiania itself appears to cover the years 1808 to 1809 given some of his comments, such as the death of Enevold de Falsen, and temperatures cited from January 1809. This work is interesting for its geographical and geological descriptions as well as for its more general comments. Many translations and re-printings of the work have occurred since the original German edition was published in 1810.

32   **Travellers discovering Norway in the last century: an anthology.**
     Edited by B. A. Butenschøn, editorial consultant Dr. Einar H.
     Schiøtz.   Oslo: Dreyer, 1968. 251p.

An anthology of accounts by Englishmen and Americans of their trips to Norway from the late 18th century until almost 1900. The volume contains selections from fourteen accounts by such well-known individuals as Mary Wollstonecraft, Thomas Malthus, Sir Humphrey Davy, and William Gladstone. The work is amply illustrated with pictures from the period of Norwegian scenery and daily life. There are also selections from Edward Price's *Norway: views of wild scenery and a journal (1834)* and a special section entitled *Norwegian painters discover Norway*. An important work containing an excellent sample of the travel literature written about Norway.

33   **Norway.**
     Philip Caraman.
     London: Longmans, 1969. 226p. maps. bibliog.

A description of the different regions of Norway visited by the author and his impressions of the country after three years of residence. There is special emphasis on his trip to North Norway in 1966. The author's position as a Catholic priest provided him with a special view of Norway and its people.

34   **The land of the midnight sun: summer and winter journeys through
     Sweden, Norway, Lapland, and Northern Finland with descriptions
     of the inner life of the people, their manners and customs, the
     primitive antiquities, etc.**
     Paul B. du Chaillu.   London: John Murray, 1881. 2 vols.

Two large volumes recounting the author's trips, beginning in 1871. Norway figures prominently in both volumes as the author visited it on several occasions and recounts his travels in the southern regions as well as his adventures among the Lapps in the North. This detailed description is perhaps the most comprehensive of the many 19th century travel accounts of Scandinavia in general and Norway in particular.

35   **Travels in various countries of Europe, Asia, and Africa. Part the
     third: Scandinavia.**
     Edward Daniel Clark.   London: T. Cadell & W. Davis, 1819. 2
     vols. maps.

Clark began his trip in 1799 along with Robert Malthus and some other Englishmen. When the party split up, Clark proceeded to Sweden while Malthus went first to Norway. The main emphasis in his account is on Trondheim and the trip from there to Christiania (Oslo) that begins in the latter part of Section the First (p. 588-743) and ends in Section the Second (p. 1-88). Interesting comparisons can be made between his account and that of Malthus because they did eventually visit many of the same places, although in reverse order, and meet the same people. Clark did not publish his account until *Travels through Norway and Lapland* . . . (q.v.), had appeared in English and he therefore refers to it occasionally, particularly to correct some errors he felt von Buch had made. A recent edition has been translated into Norwegian by Johnny Johnsen, *Reise i Norge* (Oslo: Universitetsforlaget, 1977).

36 The Spanish story of the Armada and other essays.

James Anthony Froude.   New York: Scribners, 1892. 344p.

The last two chapters, 'The Norway fjords,' and 'Norway once more,' are a description of the noted historian's trips to Norway in 1881 and 1884. The main subjects discussed in the chapters include a trip from Bergen to Trondheim through the fjords, Norwegian society and religion, and salmon fishing.

37 Mission to the North.

Florence Jaffray Harriman, foreword by Johan Nygaardsvold.

London: Harrap, 1941. 236p. map.

Florence Harriman was the United States Minister to Norway from 1937 to 1940 and her memoirs of that period are an interesting account not so much of her official duties but of her personal experiences and life in Norway. The final section does, however, discuss the diplomatic crises in Norway prior to the German invasion of April 1940 and her resultant hurried departure from Scandinavia.

38 The travel diaries of Thomas Robert Malthus.

Edited by Patricia James.   Cambridge, England: Cambridge University Press, 1966. 316p. maps. bibliog.

Although brief parts of the book contain Malthus' notes from other travels, the main section focuses on Malthus' visit to Norway in 1799. He was particularly interested in the country as a result of his demographic studies and his description is one of the most interesting and serious accounts. An appendix to the work quotes from Malthus' chapter on Norway in the second edition of the *Essay on the principle of population* published in 1826 with relevant passages from the *Scandinavian Journal* printed on the opposite page.

39 Three in Norway by two of them.

J. A. Lees, W. J. Clutterbuck.   Oslo: Tanum-Norli, 1984. 205p.

(Tokens of Norway).

Considered a classic of its genre, this work was first published in 1882 and has been repeatedly re-issued ever since. It is an account of three Englishmen as they traveled, fished, and hunted through much of the country, providing both humour and insight along the way. Lees also wrote *Peaks and pines: another Norway book* in 1899 as an account of a second trip to Norway. This was also published by Tanum, 1970, in the Tokens of Norway Series.

40 **Unprotected females in Norway; or the pleasantest way of travelling there, passing through Denmark and Sweden with Scandinavian sketches from nature.**
[Emily Lowe].   London: Routledge, Warne & Routledge, 1864. 283p.

A travel book recounting a trip through Norway by two English ladies with no fear of being unprotected. Interesting for its description of life and manners in Norway and the self-description of the author.

41 **Norwegian holiday.**
Harlan Major.   New York: Funk & Wagnalls, 1950. 268p.

Originally written as a tourist guide, but no longer valid as such, it remains valuable for its observations about the country and its information that is still correct. The volume also provides an interesting example of the changes in value and usage a book can have. For another account of Norway by the same author see *Norway: home of the Norseman* (New York: David McKay, 1957).

42 **Norway: changing and changeless.**
Agnes Rothery.   London: Faber & Faber, 1939. 294p. map. bibliog.

In its own time, this may have been considered a general account of the country. Given the changes that have occurred since then, it can now be considered a travel work, describing many interesting places and topics. It is also interesting for the picture it presents of Norway immediately prior to the Second World War, which allows the reader to compare Norway's past with its present-day situation.

43 **Norway the Northern playground.**
W. Cecil Slingsby.   Oxford: Basil Blackwell, 1941. 227p. map. (Blackwell's Mountaineering Library).

First published in 1903, this volume was re-issued and edited nearly forty years later. Slingsby was a noted mountaineer and the work records several of the climbs that he made in Norway.

44 **Ways of Norway: rambling through past and present.**
Susan Tyrell.   Oslo: Grøndahl & Søn, 1984. 144p. map. bibliog.

A travel book describing such places as Arendal, Stavanger, Bergen, the Sognefjord, Trondheim, and Northern Norway not only as they are today but also in the light of the past. It is amusing, perceptive, and entertaining. Another interesting work by a frequent traveller to Norway that, unfortunately, has not been translated into English is Hans Magnus Enzensberger's *Norsk utakt* (Norwegian anachronisms) (Oslo: Universitetsforlaget, 1984), a collection of essays that reflect as much affection for Norway and its inhabitants as Tyrell demonstrates, but with a more critical eye.

45 **Letters written during a short residence in Sweden, Norway, and Denmark.**
Mary Wollstonecraft, edited with an introduction by Carol H. Poston. Lincoln, Nebraska: University of Nebraska Press, 1976. 200p.

Mary Wollstonecraft, best known for *A vindication of the rights of women*, spent the summer of 1795 in Scandinavia and one year later published the letters which she wrote during the trip. Letters V-XV (p. 37-134) concern her trip to Norway on both sides of the Oslofjord, and provide a perceptive and interesting view of Norwegian society. First published in London in 1796 and translated into Norwegian in 1976 by Per A. Hartun as *Min nordiske reise: beretninger fra et opphold i Sverige, Norge og Danmark 1795* (Oslo: Gyldendal Norsk Forlag, 1976). A valuable reference work that should be consulted in connection with her *Letters* is Per Nyström's *Mary Wollstonecraft's Scandinavian journey* (Gothenburg, Sweden: Kungl. Vetenskaps-och Vitterhets-Samhället, 1980).

Norwegian life and literature: English accounts and views especially in the 19th century.
See item no. 685.

The land of the long night.
See item no. 748.

Itineraria Norvegica: a bibliography of foreigners' travels in Norway until 1900.
See item no. 942.

Geography

General

46 **Norwegen**. (Norway.)
Ewald Glässer.   Darmstadt, GFR: Wissenschaftliche Buchgesell-
schaft, 1978. 289p. maps. bibliog.

Provides an informed and scholarly examination of the physical and economic
geography of Norway in the first half of the book and then presents six studies of
different regions of the country. An extensive bibliography contains references to
many German works on Norway which are not found in other bibliographies.

47 **Norway: land, people, industries: a brief geography.**
Magne Helvig, Viggo Johannessen.   Oslo: Johan Grundt Tanum
Forlag, 1974. 4th ed. 142p. maps. bibliog. (Tokens of Norway).

A geographical description of Norway that briefly outlines the geological
development of the country and its population and discusses the different parts of
the Norwegian economy.

48 **Norway, Svalbard and Jan Mayen: official standard names approved
by the United States Board on Geographic Names.**
Washington, DC: Office of Geography, Department of Interior,
1963. 1029p. map. (Gazetter no. 77).

Contains 72,550 entries listing places and features in Norway and the territories of
Jan Mayen and Spitsbergen (Svalbard). Entries are made by name; nature, such
as airport, populated area; location by longitude and latitude; location by *fylke*
(county) or territory; and there is a referenced code for the source of information.

Norway as a part of Northern and Western Europe

49 **Scandinavia: an introductory geography.**
Brian Fullerton, Alan F. Williams. New York: Praeger; London:
Chatto & Windus, 1972. 374p. maps. bibliog. (Praeger Introductory
Geographies).

The first section discusses the physical geography of Denmark, Sweden, Finland,
and Norway. This is followed by a study of each country in turn, providing an
economic introduction and a discussion of its various regions. Norway is covered
on p. 275-341, including short chapters on the Oslofjord area, Eastern Norway,
Southern Norway, the Trøndelag, and Northern Norway. The
emphasis placed on physical and economic geography varies between chapters.
Most chapters contain suggestions for further reading in addition to the
bibliography at the end of the book.

50 **An advanced geography of Northern and Western Europe.**
R. J. Harrison Church, Peter Hall, G. R. P. Lawrence, William R.
Mead, Alice F. A. Mutton. Amersham, England: Hulton
Educational Publications, 1980. 3rd ed. 480p. maps. bibliog.

Three introductory chapters discussing the physical geography, population, and
economic development of the entire region precede several chapters devoted to a
study of the individual counties. The chapter on Norway by William R. Mead (p.
92-114) outlines Norway's physical geography and its impact upon economic
developments.

51 **Historical geography in Scandinavia.**
Staffan Helmfrid. In: *Progress in historical geography*. Edited by
Alan R. H. Baker. Newton Abbot, England: David & Charles,
1972, p. 63-89. maps. bibliog.

A bibliographic essay discussing the research undertaken by Scandinavian
historical geographers during the 1950s and 1960s.

52 **Scandinavia: a new geography.**
Brian S. John. London, New York: Longmans, 1984. 365p. maps.
bibliog.

John does not devote separate chapters to each of the Scandinavian states.
Instead, he studies them topically in twenty-three chapters arranged around five
main themes: the physical and cultural environment; spatial expressions of the
human economy; regional inequities between the 'heartland' and outlying regions;
sample studies of local landscapes (including a chapter on Fjærland, a fjordside
settlement); and recent examples of cooperation that stand in contrast to
continued differences of opinion and national policy. The work is supplemented
by an excellent and extensive bibliography.

14

Geography. Norway as a part of Northern and Western Europe

53 **Norden: crossroads of destiny and progress.**
Vincent H. Malmström. Princeton, New Jersey: D. Van Nostrand,
1965. 128p. maps. bibliog.
A brief survey of the geography and culture of the Nordic region followed by
chapters on each of the five states. The chapter entitled 'Norway: maritime giant',
(p. 51-63) provides a historical-geopolitical sketch of the country from the Viking
period until the mid-1960s.

54 **Northern Europe.**
Vincent H. Malmström. In: *A geography of Europe: problems and
prospects*. Edited by George Hoffman. New York: John Wiley,
1983. 5th ed. p. 306-44. maps. bibliog.
First published in 1953, this article has been revised to provide a brief up to date
description of the physical and economic geography of Scandinavia, ending with a
concise but cogent view of contemporary problems.

55 **An economic geography of the Scandinavian states and Finland.**
William R. Mead. London: University of London Press, 1958.
302p. maps.
Mead divides the work into three main sections: the resource variable, the human
variable, and some primary economic activities. The first is a discussion of
physical geography, the impact of changes that have occurred, and the effects of
snow and ice. The middle section studies population growth and movement along
with a consideration of land and resource exploitation and industrialization. The
third is a description of economic activities such as farming, fishing, mining, and
energy.

56 **Scandinavia and Scandinavians in the annals of the Royal Geogra-
phical Society, 1830-1914.**
William R. Mead, C. Wadel. *Norsk Geografisk Tidsskrift*, vol. 18,
nos. 3-4 (1961), p. 99-143.
Describes the links between Scandinavian geographers and explorers and the
Royal Geographical Society through personal contacts and participation by the
Scandinavians in the society's activities and publications.

57 **An historical geography of Scandinavia.**
William R. Mead. London: Academic Press, 1981. 313p. maps.
bibliog.
A chronological study of the human and physical geography of Scandinavia.
Emphasis is placed on environment, geopolitics, rural and urban settlements,
communication and transportation patterns, and principal economic activities. A
unique and interesting feature is the discussion of the pattern of daily life during
the different periods. The work is profusely illustrated with maps and diagrams
and extensive bibliographies follow each chapter.

58 **Norden: destiny and fortune.**
William R. Mead. *Daedalus*, vol. 113, no. 1 (1984), p. 1-27.
(Nordic Enigma).

A thoughtful essay discussing the physical geography of the Scandinavian countries and the cultural characteristics of the region.

59 **The Scandinavian lands.**
Ray Millward. New York: St. Martin's Press; London: Macmillan, 1965. 488p. maps. bibliog.

A basic geographical introduction to Scandinavia. A chapter is devoted to each of the four continental Scandinavian countries in the first section, including one on Norway (p. 11-43). It provides brief surveys of the geological, geographical, historical, and economic features of Norway's main regions. Subsequent chapters in part two discuss these topics in more detail and within a general Scandinavian context.

60 **The countries of north-western Europe.**
F. J. Munkhouse. London: Longmans, 1971. 526p. maps. bibliog.
(Geographies: an Intermediate Series).

The chapter on Norway, (p. 59-91), provides brief descriptions of its physical geography, climate, economic resources, and means of communication.

61 **The Scandinavian world.**
Andrew C. O'Dell. London: Longmans, Green, 1957. 549p. maps. bibliog. (Geographies for Advanced Study).

The opening chapters discuss the geological structure, climate, the seas surrounding Scandinavia and the early development of man. The chapter on Norway, (p. 213-77), is one of several covering the individual Nordic states with an emphasis both on the physical and economic features. The work includes an extensive coverage (p. 278-301) of Norway's Arctic islands, Jan Mayen and Spitsbergen (Svalbard). O'Dell concludes with a thorough survey of economic geography which uses a comparative approach and discusses topics in more detail and more analytically than the other sections. There are more richly illustrated or more readable geographies of Scandinavia, but O'Dell's work is distinguished by its data and scholarship.

62 **A geography of Norden: Denmark, Finland, Iceland, Norway, Sweden.**
Edited by Axel Sømme. Oslo: J. W. Cappelen Forlag, 1968. new ed. 363p. maps. bibliog.

A collaborative work first published in 1960. Seven chapters by different scholars discuss basic geographical and geological factors affecting all of the Nordic states, such as climate, natural resources, the surrounding seas, and plant life. In the series of chapters that follow dealing separately with each nation, Tore Sund writes on Norway and her economic and natural resources. Werner Werenskøld has appended a brief overview of Norway's islands in the Atlantic, Jan Mayen and Spitsbergen (Svalbard). In addition to the maps and tables in the text, the volume also includes an appendix of twelve plate maps of the region illustrating various factors discussed in the text.

Regional studies

North Norway

63 **The revival of Northern Norway.**
Diderich H. Lund. *Geographical Journal*, vol. 109, nos. 4-6 (1947), p. 185-97. map.

Lund, the director of the Finnmark Reconstruction Office, provides a thorough survey of Northern Norway before the Second World War, discusses the physical damage to the area during the war as a result of the German occupation, and studies the immediate post-war reconstruction efforts, particularly with respect to housing.

64 **The Scandinavian northlands.**
William R. Mead. Oxford: Oxford University Press, 1974. 48p. maps. bibliog. (Problem Regions in Europe).

This study of *Nordkalotten*, the North Cape regions of Norway, Sweden, and Finland within the Arctic Circle treats the three Norwegian *fylker* (counties) of Nordland, Troms, and Finnmark. The volume examines the political, economic, and social problems of the region as a product and interaction of four variables: the physical environment, population, technology, and organization.

65 **The North Cape and its hinterland.**
Sigurd Senje. [Oslo]: Tanum-Norli, 1979. 53p. maps. (Tokens of Norway).

A description of everyday life on the island of Magerøy. There is discussion of the geographical setting, the settlements, the Lapps, and a brief study of the region's history. The account is richly-illustrated with many photographs and presents a franker and more realistic portrayal of the area than is normally found in such surveys for the general reader.

66 **Norway North of 65.**
Edited by Ørnulf Vorren. Oslo: Oslo University Press; London: George Allen & Unwin, 1960. 271p. maps. bibliog. (Tromsø Museums Skrifter, no. 8).

A collection of sixteen articles dealing with the people, climate, economy, systems of communication, transportation, and education of the three northern *fylker* (counties) of Troms, Nordland, and Finnmark.

Spitsbergen

67   **Svalbard: Norway in the Arctic.**
Tim Greve.   Oslo: Grøndahl, 1975. 85p. maps.
A brief introduction to the island of Spitsbergen (Svalbard). Topics covered
include its geography and climate, history, the treaty of 1920 providing conditions
for the exploitation of its natural resources, principally coal, its present
administration, and living conditions.

Political and economic geography

68   **The Norwegian-Soviet boundary: a study in political geography.**
Trevor Lloyd.   *Norsk Geografisk Tidsskrift*, vol. 15, nos. 5-6
(1955/56), p. 187-242. maps. bibliog.
An article dealing primarily with the history of the border between the two
countries and its administration by them in the decade after the Second World
War.

69   **The political geography of the Arctic.**
Trevor Lloyd. In: *The changing world: studies in political geography*. Edited by W. Gordon East, A. E. Moodie.   London:
Harrap, 1956, p. 960-81. maps. bibliog.
Places Norwegian possession of Spitsbergen (Svalbard) and Jan Mayen islands
within the context of the entire Arctic region. The main subjects considered are
economic development, logistics, and strategy.

70   **Sogn and Fjordane in the fjord economy of Western Norway.**
William R. Mead.   *Economic Geography*, vol. 23 (1947), p. 155-66.
maps.
A study in economic geography emphasizing the interplay between the main
farm, the summer pasture (*seter*), and fishing in order to provide a living for the
people of this region.

Climatology and physical geography

71 The present climatic fluctuation.
Hans Ahlmann. *Geographic Journal*, vol. 102 (July-Dec. 1948), p. 165-95. maps.

Reproduces a paper read at the Royal Geographical Society in London on May 3, 1948, and the discussion that followed. The author points out the significant changes which have taken place in temperature and precipitation since regular records have been kept. Although the author provides data from several European countries, much of his evidence comes from Scandinavia, including Norway.

72 Climate in North Norway.
Sigurd Winther Hansen. In: *Norway North of 65*. Edited by Ørnulf Vorren. Oslo: Oslo University Press; London: George Allen & Unwin, 1960, p. 37-49. map. (Tromsø Museums Skrifter, no. 8).

The climate of North Norway is discussed including some explanations for it. Comparisons are made with the climate of other parts of the country.

73 Notes on the formation of fjords and fjord-valleys.
Hans Holtedahl. *Geografiska Annaler*, vol. 49A (1967), p. 188-203. maps. bibliog.

A scholarly study of the impact of erosion on the Hardangerfjord and Sognefjord and the surrounding valleys, particularly the Flåm and Fossli areas.

74 Glacier dammed lakes in Norway.
Olav Liestøl. *Norsk Geografisk Tidsskrift*, vol. 15, no. 3-4 (1955-56), p. 122-49. maps. bibliog.

Discusses the factors causing the leakage of water in glacier dammed lakes and outlines several case studies to illustrate the explanations for leakage that occurred earlier.

75 Jotunheimen: challenge of a mountain wilderness.
Edited by Finn P. Nyquist with contributions by Vera Henriksen, Torgeir T. Garmo, Claus Helberg, Bjørn Halvorsen, Rie Bistrup, Knut A. Nilsen. Olso: North Sea Press/Grøndahl Production, 1977. 200p.

A work combining a scholarly geographic study with a picture book created solely to entertain. It contains ten informative articles and excellent photographs of the mountain, its environment, and the people who live and visit there.

76 **Sørfjord in Inner Hardanger.**
Axel Sømme. *Norsk Geografisk Tidsskrift*, vol. 17, no. 1 (1959-
60), p. 168-75. maps.
Summarizes the main physical geographical features of this fjord south of Bergen.

77 **The Norwegian coast.**
Kaare Strøm. *Norsk Geografisk Tidsskrift*, vol. 17, no. 1 (1959-
60), p. 132-37. maps.
A brief article dividing the Norwegian coast into distinct geographical-
geomorphological subdivisions based on natural landscape types.

78 **Fjord land and coast land of Western Norway.**
Tore Sund. *Norsk Geografisk Tidsskrift*, vol. 17, no. 1 (1959-60),
p. 176-86.
A geographical excursion through the fjord *fylke* (county) of Sogn-og-Fjordane
on the way from Oslo to Bergen.

Maps and atlases

79 **Cappelens bilatlas Norden**. (Cappelen's car atlas of the Nordic
states.)
Oslo: J. W. Cappelens Forlag, 1981. 287p. maps.
An atlas published in cooperation with Norges Automobil-Forbund (the
Norwegian Automobile Association) providing detailed maps of Norway,
Denmark, Sweden, and Finland on a scale of 1:6000000. Maps of Oslo, Helsinki,
Copenhagen, Stockholm, and Gothenburg are also included. A text is provided at
the beginning in the Scandinavian languages, and in English, German, French,
and Dutch and a section provides a translation of road traffic signs into the same
languages.

80 **Cappelens kartbok for Oslo og omegn med kartgrunnlag fra
Fylkeskart-kontoret i Oslo og Akershus og Oslo oppmålingsvesen.**
(Cappelen's map book for Oslo and the surrounding region based
upon the county mapping office in Oslo and Akershus and the Oslo
mapping survey.)
Oslo: J. W. Cappelens Forlag, 1985. 201p. maps.
A detailed atlas of Oslo and the surrounding region. An extensive index enables
easy use of the maps. There is some extremely helpful information regarding the
capital's public transportation system which is also included in English and
German and there is a directory of hotels, restaurants, museums, and other places
of interest.

81 **Norge i kart gjennom 400 år med opplysninger om den som utformet kartbildet.** (Norway in maps through 400 years with information on those who prepared the maps.)
Sigurd Engelstad, introduction by Kristian Nissen. Oslo: J. W. Cappelens Antikvariat, 1952. 112p. bibliog. (Katalog. no. 15).

The work is divided into sections for atlases, world maps, the Polar region, Scandinavia, Norway, and sea maps. The maps are indexed in the language in which they were published. A brief annotation is in Norwegian but a foreword in English is also provided.

82 **Gamle Norske kart: samkatalog over utrykte kart fra de siste 300 år.** (Old Norwegian maps: a common catalogue of unpublished maps from the last 300 years.)
Edited by Rolf Fladby. Oslo: Universitetsforlaget, 1979-1984. 17 vols.

A catalogue of unpublished maps of the different counties of Norway from ca. 1600 until ca. 1900. Maps of local areas, however, are registered until the 1970s. Each map is listed by name, its scale, date, and location.

83 **Norsk historisk atlas.** (Norwegian historical atlas.)
Rolf M. Hagen, Knut Johannessen, Liv Marthinsen, Egil Mikkelsen, Harald Skram. Oslo: J. W. Cappelens Forlag, 1980. 386p. maps. (Norges Historie, no. 15).

This is the final volume in a series on Norway's history written by some of the country's leading historians. Ninety-six pages of historical maps and commentary upon them are followed by tables and outlines on a number of important topics prepared by Anne-Hilde Nagel. Although the maps are labelled in Norwegian, they are useful to scholars with access to Norwegian dictionaries.

84 **I Norge med campingvogn.** (In Norway with camping trailers.)
Oslo: [Grøndahl & søner], 1985.

A map issued by the Vegdirektorat, Norway's Department of Highways, on a scale of 1:170000. It indicates caravan sites in Norway with a special insert for the Oslo area, a basic road map of the country, and driving suggestions in Norwegian, English and German.

85 **Katalog over norske sjøkart og nautiske publikasjoner.** (Catalogue of Norwegian charts and nautical publications.)
Oslo: Norges Sjøkartverk og Norsk Polarinstitutt, 1977. 29p. map.

A catalogue in Norwegian and English listing nautical charts and sailing information on the Norwegian coast and adjacent waters.

86 **Norge: fjerde bind: atlas register.** (Norway: volume 4: atlas
register.)
Edited by Hallstein Myklebost, Sigurd Strømme, Waldemar
Brøgger, Anders Rohr, Kristian Gleiditsch, Fridtjov Isachsen.
Oslo: J. W. Cappelens Forlag, 1963. maps.
This is the last in a series of major geographical reference works. The first three
volumes provide a wide range of information about the regions of Norway for
those who can read Norwegian. This volume contains detailed maps of the
Oslofjord area, Bergen, Trondheim, Stavanger, and Kristiansand. The signs used
on the maps are not translated into English but in some cases can be deduced
without resorting to a dictionary. A special feature is a thirteen page introductory
section by Kristian Nissen, 'Norge i kart: en kort historisk oversikt,' (Norway in
maps: a short historical overview) that discusses and reproduces early maps of
Scandinavia and Norwegian provinces.

87 **Norge.** (Norway.)
Oslo: J. W. Cappelens Forlag, 1979. 13 maps.
A set of seven detailed maps of Norway. The first six are of the different regions
and there is one of the entire country drawn on a scale of 1:325,000-400,000. The
company also publishes a separate detailed map of Oslo and its suburbs that is
essential for all visitors to the capital. The text is provided in Norwegian, English,
German, and French.

88 **Jordbrukets geografi i Norge: B: atlas.** (Geography of Norwegian
agriculture: B: atlas.)
Axel Sømme. Bergen, Norway: J. W. Eides Forlag, 1949. 109p.
maps. (Skrifter fra Norges Handelshøyskole).
A collection of maps, charts, and tables explaining various aspects of Norwegian
agriculture and the factors such as temperature and rainfall that have a profound
effect on it. Sømme's statistical data ends in 1939, thus limiting its value in the
1980s.

89 **Norway in maps.**
Edited by Tore Sund, Axel Sømme. Bergen, Norway: John
Griegs, 1947. 3 vols. maps. (Skrifter fra Norges Handelshøyskole).
An attempt to provide the reader with an understanding of Norwegian geography
through narrative maps, sketch maps and photographs, which were selected in
order to represent the different landscape types and chief settlement forms.

Geology

90 **The Quaternary of Norway.**
Bjorn G. Andersen. In: *The Quaternary, Volume I.* Edited by
Kalervo Rankama. New York: Interscience Publishers (John
Wiley), 1965, p. 91-138. maps. bibliog. (Geologic Systems Series).
A description of the moraine regions of Norway, the glaciation history of the
country, and shorelines and their displacement, along with a brief study of
Quaternary sediments, geomorphology, earthquakes, and early archaeology.

91 **Glacial geology in Western Troms, North Norway.**
Bjorn G. Andersen. Oslo: Universitetsforlaget, 1968. 160p.
(Norges Geologiske Undersøkelse, no. 256.)
This detailed description of the glacial development of North Norway provides a
good example of the geological work that has been undertaken by Norwegian
scholars in this field.

92 **Guide book to excursions in Norway.**
Edited by Johannes A. Dans. Oslo: Wittusen & Jensen, 1960. 17
parts. maps. bibliog.
A collection of papers presented during seventeen excursions begun at the
International Geological Congress in Oslo in 1960. All dealt with specifically
Norwegian geological topics produced by Norwegian scholars. An important
study of the nature of past geological research in Norway.

93 **The geology of parts of southern Norway.**
Olaf Holtedahl, Arne Bugge, Carl Fred. Koldering, Halvor
Rosendahl, Jakob Schetelig, Leif Størmer. *Proceedings of the
Geologists' Association*, vol. 45, no. 3 (1934), p. 307-88. maps.
bibliog.
The article is divided into four main sections in which the authors discuss
geological formations unique to the regions near Kongsberg, Oslo, the Finse
district, and the Bergen area.

94 **Geology of Norway.**
Edited by Olaf Holtedahl. Oslo: H. Aschehoug, 1960. 2 vols.
maps. bibliog. (Norges Geologiske Undersøkelse, no. 208).
Holtedahl, Norway's foremost geologist of the 20th century, edited this extensive
introduction to Norway's geological structure and development. The basic
objective was to provide a survey useful to both novices and experts in the field.
The first illustrated volume consists of several articles by prominent scholars. The
second volume contains a geological (bedrock) map of Norway and nineteen
plates. The work is based on *Norges geologi* [Norway's geology], a two-volume
work by Holtedahl published in 1953 (Norges Geologiske Undersøkelse no. 164).
This was translated into Russian in 1957-8.

95 **Geology of the North Atlantic borderlands.**
    J. William Kerr, A. J. Ferguson.   Calgary, Canada: Canadian
    Society of Petroleum Engineers, 1981. 743p. maps. bibliog.
    (Memoir 7: Papers Presented at the St. John's Symposium of the
    Canadian Society of Petroleum Engineers).
This work of technical scholarship includes four articles on the geology of
Spitsbergen and Norway.

96 **Rocks and land forms in North Norway.**
    Kåre Landmark. In: *Norway North of 65*. Edited by Ørnulf
    Vorren.   Oslo: Oslo University Press; London: George Allen &
    Unwin, 1960, p. 16-36. bibliog. (Tromsø Museums Skrifter, no. 8).
Describes the geological formation, structure, and chief characteristics of North
Norway.

97 **Petrology of the Holterkollen plutonic complex, Oslo region, Norway.**
    Thomas R. Neff, Sobhy O. Khalil.   *Norsk Geologisk Tidsskrift*,
    vol. 60 (1980), p. 53-70. maps.
This detailed, scholarly study is an excellent example of the important research
material available in English on the subject.

98 **The North Sea.**
    R. M. Pegrum, G. Rees, D. Naylor.   London: Graham, Trotman,
    Dudley, 1965. 225p. maps. bibliog. (Geology of the North-West
    European Continental Shelf, no. 2).
A discussion of the geology of the North Sea with a particular emphasis on those
areas where oil and gas have been discovered, with due reference to the
Norwegian sector. It uses less technical terms than some other works on the
subject and contains a glossary which will be useful to the non-specialist.

99 **The geomorphology of Norway.**
    Kaare Munster Strøm.   *Geographical Journal*, vol. 102 (July-Dec.
    1948), p. 19-27. maps.
Presents a paper read to the Royal Geografhical Society in London on March 22,
1948, and the discussion that followed on the surface features of Norway. It is
well-illustrated with maps and several photographs of the geological features that
were discussed.

**Travels through Norway and Lapland during the years 1806, 1807, and
1808.**
See item no. 31.

**The Iron Age settlement of Arctic Norway: a study in the expansion of
European Iron Age culture within the Arctic Circle.**
See item no. 134.

North Norway: a history.
See item no. 154.

The heart of Norway: a history of the central provinces.
See item no. 155.

West Norway and its fjords: a history of Bergen and its provinces.
See item no. 156.

East Norway and its frontiers: a history of Oslo and its uplands.
See item no. 157.

South Norway.
See item no. 158.

In Northern mists: Arctic exploration in early times.
See item no. 212.

Norsk Geografisk Tidsskrift.
See item no. 887.

Norsk Geologisk Tidsskrift.
See item no. 888.

Scandinavia in social science literature: an English language bibliography.
See item no. 920.

Tourism and Travel Guides

100 **Bergen Guide: English Edition.**
Bergen, Norway: Bergen Tourist Board, annual. maps.
A brief tourist guide to the city containing outline maps of its attractions, fjord tour information, the location of interesting places and time when they are open, along with other useful addresses and telephone numbers.

101 **Living in Norway: a practical guide.**
Patricia A. Bjaaland. Minneapolis, Minnesota: Sons of Norway, 1983. 111p.
This is the most useful guide for those planning to travel to Norway as permanent or temporary residents, as informed tourists, or for those who simply wish to know more about the country. The author has arranged her material alphabetically, included several vocabulary lists and conversion tables, and provided helpful hints for a number of occasions and situations.

102 **Introducing Oslo: a short guide book with comments.**
T. K. Derry. Oslo: Johan Grundt Tanum Forlag, 1969. 182p. maps.
A detailed description of Norway's capital. Ten chapters provide a historical outline, a brief walking tour of central Oslo, and a description of the main public buildings, museums, and other places of interest to the visitor. A final section provides brief outlines of many individuals and locations within Oslo that are organized alphabetically for ready reference.

103 **Facts About Norway.**
Oslo: Schibsteds, 1948-. annual.
Provides extensive facts and figures which are useful for the traveller and thumbnail sketches of Norwegian institutions. *Aftenposten*, Norway's second largest newspaper is also published by Schibsteds.

104   **The world's largest passenger ship *S.S. Norway*: a tribute in words and pictures.**
Oddvar Nilsen, Alf G. Andersen, Dag Lausand, Peter Otto Dybvik, translated from the Norwegian by J. Basil Cowhshaw.
Ålesund, Norway: Forlaget Nordvest, 1985. 176p.

A photographic and narrative journey abroad the *S.S. Norway* from Amsterdam to the North Cape and then to Oslo, which is a description not only of the ship and life aboard but also of the Norwegian landscape along the way. It is also available in a Norwegian edition.

105   **Oslo Guide: English Edition.**
Oslo: Reisetrafikkforeningen for Oslo og Omegn (Oslo Tourist Board), annual. maps.

Useful information regarding local attractions, museum locations and opening hours, and a sketch of the city's tram, subway, and bus systems.

106   **Oslo This Week.**
Oslo: Reisetrafikkforeningen for Oslo og Omegn (Oslo Tourist Board), monthly.

This pamphlet provides information on museums, special events and performances of all types in the capital and adjacent areas. Distributed on a complimentary basis at several locations such as the *Rådhus* (City Hall) and travel agencies.

107   **Once upon a town: Susan Tyrell about Stavanger.**
Susan Tyrell.   Stavanger, Norway: Dreyer, 1979. 160p

A tour of Stavanger, in a parallel English and Norwegian text, illustrated with several photographs. The author outlines the city's history, and describes its streets, buildings, and the surrounding countryside. Special consideration is given to Stavanger's importance in the development of North Sea oil and the consequent influx of Americans to the area.

108   **Of Norwegians ways.**
Bent Vanberg.   Minneapolis, Minnesota: Dillon Press, 1971. 227p. map.

This wide-ranging work is particularly useful to those planning a trip to Norway. It includes chapters on a variety of subjects such as the nation's history, interest in sports, art, and language. It considers etiquette and food, and provides useful phrases and expressions.

109   **A journey to the northern capitals.**
Oliver Warner.   London: George Allen & Unwin, 1968. 157p.

Provides brief introductions to the four Scandinavian capitals and some of the main areas of interest. Although it does not include all tourist attractions, and is now somewhat dated, the section on Oslo (p. 44-67) provides useful information on the museums on Bygdøy, the Munch Art Museum, Akershus Castle, and the Oslo City Hall.

110 **2,500 miles on the Norwegian coastal steamer.**
Erling Welle-Strand, translated by Christopher Norman. Bergen,
Norway: J. W. Eide, 1972. 63p.

A description of the twelve-day trip from Bergen to Kirkenes and back on the
popular coastal steamer. A sketch is provided of the trip one might expect on
board and the volume focuses on the scenery and towns along the route.

111 **Motoring in Norway.**
Erling Welle-Strand, Per Prag. [Oslo]: Norway Travel
Association, 1972. 127p. maps.

Presents a number of alternative routes that one may take through Norway and
into neighbouring Sweden. The official number of each road according to the
European and Norwegian systems is provided, along with its driving conditions,
mileage to places along the route in both miles and kilometres, places of interest,
and services available at various locations and a sketch map is included.

112 **Tourist in Norway.**
Edited by Erling Welle-Strand. Oslo: Schibsteds, 1980. 6th ed.
141p. maps.

This useful guidebook contains important sections covering branches of the
Norway Travel Association outside the country, travel agencies in several
Norwegian towns, different modes of travel available in Norway, and twenty-
three basic tours (with variations) that can be taken. Special chapters have been
prepared on Oslo, Bergen, Trondheim and Stavanger.

Jotunheim: challenge of a mountain wilderness.
See item no. 75.

Flora and Fauna

113 **Fauna.**
Bengt Christiansen. In: *Norway North of 65*. Edited by Ørnulf
Vorren. Oslo: Oslo University Press; London: George Allen &
Unwin, 1960, p. 73-99. bibliog. (Tromsø Museums Skrifter, no. 8).
A survey of the land animals, birds, fresh fish and marine life in and around
North Norway.

114 **Norges fisker.** (Norway's fish.)
Bengt Christiansen. Oslo: J. W. Cappelens Forlag, 1976. 168p.
A brief description of the fish found in Norway with many illustrations. The Latin
name for each species is also provided.

115 **Maps of distribution of Norwegian plants: the coast plants.**
Knut Fægri. Oslo: Oslo University Press, 1960. 174p. maps.
bibliog. (Universitet i Bergen Skrifter, no. 26).
Specific coastal plants are described, and a map indicates their location. The text
denotes places where the species has previously been sighted, the first record of
its existence in Norway, doubtful reports of its existence, altitude limits, habitat,
and other relevant information. An extensive bibliography makes it particularly
valuable given the dearth of generally available material in English.

116 **Norges dyr.** (Norway's animals.)
Edited by Ragnar Fislid, Arne Semb-Johansson. Oslo: J. W.
Cappelens Forlag, 1980-82. 6 vols. 2nd rev. ed. maps.
A massive work, first published in 1969, that describes Norway's animals, fish,
and birds. It contains articles by recognized scholars on each of these forms and
includes many maps, photographs and illustrations. The sixth volume contains an

index with the Latin name for all the species mentioned in the work as well as the Norwegian form.

117   **Mountain flowers of Scandinavia.**
      Olav Gjærevall, Reidar Jørgensen.   Trondheim, Norway:
      Trondhjems Turist Forening, 1978. 175p. maps.

The authors introduce their subject with a brief discussion of the plant forms of Scandinavia's mountainous regions, their origins in the area and their distribution. Contains colour illustrations of 164 flowers of the region. A good introduction for the general reader or the traveller.

118   **Norges fugler.** (Norway's birds.)
      Svein Haftorn.   Oslo: Universitetsforlaget, 1971. 862p. maps.

A detailed reference work on Norway's birds. Species and sub-species are listed by their Norwegian and Latin names in larger type and their names in Swedish, Danish, English, and German are also provided. Information includes their markings, sound, habitats in general and in Norway, sightings, and their diet.

119   **The world of the polar bear.**
      Thor Larsen, foreword by Sir Peter Scott.   London: Hamlyn,
      1978. 93p. map. bibliog.

This work for the general reader by a leading authority on the subject, discusses the animal throughout the Arctic. The study is well illustrated and discusses important topics with respect to features and characteristics.

120   **Norsk og svensk flora.** (Norwegian and Swedish flora.)
      Johannes Lid.   Oslo: Norske Samlaget, 1963. 800p.

Most entries in the table of contents, the main portion of the book, and the index references are made by the Latin name as well as by the Norwegian and Swedish name. Entries contain information regarding size, appearance, and the places in both countries where each species is most likely to exist. Many black-and-white illustrations are included. The book was published in two editions beginning in 1944 as *Norsk flora* (Norwegian flora).

121   **The polar bear (Ursus maritimus Phipps) in the Svalbard area.**
      Odd Lønø.   Oslo: Norsk Polarinstitutt, 1970. 104p. maps. bibliog.
      (Norsk Polarinstitutt Skrifter, no. 149).

A scholarly study of the polar bear discussing the catching of polar bears on Spitsbergen (Svalbard) in the past, their food, age determination, and their breeding biology and population structure.

122   The natural history of Norway: containing an accurate account of
the temperature of the air, the different soil, waters, vegetables,
metals, minerals, stones, beasts, birds, and fishes; together with the
descriptions, customs, and manners of living of the inhabitants;
interspersed with physiological notes from eminent writers, and
transactions of academics in two parts.
Erich Pontoppidan.   London: A. Linde, 1755. 2 vols. in 1. map.
The work does discuss at least to a limited extent everything mentioned in the
title but the author's greatest contribution was his description of both Norway's
fauna and flora throughout the work. Originally published in Copenhagen in
1752-55 and recently republished in Norwegian in 1977 as a facsimile of the 1755
edition.

123   **Vegetation.**
Olaf I. Ronning. In: *Norway North of 65.* Edited by Ørnulf
Vorren.   Oslo: Oslo University Press; London: George Allen &
Unwin, 1960, p. 50-72. maps. bibliog. (Tromø Museums Skrifter,
no. 8).
A description of the vegetative regions of North Norway and the distinctive plant
life found in them. An index of the English equivalents of the Latin names used in
the text is provided at the end of the article.

124   **Arctic summer: birds in North Norway.**
Richard Vaughan.   Shrewsbury, England: Anthony Nelson, 1979.
132p. map. bibliog.
Describes the author's journey through North Norway. The work emphasizes the
birds he observed and is illustrated with many photographs. A systematic list of
the birds of the Varanger Peninsula is included as an appendix to the work.

Lapland: the world's wild places.
See item no. 25.

**Sport in Norway and where to find it together with a short account of the
vegetable productions of the country to which is added a bit of the alpine
flora of the Dovre Fjeld and of the Norwegian ferns, etc.**
See item no. 29.

Nordic Journal of Botany.
See item no. 885.

Prehistory and Archaeology

125 **The Northmen.**
Thomas Froncek, introduced by Birgitta L. Wallace. New York:
Time-Life, 1974. 160p. maps. bibliog. (Emergence of Man Series).

A study of life in Scandinavia from ca. 2,000-500 BC. Much of the research was
done in Denmark but represents developments and conditions that also prevailed
in Norway. Colourful, informative, and a good introduction for the general
reader.

126 **Rock carvings in Norway.**
Anders Hagen, translated by Marie Killingen.   Oslo: Johan
Grundt Tanum, 1965. 55p. (Tokens of Norway).

Hagen divides prehistoric rock carvings into those produced by hunting and
fertility groups. He analyses each form with respect to technique and meaning.
Several black-and-white photographs of the rock carvings illustrate the work.

127 **Norway.**
Anders Hagen, translated by Elizabeth Seeburg.   London:
Thames & Hudson, 1967. 205p. maps. bibliog. (Ancient Peoples
and Places).

A basic introduction to the prehistory and archaeology of Norway. Hagen
provides a chronological account of the first inhabitants of Norway, Neolithic Age
farmers, sub-Neolithic cultures, and Bronze and Iron Age inhabitants until the
Viking period. He also provides an explanation of some of the archaeological
evidence that supports these developments. Seventy-five photographs and sixty-
eight drawings supplement the narrative.

128 **Archaeological contributions to the early history of urban communities in Norway.**
Asbjørn E. Herteig, Hans-Emil Lidén, Charlotte Blindheim.
Oslo: Universitetsforlaget, 1975. 175p. maps. bibliog. (Instituttet
for sammenlignende kulturforskning).

Herteig presents a brief discussion of the development of urban communities in
Western Europe and Scandinavia. After this the three authors describe
archaeological work undertaken in four early Norwegian communities of Bergen,
Borund in Sunnmøre, Oslo, and Kaupsang and they explain the significance of
this work.

129 **Problems relating to the early Mesolithic settlement of Southern
Norway.**
Svein Indrelid. *Norwegian Archaeological Review*, vol. 8, no. 1
(1975), p. 1-18. map. bibliog.

Discusses previous research on the settlement of Southern Norway during the
Mesolithic period as well as the arguments pointing to the development of the
earliest Nøstvet elements in Western Norway from the period 5,600-6,100 BC.
For a parallel study in the same issue of the journal on Southeastern Norway, see
Egil Mikkelsen's 'Mesolithic in south-eastern Norway,' p. 19-35.

130 **A history of Scandinavian archaeology.**
Ole Klindt-Jensen. London: Thames & Hudson, 1975. 144p.
maps. bibliog. (The World of Archaeology).

A survey of the nature and development of Scandinavian archaeology since the
16th century. A chronological approach is used for the most part, incorporating
the work carried out in all of the countries together. Separate chapters, however,
deal with the research activities conducted in each of the Scandinavian states
during the 20th century, including a brief chapter on Norway, (p. 97-104).

131 **Farms and fanes of ancient Norway: the place-names of a country
discussed in their bearings on social and religious history.**
Magnus Olsen. Oslo: H. Aschehoug, 1926. 349p. maps. (Instituttet for sammenlignende kulturforskning, Series A, no. 9).

A detailed study of Norwegian place-names that indicates the existence of farming
in these areas during prehistoric times. The book is organized according to the
end suffix of the place-names, thus indicating the type of agriculture, social forms,
and religious significance of the places discussed.

132 **The world of the Norseman.**
Eric Oxenstierna, translated from the German by Janet Sond-
heimer. New York: World Publishing; London: Weidenfeld &
Nicolson, 1967. 163p. map. bibliog. (Ancient Civilizations).

Originally published in Stuttgart in 1957, this is a discussion of the archaeological
work done in Scandinavia mainly on the pre-Viking period. Most of the examples
are taken from Denmark and Sweden but Norwegian cases are also cited. The
work is informative, scholarly, but also anecdotal in style.

Prehistory and Archaeology

133 **Scandinavian archaeology.**
Haakon Shetelig, Hjalmar Falk, translated by E. V. Gordon.
Oxford: Clarendon Press, 1937. 458p.

A discussion of the archaeological remains in Norway from its first settlement to the Viking period. The major portion of the book is organized on a chronological basis describing the different archaeological periods and their characteristics. In the last section, however, several topics are discussed including decorative art, subsistence, dwellings, costume, seafaring, weapons, and religion. This was the standard work on the subject for decades and is still an important study. For an earlier and somewhat briefer account in French by Shetelig alone, see *Préhistoire de la Norvège* (Oslo: H. Aschehoug, 1926).

134 **The Iron Age settlement of Arctic Norway: a study in the expansion of European Iron Age culture within the Arctic Circle.**
Thorleif Sjøvold. Tromsø, Norway; Oslo: Norwegian Universities Press, 1962-1974. 2 vols. maps. bibliog. (Tromsø Museums Skrifter, vol. 10: 1-2).

Volume one covers the Roman and migration periods and volume two deals with the Merovingian and Viking periods. In both works Sjøvold catalogues the archaeological finds that were made in each period; describes the burial customs based on time and location within Northern Norway; and studies the artifacts according to type and material. On the basis of this analysis he attempts to draw conclusions regarding the character of these Iron Age settlements. Appended to volume two are brief notes by Johan Torgersen on 'Skeletal material', (p. 373-77) and 'The Viking Age coin finds in North Norway', by Kolbjørn Skaare, (p. 378-83).

The Vikings.
See item no. 160.

The Vikings: an illustrated history of their voyages, battles, customs, and decorative arts.
See item no. 167.

The Viking achievement: a survey of the society and culture of early medieval Scandinavia.
See item no. 170.

The excavations at York: the Viking dig.
See item no. 173.

The discovery of a Norse settlement in America: excavations at L'Anse aux Meadows, 1961-1968.
See item no. 176.

Land under the Pole Star: a voyage to the Norse settlements of Greenland and the saga of the people that vanished.
See item no. 177.

Westward to Vinland: the discovery of pre-Columbian house-sites in

North America.
See item no. 178.

Viking expansion westwards.
See item no. 187.

The Norsemen.
See item no. 191.

The age of the Vikings
See item no. 194.

The Viking world.
See item no. 196.

The Vikings and their origins: Scandinavians in the first millenium.
See item no. 203.

The Scandinavians in England.
See item no. 204.

Lapps and Norsemen in olden times.
See item no. 321.

Old art and monumental buildings in Norway restored during the last fifty years.
See item no. 783.

Ancient Norwegian design: pictures from the University Museum of National Antiquities, Oslo.
See item no. 822.

Acta Archaeologica.
See item no. 876.

Norwegian Archaeological Review.
See item no. 891.

Bibliographies des science prehistorique en Norvège 1900-1935. (Bibliography of prehistory in Norway 1900-1935.)
See item no. 912.

History

General

135 A short history of Norway.
  T. K. Derry.   London: George Allen & Unwin, 1957. 281p. map.
  bibliog.
This concise survey of Norway up to 1956 is still a valuable reference work.

136 A history of modern Norway 1814-1972.
  T. K. Derry.   London: Oxford University Press, 1973. 503p.
  maps. bibliog.
A solid survey of the development of modern Norway, which pays due attention
to all parts of the period. Includes short sketches of Norwegians prominent in
politics and in a variety of other fields.

137 History of the Norwegian people.
  Knut Gjerset.   New York: AMS Press, 1969. 2 vols in 1. maps.
A reproduction of the original edition published in 1932. The Viking age and the
years of independence during the Middle Ages (to 1319) are covered in the first
volume. Volume two contains a chronological account of Norway up to 1914. This
is one of the oldest accounts of Norwegian history which is still in frequent use,
and it possesses much of the detail and flair missing in shorter accounts.

138 **Norwegian history simplified.**
Zinken Hopp [Signe Marie f. Brochmann], translated from the
Norwegian by Toni Ramholt.   Bergen, Norway: John Griegs
Forlag, 1961. 104p.

A light-hearted and anecdotal sketch of Norwegian history which looks at the
Vikings and other prominent people and events.

139 **Norway in world history.**
Wilhelm Keilhau.   London: MacDonald, [1944]. 206p. (Cross-
Roads Series).

A survey of Norwegian history by an outstanding 20th-century economic
historian. About half the work deals with the Viking and mediaeval periods while
most of the remaining section is devoted to the 19th century.

140 **A history of Norway.**
Karen Larsen.   Princeton, New Jersey: Princeton University Press
for the American-Scandinavian Foundation, 1950. 573p.

A well-written account covering Norwegian history up to 1945. It is particularly
important for its thorough coverage of Norway during the Middle Ages and the
Early Modern period.

141 **A brief history of Norway.**
John Midgaard.   Oslo: Tanum, 1979. 10th ed. 149p. maps.
bibliog. (Tokens of Norway).

A short survey of Norwegian history with emphasis on the Viking period, the
1814 crisis, independence in 1905, the Second World War, and the post-war reconstruction period. A useful introduction to the general development of Norway,
although there is little mention of such subjects as culture and economics.

Norway in Scandinavian history

142 **Scandinavia during the revolutionary era, 1760-1815.**
H. Arnold Barton.   Minneapolis, Minnesota: University of Minnesota Press, 1985. 435p. maps. bibliog. (Nordic Series, no. 12).

Emphasis is placed on economic and cultural developments as well as on internal
political affairs and the involvement of the Scandinavian states in the Napoleonic
Wars. Topics affecting Norway in particular include Scandinavian neutral wartime
shipping, the Lofthus uprising of 1787, the Haugean religious revival, the 1809
crisis, and Norway's independence movement of 1814.

143 **A history of Scandinavia: Norway, Sweden, Denmark, Finland and Iceland.**
T. K. Derry.   Minneapolis, Minnesota: University of Minnesota Press, 1979. 447p. map. bibliog.

This single volume survey of Scandinavian history in English fills a long felt need. Derry provides a brief account of the Vikings and of Norway during the Kalmar Union and the period of Danish rule to 1814. About one-half of the work covers the period from 1814 to the mid-1970s with Norway receiving her share of consideration. Emphasis is on politics but two chapters discuss cultural and other contributions by Scandinavians during the 19th and 20th centuries.

144 **The Scandinavian countries, 1720-1865: the rise of the middle classes.**
Brynjolf Jakob Hovde.   Port Washington, New York, London: Kennikat Press, 1972. 2 vols.

First published in 1943, this is a most thorough and knowledgeable survey of the period. Political history is included, although Hovde emphasizes economic, social, and cultural developments. Consideration is given to agriculture, trade, religion, philosophy, literature, education, and the origins of the popular folk movements that had a considerable impact then and throughout the 19th century.

145 **The Nordic countries 1850-1914.**
Lennart Jörberg, translated by Paul Britten Austin. In: *The emergence of industrial societies*. Edited by Carlo M. Cipolla. New York: Barnes & Noble; Sussex, England: Harvester Press, 1976, p. 375-485. bibliog. (Fontana Economic History of Europe, Vol. 4, Pt. 2).

Considers the Industrial Revolution in Finland, Sweden, Norway, and Denmark. Basic factors such as population growth, agricultural change, and industrial development are discussed by individual country and on a comparative basis. First published in 1970. For a discussion of this topic with special reference to Norway see 'The Industrial Revolution in Norway' by Francis Sejersted, *Scandinavian Economic History Review*, vol. 20, no. 2 (1972), p. 153–64.

146 **Scandinavia 1914-1970.**
Lennart Jörberg, Olle Krantz, translated by Paul Britten Austin. In: *Contemporary economics*. Edited by Carlo M. Cipolla. New York: Barnes & Noble; Sussex, England: Harvester Press, 1977, p. 377-459. bibliog. (Economic History of Europe, Vol. 6, Pt. 2).

An outline of the main trends in the economic development of Finland, Sweden, Norway, and Denmark during the period. The authors discuss economic growth, population developments, foreign trade, agricultural and industrial development, and the role of the state in economic policy. A concise summary of developments that is enhanced by numerous tables, diagrams, and an extensive bibliography.

147 **Les peuples scandinaves au moyen âge.** (The Scandinavians in the
Middle Ages.)
Lucien Musset.   Paris: Presses Universitaires de France, 1951.
342p. maps. bibliog.
The most detailed discussion of the Scandinavian countries during the Middle
Ages in a non-Scandinavian language. Musset begins with an account of pre-
Viking Scandinavia and the activities of the Vikings abroad but most of the work
studies the development of the Scandinavian states from ca. 1,000 until the
Kalmar Union of 1397. Although the author concentrates chiefly on politics,
attention is also given to religious, commercial and social developments.

148 **Nordic societies.**
Henrik Nissen. In: *Scandinavia during the Second World War.*
Edited by Henrik Nissen.   Minneapolis, Minnesota: University of
Minnesota Press, 1983, p. 3-52. (Nordic Series no. 9).
An introduction to the Scandinavian countries during the 1930s, emphasizing
economic structures and developments, the political structures of the different
states, and providing a brief outline of their foreign policies on the eve of the
Second World War.

149 **The decline of neutrality 1914-1941 with special reference to the
United States and the Northern neutrals.**
Nils Ørvik.   Oslo: Johan Grundt Tanum Forlag, 1953. 294p.
bibliog.
Studies the different forms of neutrality practiced during the period, offering the
United States and the Scandinavian countries as contrasting studies. Norway
figures prominently in the work as the country's neutrality was tested severely
during the First World War (part one, chapter two), and it was unable to remain
neutral in 1940, due to the German invasion outlined in part four chapter two.

150 **Agrarian structure and peasant politics in Scandinavia: a comparative study of rural response to economic change.**
Øyvind Østerud.   Oslo: Universitetsforlaget, 1978. 279p. bibliog.
An extended discussion of the theoretical framework of the book is followed by a
detailed description of the agrarian structure of society, landholding and the
transformations that took place in it through enclosure and other forms of
agricultural change during the 19th century. The work concludes with a discussion
of the nature of peasant participation in politics in each of the Scandinavian
countries during the 19th century and the peasant movements that arose during
the same period.

151 **The Scandinavian states and the League of Nations.**
S. Shepard Jones.   New York: Greenwood Press, 1969. 298p.
bibliog.
Although first published in 1939 (Princeton, New Jersey: Princeton University
Press for the American-Scandinavian Foundation), the volume remains the major

study of this subject. Themes discussed include: the role of the Scandinavian states in the founding of the League; their positions in the League on questions of its structure; and their role on matters of conciliation, disarmament, and mandate and international territories.

Regional history

152 **Svalbard in international politics 1871-1925: the solution of a unique international problem.**

Trygve Mathisen. Oslo: Brøggers, 1954. 211p. map. bibliog. (Norsk Polarinstitutt Skrifter, no. 101).

A study of the early exploration and increasing interest over the economic exploitation of Spitsbergen by the USA and the USSR that led to the treaty of 9 February 1920 recognizing Norwegian sovereignty over the island.

153 **Svalbard in the changing Arctic.**

Trygve Mathisen. Oslo: Gyldendal Norsk Forlag, 1954. 112p. maps. bibliog.

A continuation of *Svalbard in international politics: the solution of a unique international problem* (q.v.). The author studies the area from the treaty of 1920 granting Norway sovereignty over the region until about 1950. Of special interest is the last half of the book which discusses the Russian proposals of 1945 for joint Soviet-Norwegian control over part of the archipelago and the impact of postwar economic and political developments.

154 **North Norway: a history.**

Frank N. Stagg, foreword by A. H. Winsnes. London: George Allen & Unwin, 1952. 204p. maps. bibliog.

A chronological account of the region. The interaction between the area and events further south is a major theme. The last third of the book provides a description of the North's three provinces, Nordland, Troms, and Finnmark, during the 19th century.

155 **The heart of Norway: a history of the central provinces.**

Frank N. Stagg, foreword by Arne Fjelba. London: George Allen & Unwin, 1953. 194p. maps.

The development of Trondheim is traced from the coming of the 'trønders' in about 400 AD until after 1814. Lesser consideration is given to the character of the counties outside Trondheim, such as Sør-Trøndelag, Nord-Trøndelag, Nordmøre, and Romsdal.

156   **West Norway and its fjords: a history of Bergen and its provinces.**
      Frank N. Stagg, foreword by G. M. Gathorne-Hardy.   London:
      George Allen & Unwin, 1954. 245p.

Most of this work studies the city of Bergen, taking an extensive look at its history
and the influence it has had on the surrounding area and on Norway as a whole.
The final portion of the book describes the provinces of Hordeland, Sogn-og-
Fjordane, and Sunnmøre.

157   **East Norway and its frontiers: a history of Oslo and its uplands.**
      Frank N. Stagg, foreword by Francis Bull.   London: George Allen
      & Unwin, 1956. 285p. maps.

Studies the historical development of Oslo and the surrounding area. The last
third of the book is devoted to a description of the four provinces of eastern
Norway: Akershus, Hedmark, Oppland, and Østfold.

158   **South Norway.**
      Frank N. Stagg, foreword by Alf Sommefelt.   London: George
      Allen & Unwin, 1958. 232p. maps.

In contrast with the rest of the series, this volume studies the history and
character of the different areas separately rather than from a common early
historical base. Firstly, Stagg discusses the province of Vestfold and the two
counties of Jarlsberg and Larvik that were independent for much of Norway's
history. After short treatments of Buskerud and Telemark, he provides an
extensive account of the counties of Aust and Vest-Agder, and of Rogaland and
its centre, Stavanger.

The Vikings 900-1066

159   **Vikings of the West: the expansion of Norway in the early Middle
      ages.**
      Per Sveaas Andersen.   Oslo: Tanum, 1971. 103p. maps. bibliog.
      (Tokens of Norway).

Much of the work studies life in Norway during the Viking period, discussing
social, economic, and political conditions, and theories based on historical
research of Viking expansion outside Scandinavia. Expansion by Norwegians is
outlined in the second half and an attempt is made to link Norwegian
development with that of the rest of Scandinavia and Europe. Based primarily on
literary and archaeological sources.

160 **The Vikings.**
    Holger Arbman, translated from the Swedish and introduced by
    Alan Binns. London: Praeger, 1961. 212p. maps. bibliog.
    (Ancient Peoples and Places).

A survey of the Vikings emphasizing archaeological evidence as well as literary
sources. Arbman describes the Scandinavian background of the Viking phenomenon, their activities in the British and North Atlantic isles, Western Europe and
Russia, with a concluding chapter on Viking art. Richly illustrated with black-and-
white photographs, drawings and maps, this is a useful introduction.

161 **The quest for America.**
    Edited by Geoffrey Ashe, Thor Heyerdahl, Helge Ingstad, J. V.
    Lucas, Betty Meggers, Birgitta L. Wallace. New York: Praeger,
    1971. 298p. maps. bibliog.

A collection of essays concerning early exploration of the Americas. Three
articles by outstanding scholars discuss different aspects of the Viking presence in
North America. Helge Ingstad's 'Norse explorers,' (p. 96-112) uses literary and
cartographic evidence to summarize Norse trips to Vinland. 'Norse sites at
L'Anse aux Meadows,' (p. 175-97), also by Helge Ingstad, describes the events
that brought him to the place on Newfoundland where evidence of a Viking
presence in the New World has been found. Birgitta L. Wallace in 'Some points
of controversy,' (p. 155-74), describes some of the alleged artifacts that were used
before Ingstad's discoveries to 'prove' the existence of Vikings in America and
their actual origin.

162 **The Kensington Rune Stone: new light on an old riddle.**
    Theodore C. Blegen, bibliography by Michael Brook. St. Paul,
    Minnesota: Minnesota Historical Society, 1968. 212p. bibliog.

Recounts the discovery of and early controversy over the famous, or infamous,
Kensington Stone. Emphasis is on the role of Olaf Ohman, together with the
other apparent conspirators in the hoax, and Hjalmar Holand as a chief promoter
of its authenticity. The text is followed by an appendix containing many primary
sources related to the case and an extensive bibliography.

163 **The Viking Age.**
    Charlotte Blindheim. Oslo: Universitets Oldsaksamling, 1974.
    34p. bibliog.

Begins with a brief historiographical sketch of the Viking Age, emphasizing the
work of Peter Sawyer and David Wilson who called for a reassessment of the
Vikings. Artifacts in the Viking Age Gallery of the Universitets Oldsaksamling
(University Museum of National Antiquities) are pointed out which illustrate, as
do Sawyer and Wilson, peaceful domestic trade instead of Viking violence.

164 **The Viking saga.**
Peter Brent. London: Weidenfeld & Nicolson, 1975. 264p. maps.
bibliog.
A discussion of Viking expansion with chapters on the Vikings in France,
England, Russia, Iceland, and Vinland. A chapter on Scandinavian mythology is
also included in this excellent introduction for the general reader.

165 **Ancient emigrants: a history of the Norse settlements of Scotland.**
Anton W. Brøgger. Oxford: Clarendon Press, 1929. 208p. maps.
bibliog.
Studies the linguistic and archaeological evidence of the Viking, clearly
Norwegian, settlements of Scotland. The Orkney and Shetland Islands receive
much of Brøgger's attention since Viking settlements there were more extensive
than on the mainland. The last portion of the book traces Norwegian rule of the
islands until 1266. Despite its age, this is still a very valuable study of this aspect
of Norwegian expansion during the Viking Age.

166 **The Viking ships: their ancestry and evolution.**
Anton W. Brøgger, Haakon Shetelig, translated from the Norwegian by Katherine Shaw. New York: Twayne, 1971. 191p.
Two pre-eminent Norwegian archaeologists discuss the earliest archaeological
findings of the pre-Viking period, providing an insight into the slow development
of boat construction. The main portion of the work consists of a detailed
description of the Gokstad, Oseberg, and Tune ships. The study was first
published in Norwegian (Oslo: Dreyers Forlag, 1950), and translated into English
in 1951. The work has retained its importance, hence its re-publication in 1971.
Two recent articles in *Proceedings of the Eighth Viking Congress* (Odense,
Denmark: Odense University Press, 1981) question some of the conclusions
drawn by Brøgger and Shetelig. The articles are by Ole Crumlin-Pedersen,
'Viking shipbuilding and seamanship.' (p. 271-86) and Alan Binns, 'The ships of
the Vikings: were they "Viking ships?" ' (p. 287-94).

167 **The Vikings: an illustrated history of their voyages, battles, customs
and decorative arts.**
Johannes Brøndsted, translated from the Danish by Kalle Skov.
Baltimore, Maryland: Penguin, 1967. 320p. maps. bibliog.
An excellent survey of the Vikings first published in 1960. Brøndsted provides a
brief chronological and country by country description of Viking activity,
connecting activities abroad with developments at home. This is followed by an
account of weapons, dress, art, religion, and a particularly interesting discussion
of the Viking way of life. A well-written work by a recognized authority.

168 **The Viking road to Byzantium.**
Hilda Ellis Davidson. London: George Allen & Unwin, 1976.
341p. maps. bibliog.
Discusses the Scandinavian penetration of Russia and the Byzantine Empire in
particular as well as their roles as pilgrims and crusaders to the Holy Land.

Although most of the Vikings who headed in this direction are presumed to have been Swedes, Norwegian and Icelandic participation is often mentioned because the literary evidence of these Viking enterprises stems from these lands. Thus Harald Hardråda and his exploits are given a solid treatment. In a concluding chapter Davidson discusses the impact that such contact with the East had upon Old Norse literature and mythology.

169 **Eaters of the dead: the manuscript of Ibn Fadlan relating his experiences with the Northmen in A. D. 922.**
     Ibn Fadlan, edited by Michael Crichton. New York: Alfred A.
     Knopf, 1976. 193p. bibliog.
Ibn Fadlan was sent by the Caliph of Baghdad as an envoy in 921 to the King of the Bulgars. Instead of fulfilling his mission, he encountered a Viking band with whom he spent three adventurous years. His account does not pertain directly to Norway or Norwegians but is an interesting view of the Vikings by an outsider. The text was first translated by Per Fraus-Delus, late Professor Emeritus of Comparative Literature at the University of Oslo.

170 **The Viking achievement: a survey of the society and culture of early medieval Scandinavia.**
     Peter Foote, David M. Wilson. New York; Washington, DC:
     Praeger, 1970. 473p. maps. bibliog. (Great Civilizations).
The subtitle describes the contents of this major work: a detailed but clearly-written book upon Scandinavian life both during and after the Viking Age. Major emphasis is given to the nature of society, including women and children, daily life (housing, clothing, cooking), trade, means of transportation, warfare, art, literature, law, and religion.

171 **The two Olafs of Norway with a cross on their shields.**
     Charles Gibson. London: Dennis Dobson, 1968. 185p. maps.
     bibliog. (People from the Past).
A brief, popular history of Norway's kings from Harald the Fairhaired to Harald Hardråda (870-1066) with a special emphasis on Olav Trygvasson and Olav Haraldsson (St. Olav). An uncomplicated, easy-to-read introduction for the general reader and the young adult.

172 **The Viking world.**
     James Graham-Campbell. New York: Ticknor & Fields; London:
     Frances Lincoln, 1980. 220p. maps. bibliog.
An excellent introduction to Viking life both in Scandinavia and abroad. It does not attempt to detail political developments or Viking expansion but does provide a good introduction for the general reader on Viking ships and their construction, home life, art, mythology, the development of Christianity, and runes. Sean McGrail, R. I. Page, and Christine Fell have contributed to the work, which is richly supplemented by photographs, illustrations and maps.

173   **The excavations at York: the Viking dig.**
Richard Hall.   London: Bodley Head, 1984. 158p. maps.
Describes the Coppergate archaeological dig undertaken in York from 1976 to
1981 and its results. Hall, the director of the project, illustrates his narrative with
numerous maps, diagrams, and photographs to reveal Scandinavian Jorvik during
the 9th and 10th centuries as well as the Roman and Anglo-Saxon remains found
on the site. For a brief article on the project by the same author, see 'The
Coppergate venture,' *Scandinavian Review*, vol. 67, no. 3 (1979), p. 6-12.

174   **Was Vinland in Newfoundland?**
Einar I. Haugen. In: *Proceedings of the Eighth Viking Congress.*
Odense, Denmark: Odense University Press, 1981, p. 3-8.
Represents the opinion that Ingstad's excavations in Newfoundland are Viking
but that the true Vinland of the sagas lies further south and is yet to be
discovered.

175   **Explorations in America before Columbus.**
Hjalmar R. Holand.   New York: Twayne, 1956. 381p. maps.
bibliog.
A classic presentation of the thesis that there was a virtually constant
Scandinavian presence in America from the Vikings until Columbus. Through the
sagas and promotion of the credibility of artifacts such as the Kensington Stone
and the Newport Tower, Holand attempts to prove this thesis which has been
rejected by most scholars. An appendix includes primary sources indicating the
authenticity of the Kensington Stone and illustrating the author's life-long dispute
over this subject.

176   **The discovery of a Norse settlement in America: excavations at
L'Anse aux Meadows, 1961-1968.**
Anne Stine Ingstad.   New York: Columbia University Press;
Oslo: Universitetsforlaget, 1977. 2 vols. maps.
A detailed report of the archaeological expeditions between 1961 and 1968 that
discovered evidence of a Norse settlement at L'Anse aux Meadows. Contains
descriptions by participating scholars of the excavation procedures, the house-
sites, the artifacts recovered, and the procedures used to determine their age and
authenticity. Many maps, diagrams, and photographs are included in this
extremely important study.

177   **Land under the Pole Star: a voyage to the Norse settlements of
Greenland and the saga of the people that vanished.**
Helge Ingstad, translated from the Norwegian by Naomi Walford.
New York: St. Martin's Press; London: Cape, 1966. 381p. maps.
bibliog.
Studies Greenland during the Viking Age. Two main themes are the ties that
Greenland had with Iceland and Norway and the possible cause of the extinction
of the Scandinavian colony there. The section on the possible location of Vinland

is significant since Ingstad discovered the L'Anse aux Meadows site not long after writing this work. The book was first published in 1959 (Oslo: Gyldendal).

178   **Westward to Vinland: the discovery of pre-Columbian house-sites in North America.**
Helge Ingstad, translated from the Norwegian by Erik J. Friis.   New York: St. Martin's Press, [1969]. 249p.
Recounts Helge Ingstad's discovery of Viking remains at L'Anse aux Meadows, Newfoundland, and the subsequent archaeological expeditions from 1961 to 1964 which unearthed evidence of the Viking presence in North America. Much of the first part is a summary of the evidence of the sagas and the early maps that argued for an investigation of Newfoundland which Ingstad had made earlier and recorded in *Land under the Pole Star* (q.v.). The rest of the work is an account in journal form of his investigation of the site.

179   **The Vikings in England: a review.**
Gillian Fellows Jensen.   *Anglo-Saxon England,* vol. 4 (1975), p. 181-206.
A detailed historiographical study of the literature produced on the subject since Sir Frank Stenton's research on the nature and impact of Scandinavian settlement in England. Valuable for its discussion and its notes that form an important bibliography for the subject from about 1945 to the mid-1970s.

180   **The Norse Atlantic saga: being the Norse voyages of discovery and settlement to Iceland, Greenland, and America.**
Edited by Gwyn Jones.   London, New York: Oxford University Press, 1964. 246p. maps. bibliog.
The first section provides a detailed account of Iceland's development during the Viking period and deals briefly with Greenland and the Norse discovery and temporary settlement of Vinland. The second section contains translations by the author of *The book of the Icelanders. The book of the settlements, The Greenlander's saga, Erik the Red's saga* and others. Writing at the time of Helge Ingstad's discovery of archaeological evidence for the Viking presence at L'Anse aux Meadows, Jones pinpointed the same general area as the site of Viking landings in North America through his examination of the literary sources. Although it does not deal specifically with Norway, this work, as do the sagas in general, discusses the settlement of Iceland by Norwegians and studies their descendants who were also in frequent touch with the old country. It should be noted that a new and considerably enlarged edition of this work is due to be published by Oxford University Press in the spring of 1986.

181   **A history of the Vikings.**
Gwyn Jones.   Oxford; New York: Oxford University Press, 1984. rev. ed. 520p. maps. bibliog.
A scholarly, detailed, and very readable presentation first published in 1968. Covers the Vikings abroad; Scandinavia's early, pre-Viking history; and Scandinavia's history during the Viking Age. Jones, Emeritus Professor of

English Language and Literature at University College, Cardiff, is a highly-regarded scholar of the Viking Age and this is probably the most informative and comprehensive single-volume study of the subject.

182   **A history of the Vikings.**
Thomas D. Kendrick.   New York: Barnes & Noble, 1968. 412p.
maps. bibliog.

An extremely detailed study emphasizing the military character of the Vikings. Extensive chapters on pre-Viking Scandinavia and political developments there during and immediately after the Viking Age, precede an account of the Viking attacks upon different parts of Europe. The major portion of the book is organized geographically by country with a chronological description of Viking activity following. First published in 1930, this remains a useful reference work.

183   **The Vikings.**
Michael Haslock Kirkby.   Oxford: Phaidon; New York: E. P.
Dutton, 1977. 207p. maps.

Aimed at the general reader this survey emphasizes Viking expansion along with a brief description of society and cultural life. Viking activity in England is discussed in the greatest detail, including an introductory chapter on Viking York, Canute's North Sea empire, and events prior to 1066.

184   **The Northern seas: shipping and commerce in northern Europe**
A. D. 300-1100.
Archibald R. Lewis.   New York: Octagon Books, 1978. 498p.
maps.

Studies the Vikings and their effect on Europe. Lewis integrates Scandinavian economic developments and trade ties into the mainstream of European developments during the period. The book was first published in 1958 (Princeton, New Jersey: Princeton University Press).

185   **The Vikings in history.**
F. Donald Logan.   London: Hutchinson, 1983. 224p. maps.
bibliog.

A readable, detailed survey of the Vikings as raiders and settlers in Europe and as explorers in the North Atlantic. Much of the work concentrates on their presence in France, Ireland, the North Atlantic, and England. Unlike, for example, *Kings and Vikings* (q.v.), it does not discuss Scandinavian developments to any great extent. It is also distinctive in its discussion of Vinland sources and problems and its use of recent research such as Helge Ingstad's archaeological work in North America and the work done at York and Dublin.

186   **The Vikings in Britain.**
H. R. Loyn.   New York: St. Martin's Press, 1977. 176p. maps.
bibliog.

Emphasizes the Viking invasions of Britain, principally England, dividing the

main part of the book into those before and after 954 AD. Loyn connects the
invasions with political developments in Scandinavia. In the latter portion of the
book Loyn discusses the degree of Scandinavian penetration of the countryside
and the evidence used for such a study. An excellent introduction to this aspect of
Viking history.

187 **Viking expansion westwards.**
Magnus Magnusson. New York: Henry Z. Walck; London:
Bodley Head, 1973. 152p. maps. bibliog. (Walck Archeology
Series).

A brief, easy-to-read introduction to Viking activity in Britain, the North
Atlantic, and Vinland. Each chapter deals with a different country and is well-
illustrated with archaeological artifacts. Suitable for beginners, especially young
adults.

188 **Vikings!**
Magnus Magnusson. New York: Dutton, 1980. 320p. maps.
bibliog.

The text of the distinguished television series by the same name shown first on
BBC television and then on American public television. An articulate description
of the Viking Age, illustrated with many photographs.

189 **The European discovery of America: the Northern voyages A. D.
500-1600.**
Samuel Eliot Morison. New York: Oxford University Press,
1971. 712p. maps.

Discusses the Vikings in a chapter entitled 'The Norsemen and Vinland c. A. D.
800-1400', (p. 32-80). The study relies chiefly on the sagas and Ingstad's
archaeological work. Approximately the last third of the chapter is an extended
bibliographical essay which covers the different aspects of the problem and the
major works on these subjects in a scholarly, informative, and entertaining
fashion.

190 **Westviking: the ancient Norse in Greenland and North America.**
Farley Mowat. Boston, Massachusetts: Little, Brown, [1965].
494p. maps.

An interesting attempt to reconstruct the Vinland voyages on the basis of the
sagas and the author's knowledge of the sea, climate, Norse ships, geographical
concepts and navigational skills. An explanation of the assumptions made in the
reconstruction are contained in a series of appendixes that also explain Mowat's
reaction to the then newly-discovered Vinland Map and to the recently-begun
excavations at L'Anse aux Meadows, Newfoundland by Helge Ingstad. Although
Mowat has not convinced all the experts in this field, his book deserves to be read
in addition to the other research on this subject.

191   **The Norsemen.**
Eric Oxenstierna, edited and translated from the German by
Catherine Hutter.   Greenwich, Connecticut: New York Graphic
Society Publications, 1965. 320p. maps. bibliog.
An examination of several aspects of Viking life, richly embellished with black-
and-white photographs and illustrations. In common with many recent works it
emphasizes the non-warlike aspects of the Viking character, at least towards
outsiders. It discusses the archaeological evidence of the period at length and
studies the way in which this material can tell us much about Viking society,
including the role of women, their festivals, and their ships. Originally published
as *Die Wikinger* (Stuttgart, GFR: Kohlhammar, 1959).

192   **The Vikings: the rise and fall of the Norse sea kings.**
Rudolf Poertner, translated by Sophie Wilkins.   London: St.
James Press; New York: St. Martin's, 1975. 313p. maps. bibliog.
A summary of the Vikings' contact with the outside world is followed by a series
of highly condensed studies of different aspects of their life. General topics
include society, warfare, sailing, trade, and mythology.

193   **Viking hoaxes in North America.**
Jeffrey R. Redmond.   New York: Carlton Press, 1979. 64p.
Recounts the hoaxes perpetrated in North America to prove a Viking presence
there, including interesting detail on the Kensington Stone, Vinland Map, and
other such enterprises.

194   **The age of the Vikings.**
P. H. Sawyer.   London: Camelot Press, 1962, 254p. maps.
bibliog.
This major work does not attempt, as its title might suggest, to paint a broad
picture of the period. Instead, it is an investigation of the various sources,
primarily treasure hoards, that underline the commercial aspects of the Vikings
and de-emphasize their warlike character. Recommended for all serious students
of the subject.

195   **Kings and Vikings: Scandinavia and Europe AD 700-1100.**
P. H. Sawyer.   London, New York: Methuen, 1982. 182p. maps.
bibliog.
A readable and valuable survey of the Vikings by an acknowledged expert.
Sawyer considers the nature of pre-Viking Scandinavia, the sources used for the
study of the subject and the raids and settlements outside Scandinavia that the
Vikings undertook. An extensive bibliography emphasizing recent literature
makes this a particularly valuable reference source. For a more detailed article by
the same author, see 'Conquest and colonization: Scandinavians in the Danelaw
and Normandy,' *Proceedings of the Eighth Viking Congress* (Odense, Denmark:
University of Odense Press, 1981), p. 123-31.

196 The Viking world.
Jacqueline Simpson. London: St. Martin's Press, 1980. 192p.

Discusses aspects of Viking life which are disregarded by those who see the Vikings as nothing more than warlike barbarians. Basing her work primarily on archaeological material, Simpson describes many aspects of the Vikings' life including their ships, weapons, homes, family life, and social relationships. Originally published as *Everyday life in the Viking age* (New York: G. P. Putnam, 1967), this is an informative and valuable introduction.

197 The Viking ships in Oslo.
Thorleif Sjøvold. Oslo: Universitets Oldsaksamling, 1979. 80p. map. bibliog.

A description of the excavation of the Oseberg and Gokstad ships, the construction of the Viking Ship Hall on Bygdøy, a detailed description of both ships, and the furniture found in the Gokstad ship.

198 Vinland and the way thither.
Herbert C. Taylor Jr. In: *Man across the sea: problems of pre-Columbian contacts*. Edited by Carroll L. Riley, J. Charles Kelley, Campbell Pennington, Robert L. Rands. Austin, Texas: University of Texas Press, 1971, p. 242-54.

The author accepts the literary and archaeological evidence that Vinland existed. He provides a brief account of the Vinland Map's discovery, its features, and the early criticism of it as a genuine document. Later, the Vinland Map was declared a forgery because of Taylor's suspicions and the belief that positive proof of the Viking presence in North America was most likely to be found in archaeological evidence such as Ingstad's discoveries at L'Anse aux Meadows.

199 Viking issue.
Scandinavian Review, vol. 68, no. 3 (1980).

A special issue devoted to the Vikings. Three articles of particular importance are James Graham-Campbell's 'The other side of the coin,' (p. 6-19) dealing with Viking trade; Peter G. Foote and David M. Wilson's study of slavery in Viking society, 'The descendants of thrall,' (p. 35-48); and Magnus Magnusson's 'End of an era,' (p. 58-69) on the significance of the English succession crisis of 1066 to Scandinavian history.

200 Vikings in the British Isles.
Harrisburg, Pennsylvania: British Heritage, 1983. 56p. maps. bibliog.

Brief but informative articles on such general topics as Viking warfare, ships, and art, along with specific presentations of the Vikings in York, Dublin, London, and the North Sea islands. Contributors include the distinguished scholars David Wilson, Richard Hall, and James Graham-Campbell.

201 **Fact and fancy in the Vinland sagas.**
Erik Wahlgren. In: *Old Norse literature and mythology: a symposium.* Edited by E. C. Polome. Austin, Texas: University of Texas Press, 1969, p. 19-80. bibliog.

A comparison of the two sagas most used as literary evidence for the existence of Vinland, *The Greenlander's saga* and *Erik the Red's saga.* Wahlgren concludes that *Erik the Red's saga* was written as a literary embellishment of the former. Reliance chiefly upon the former as a historical source therefore leads to a clearer picture of Viking Vinland. The bibliography lists many of the most significant research works on the subject until the date of its publication.

202 **Social Scandinavia in the Viking Age.**
Mary W. Williams. New York: Macmillan, 1920. 451p. map. bibliog.

Despite its age, this work is still highly recommended, as its treatment of many topics regarding society and social life has not been superseded. Coverage includes the position of women, childhood, marriage, and the home.

203 **The Vikings and their origins: Scandinavia in the first millennium.**
David M. Wilson. London: Thames & Hudson; New York: McGraw-Hill, 1970. 144p. maps. bibliog. (Library of Early Medieval Civilizations).

An excellent introduction to pre-Viking Scandinavia and the Vikings for the general reader. Includes numerous photographs of archaeological digs and artifacts.

204 **The Scandinavians in England.**
David M. Wilson. In: *The archaeology of Anglo-Saxon England.* Edited by David M. Wilson. London: Methuen, 1976, p. 393-403. map.

A brief introduction to the archaeological evidence of the Scandinavian presence in Anglo-Saxon England by an expert in the field. The author's extensive notes refer to the useful bibliography at the end of the book.

The Middle Ages 900-1530

205 **The Hanseatic control of Norwegian commerce during the late Middle Ages.**
John Allyne Gade. Leiden, Netherlands: E. J. Brill, 1951. 139p. bibliog.

Studies the economic influence the Hansa was able to exert on Norway during the first half of the 15th century as the result of its control of Bergen, Norway's chief port at the time. The Hanseatic League was a mercantile group of German towns, which established a virtual trade monopoly in Scandinavia between 1370 and 1441.

206 **A royal imposter: King Sverre of Norway.**
Geoffrey M. Gathorne-Hardy. Oslo: H. Aschehoug (W. Nygaard), 1956. 305p.

The story of Norway's King Sverre from the mid-12th century political crisis and civil war that catapulted him into power until his death in 1202. It is a literary treatment based on Sverre's saga and other early sources.

207 **Desertion and land colonization in the Nordic countries c.1300-1600: comparative report from the Scandinavian Research Project on Deserted Farms and Villages.**
Svend Gissel, Eino Jutikaala, Eva Österberg, Jørn Sandnes, Björn Teitsson. Stockholm: Almqvist & Wiksell, 1981. 304p. maps. bibliog.

A report by the national leaders on the research project established by the historical associations of the respective countries. The report deals with the planning undertaken to create the project, the methods, hypotheses, and study areas established in each country, and some of the comparisons that can be made as a result of the research. This is a valuable addition to recent knowledge of Scandinavia during the late Middle Ages and is indicative of the intensive research on this subject in recent years. Its extensive bibliography and list of works published as a result of participation in the project are also helpful.

208 **Defining a new society: the Icelandic Free State between two worlds.**
Kirsten Hastrup. *Scandinavian Studies*, vol. 56, no. 3 (1984), p. 235-55.

A political and cultural study of Iceland from 930 to to 1264 and the impact of Norway on both aspects of Icelandic life. The Icelandic authors of the 12th and 13th centuries created the illusion of an Icelandic Free State that, in fact, did not exist. Instead it was constantly affected by outsiders, particularly Norway, until it finally fell under the rule of the latter in 1264. This scholarly discussion of the 'Icelandic-Norwegian connection' should be read by those interested in either country during the Middle Ages.

209 **The King's mirror.** (Speculum Regale-Konungs Skuggsjá.)
Translated by Laurence M. Larson. New York: Harvard University Press for the American-Scandinavian Foundation; London: Oxford University Press, 1917. 388p. bibliog.

Written by an unknown author of the 13th century, it is not unreasonable to call this a combination of *The book of knowledge* and *The book of the courtier*, necessary to the success of any mediaeval Norwegian young man. It was apparently written to introduce the four main groups within society, the merchant, the king and his court, the clergy, and the peasantry. Only the accounts of the first two remain and that concerning the peasantry was probably never written. A remarkable document which provides an insight into Norway during the Middle Ages.

210 **The household of the Norwegian kings in the thirteenth century.**
Laurence M. Larson. In: *Changes in medieval society: Europe North of the Alps, 1050-1500.* Edited by Sylvia L. Thrupp. New York: Appleton-Century-Crofts, 1964, p. 133-51.
A study of the Norwegian royal household officials and their duties during the period. The article was first published in *American Historical Review*, vol. 13 (1908).

211 **Canute the Great 955 (circa) -1035 and the rise of Danish imperialism during the Viking Age.**
Laurence M. Larson. New York: AMS Press, 1970. 375p. maps. bibliog.
The conflict between Denmark and Norway during this period and Canute's rule of Norway are as much a part of this work as events in Denmark and England. Published originally in 1912 by one of the noted first-generation American scholars on Scandinavia.

212 **In Northern mists: Arctic exploration in early times.**
Fridtjof Nansen, translated by A. G. Chater. Westport, Connecticut: Greenwood Press, 1970. 2 vols. maps.
Nansen studies four basic subjects: the early European concepts of Northern Europe; the North Atlantic voyages of the Vikings to Iceland, Greenland, and Vinland; late mediaeval geographic and cartographic knowledge of Northern Europe; and the first 'modern' European voyages of exploration to North America. The work is important for the views it expresses on Viking expansion westward, particularly to Vinland, and it is also significant for its discussion of early cartographic work in and around Scandinavia.

213 **Monarchy and nobility in Norway in the period around 1500.**
E. Ladewig Petersen. *Mediaeval Scandinavia*, vol. 7 (1974), p. 125-55.
Deals specifically with the contrast between the Kalmar Union monarch King Hans and his son and eventual successor Christian II during the early 1500s with respect to the strict constitutional programme promoted by the Norwegian nobles and the other union kingdoms. It is one of the few scholarly journal articles that discusses Norway's political history during this period.

214 **Coins and coinage in Viking Age Norway: the establishment of a**
     national coinage in Norway in the XI century, with a survey of the
     preceding currency history.
     Kolbjørn Skaare. Oslo: Universitetsforlaget, 1976. 272p. maps.
     bibliog.

A detailed study of Norwegian coinage issued during the 11th century as well as
its foreign and early Norwegian predecessors. Approximately one-half of the
book is a catalogue of these coins, maps indicating the locations where they were
found, and plates of photographs.

215 **The historical context of the first towns in northern and eastern**
     Europe.
     Inge Skovgaard- Petersen. In: *Proceedings of the Eighth Viking*
     Congress. Odense, Denmark: Odense University Press, 1981, p.
     9-18.

A brief scholarly discussion relating hypotheses on the development of towns
during the Middle Ages in Scandinavia to current, more general literature on the
subject.

216 **Heimskringla.** (Circle of the world.)
     Snorri Sturluson, translated and with an introduction by Lee M.
     Hollander. Austin, Texas: University of Texas Press for the
     American-Scandinavian Foundation, 1964. 854p. maps. bibliog.

The sagas written by the great mediaeval Icelandic poet, Snorri Sturluson (1178-
1241), with Norway's kings of the Middle Ages as their theme. The sagas included
in the collection are 'The Ynglinga saga', 'Halfdon the Black', 'Harald the
Fairhaired', 'Hakon the Good', 'The sons of Erik', 'Earl Hakon', 'King Olaf
Trygvasson', 'King Olaf the Saint', 'Magnus the Good', 'Harald the Stern', 'Olaf
the Quiet', 'Magnus the Barefoot', 'The sons of Magnus', 'Magnus the Blind' and
'Harald Gille', 'The sons of Harald', 'Hakon the Broad-Shouldered', and 'Magnus
Erlingsson'. They are powerful, captivating, and entertaining. Although sometimes questioned as completely reliable historical sources, the sagas enhance our
knowledge of the events of this period, its value and its spirit. They ought also to
be appreciated as literary masterpieces. Several translations of them have been
made, particularly during the last century. Samuel Laing presented a three-
volume edition that was first published in 1844 and has been re-published at least
twice since then. For an extensive listing of the various forms and editions that
have contained part of the *Heimskringla*, see *Norse sagas translated into English:
a bibliography* (q.v.).

Union with Denmark 1530-1814

217 **Admiral Thunderbolt: the spectacular career of Peter Wessel, Norway's greatest sea hero, who in eight years of naval warfare sailed, shot, and stormed his way from sea cadet to vice-admiral (AD 1711 to 1718).**
Hans Christian Adamson.   Philadelphia: Chilton, 1959. 336p. maps.

A semi-fictional account of Admiral Tordenskiold, Peter Wessel, who became a hero of the Dano-Norwegian state during the Great Northern War (1700-1721), against Sweden. The study illustrates the influence Norwegians could obtain in the state run from Copenhagen.

218 **Nordic students at foreign universities until 1660.**
Sverre Bagge.   *Scandinavian Journal of History*, vol. 9, no. 1 (1984), p. 1-29.

A comparative country by country and chronological study of the universities that Nordic students attended, with explanations of the changes in pattern that occurred.

219 **The satellite state in the seventeenth and eighteenth centuries.**
Edited by Ståle Dyrvik, Knut Mykland, Jan Oldervoll.   Bergen, Norway: Universitetsforlaget, 1979. 199p.

A collection of thirteen essays based on a seminar held in Norway in 1977 on the theme 'Satellite states: a comparative study of the economic, social, political, and cultural conditions of countries in union with greater neighbours.' Four important articles deal with Norway in the 18th century and its role within the union with Denmark. Dyrvik's contribution 'The social structure of Norway and Denmark', (p. 63-71) compares the social structures of the two countries, emphasizing the differences between them and the conditions that had disrupted the Danish-Norwegian union by 1814. Oldervoll's essay (p. 72-79), 'The rural society of Norway,' compares the agricultural systems of the two countries, and Gudmund Sandvik in 'The Norwegian economy in the eighteenth century: a satellite of Denmark?', (p. 36-48) investigates the influence of Danish mercantile legislation and the vested interest Danish officials had in the state's financial system. Mykland in 'The growth of Norwegian national consciousness in the Age of the Enlightenment: the economic, social, and cultural factors,' (p. 185-98) describes the manifestations of national self-consciousness that developed in Norway from the late 18th century until 1814.

220 **War and trade in Northern seas: Anglo-Scandinavian economic relations in the mid-eighteenth century.**
Heinz Sigfrid Koplowitz Kent.   Cambridge, England: Cambridge University Press, 1973. 240p. bibliog.

Discusses many facets of the trade between Scandinavia and Great Britain during the 18th century and the diplomatic repercussions of it during war. The chapter on the timber trade indicates Norway's important contribution to Helstat economics and the entire work reflects Norwegian commercial interests during the period.

221 **Norwegian independence and British opinion: January to August 1814.**
Terje I. Leiren. *Scandinavian Studies*, vol. 47, no. 3 (1975), p. 364-82.
Studies both public and private British sentiment regarding Norway's attempt to become independent during those critical months of 1814. Failing to secure the necessary support for independence, Norway was forced to agree to the Act of Union with Sweden in November of that year.

222 **The geography of peasant ecotypes in pre-industrial Scandinavia.**
Stewart P. Oakley. *Scandia*, vol. 47, no. 2 (1981), p. 199-223. map.
The author divides the region into various economic and social regions based on prevailing peasant society forms during the 18th and early 19th centuries.

223 **Norway and Sweden in 1814: the security issue.**
David C. Pugh. *Scandinavian Journal of History*, vol. 5, no. 2 (1980), p. 121-36.
Analyses the union of Sweden and Norway in 1814 with particular reference to the debate in the extraordinary first *Storting* (Parliament) of October 1814 regarding the acceptance of the union from the standpoint of the king's military powers. One of the most detailed studies in English of the situation.

224 **The proper prince: the rearing of Christian August.**
Leland B. Sather. *Scandinavian Studies*, vol. 54, no. 2 (1982), p. 103-22.
A study of the early life and education of Prince Christian August of Schleswig-Holstein-Sunderburg-Augustenburg. Although he grew up in another region of the 18th century Helstat, the prince's education was of significance after he became a military commander in Norway in 1804 and during his term as the head of the *Regjeringskomisjon* (Government Commission) during the critical years of 1807 to 1809.

225 **Castlereagh, Bernadotte and Norway.**
Lars Tangeraas. *Scandinavian Journal of History*, vol. 8, no. 3 (1983), p. 193-223.
Describes the origin during the Napoleonic Wars, of the 'Norwegian question' or the possibility of separating Norway from Denmark and uniting it with Sweden; Crown Prince Karl Johan of Sweden's determination to achieve this goal; his activities in 1813 and 1814 that led to the Treaty of Kiel in January 1814; the apparent success of this objective; and Norwegian resistance in 1814 that complicated the British position on this matter.

56

Union with Sweden 1814-1905

226 **The genesis of Norwegian nationalism.**
Andreas Elviken. *Journal of Modern History*, vol. 3, no. 3
(1931), p. 365-91.
A review of the events and individuals in Norway that encouraged the growth of
nationalism from Ludvig Holberg in the early 18th century to the linguist Ivar
Aasen in the mid-19th century. For a more extensive treatment of the subject by
Elviken see *Die Entwicklung des norwegischen Nationalismus* (Vaduz, Liechten-
stein: Kraus Reprint, 1965, 132p.), a reprint of a work first published in Berlin in
1930 as vol. 198 of *Historische Studien*.

227 **National romanticism in Norway.**
Oscar J. Falnes. New York: AMS Press, 1968. 398p. bibliog.
A study of Norwegian nationalism during the age of romanticism in the 19th
century. It is an important treatment of the conflicting attitudes towards
nationalism and Scandinavianism that developed, and particularly of the
development of historical writing in Norway through the interest of 'amateurs'
such as Jakob Aall and the work of Jakob Rudolf Keyser and Peder Andreas
Munch. The work also discusses the interest in folklore that occurred because of
P. C. Asbjørnsen and Jørgen Moe and the origins of Norwegian linguistic
research and controversy through the studies of Ivar Aasen and others. First
published in New York by Columbia University Press in 1933, this remains an
important study.

228 **The old Norwegian peasant community: investigations undertaken
by the Institute for Comparative Research in Human Culture, Oslo.**
Andreas Holmsen, Halvard Bjørvik, Ragmar Frimannslund.
Scandinavian Economic History Review, vol. 14, no. 1 (1956), p.
16-81. maps.
A collection of three essays by noted Norwegian scholars on the method of
Norwegian agriculture, land-holding patterns, and peasant society. Emphasis is
given to 19th-century evidence but the descriptions and conclusions of the article
are valid for several centuries before that as well. For discussion of another major
issue in landholding patterns in Norway during the 17th and 18th centuries in the
same journal see Holmsen's 'The transition from tenancy to freehold peasant
ownership in Norway,' vol. 9, no. 2 (1961), p. 152-64.

229 **Norway's relation to Scandinavian unionism 1815-1871.**
Theodore Jorgenson. Northfield, Minnesota: St. Olaf College
Press, 1935. 530p. bibliog.
The author weaves together the different threads that created and then destroyed
in Norway the hopes for a Scandinavian union. He emphasizes the friction within
the Swedish-Norwegian union, the two generations of Scandinavianists in the 19th
century and the clash in Norway between those desiring a union of Denmark,
Norway, and Sweden and those fearing further Swedish encroachment within the
union and hoping for independence. The work also includes ten appendixes.

230 **British views on Norwegian-Swedish problems 1880-1895: selections from diplomatic correspondence.**
Edited by Paul Knaplund. Oslo: Jacob Dybwad, 1952. 269p.
(Norsk Historisk Kjeldeskrift-Institut).

Edited correspondence between British diplomatic officials in Stockholm and Christiania (Oslo) and the Foreign Office during a period of increasing stress between Norway and Sweden. An interesting presentation of the political history of Norway during this critical era.

231 **Sigurd Ibsen and the origins of the national monarchy in Norway.**
Terje I. Leiren. *Scandinavian Studies*, vol. 51, no. 4 (1979), p. 392-412.

Discusses the part played by Sigurd Ibsen, the famous playwright's son, in the promotion, during the late 1890s, of an independent Norway governed by a 'national' monarchy. His major contribution was to make such an idea acceptable to a large number of Norwegians and he was therefore instrumental in the creation of such a government in 1905.

232 **The industrialization of Norway 1800-1920.**
Sima Lieberman. Oslo: Universitetsforlaget, 1970. 222p. bibliog.

A detailed study of the industrialization process in Norway during the period. A chronological approach is used to describe developments with many tables to illustrate points made in the narrative.

233 **Norway-Sweden: union, disunion and Scandinavian integration.**
Raymond E. Lindgren. Westport, Connecticut: Greenwood Press, 1979. 298p. bibliog.

The theme is the pressure in Norway on the union with Sweden during the 19th century and its dissolution in 1905. First printed in 1959 (Princeton, New Jersey: Princeton University Press) this is the chief source in English on the subject. The final chapter considers the crisis from 1905 to 1908 over Norway's desire for an integrity treaty from the Great Powers and Nordic co-operation from that time until the late 1950s.

234 **The economic development of continental Europe 1780-1870.**
Alan S. Milward, S. B. Saul. London: George Allen & Unwin, 1973. 2nd ed. 548p. maps. bibliog.

Three chapters discuss general trends and developments and there are also several chapters on specific parts of Europe. The section on Scandinavia (p. 467-535) includes coverage of Norway (p. 516-31) describing basic economic developments of the period. A brief bibliography of materials in English relating to Scandinavia is included.

235 **The roots of nationalism: studies in Northern Europe.**
Edited by Rosalind Mitchison. Edinburgh: John Donald
Publishers, 1980. 175p.

Contains papers presented at a conference at the University of Wales Conference
Centre in September 1979 and includes two by Norwegian scholars which are
relevant to Norway. That by Alf Kaartvedt discusses 'The economic basis of
Norwegian nationalism in the nineteenth century,' (p. 11-19) and Kjell Haugland
provides 'An outline of Norwegian cultural nationalism in the second half of the
nineteenth century,' (p. 21-29).

236 **Motive forces behind the new social policy after 1870: Norway on
the European scene.**
Anne-Lise Seip. *Scandinavian Journal of History*, vol. 9, no. 4
(1984), p. 329-41.

Examines the impact of German economic and social thought on the Norwegian
medical profession, popular movements advocating health, and politicians to
produce health reform legislation in Norway chiefly in the period 1870 to 1920.

237 **The dissolution of estate society in Norway.**
Ingrid Semmingsen. *Scandinavian Economic History Review*,
vol. 2, no. 2 (1954), p. 166-203.

Concentrates on the elimination of mercantilistic legislation during the 19th
century that had provided powerful leverage to towns and merchants in the past,
agricultural reform, and the degree of social mobility in Norway at the time.

Independence 1905-1940

238 **Haakon VII, the man and the monarch.**
Tim Greve, edited and translated from the Norwegian by T. K.
Derry. New York: Hippocrene Books, 1983. 212p. (Library of
Nordic Literature).

A biography of Norway's first modern king (1905-52), covering his entire life but
emphasizing his role as a constitutional monarch and his views on Norwegian
foreign policy. A somewhat abrreviated version of the original.

239 **Sweden, Norway, Denmark and Iceland in the World War.**
Eli Heckscher, Knut Bergendal, Wilhelm Keilhau, Einar Cohn,
Thorstein Thorsteinsson. New Haven, Connecticut: Yale
University Press; London: Humphrey Milford, Oxford University
Press, 1930. 593p. (Economic and Social History of the World
War).

Published for the Carnegie Endowment for International Peace, this is an

59

abridgement of the Scandinavian Series of nine monographs edited by Eli Heckscher and Harald Westergaard. Keilhau contributed the section on Norway (p. 281-407) emphasizing the difficulties in maintaining neutrality during the First World War and the economic implications of Norway's position.

240 **Hjort, Quisling, and Nasjonal Samling's disintegration.**
Oddvar Høidal. *Scandinavian Studies*, vol. 47, no. 4 (1975), p. 467-97.

A study of the breach that developed between Vidkun Quisling and his second-in-command, Johan B. Hjort during 1936. Hjort's resignation from the party in the following year was a major factor in the disintegration of the small Norwegian Fascist Party.

241 **Who were the Fascists? Social roots of European Fascism.**
Edited by Stein Ugelvik Larson, Bernt Hagtvet, Jan Petter Myklebust. Bergen, Norway: Universitetsforlaget, 1980. 816p. maps.

Contains articles discussing the development of Fascism in different parts of Europe and comparative studies seeking to establish common factors in the various movements. Ten of the articles (p. 586-750) deal with the development of Fascism in Scandinavia and five of those concern the development of the Nasjonal Samling (NS) party in Norway in the 1930s and its leader, Vidkun Quisling. Emphasis is on the groups and geographical regions that gave greatest support to the NS. Extensive notes at the end of each chapter indicate further reading that can be done on the subject. The authors of the articles on Norway are Stein Ugelvik Larsen, Jan Petter Myklebust, Bernt Hagtvet, Hans Hendriksen, Sten Spare Nilson, and Hans-Dietrich Loock.

242 **Scandinavia in great power politics 1905-1908.**
Folke Lindberg. Stockholm: Almqvist & Wiksell, 1957. 333p.
(Acta Universitatis Stockholmensis: Stockholm Studies in History).

The first part of this study is of the greatest interest as far as Norway is concerned because it deals with Norway's declaration of independence in 1905 and the Integrity Treaty that it eventually negotiated with the Great Powers. The second part describes Sweden's difficulties as it was caught between competing Russian and German interests in the Baltic during the same period.

243 **Haakon: King of Norway.**
Maurice Michael. New York: Macmillan; London: Allen & Unwin, 1958. 207p.

A biography linking Norway's first modern king (1905-1952) with the important events of his reign. Much of the work deals with the events in 1905 surrounding the proclamation of Norwegian independence from Sweden and Haakon's selection as king. Other events covered in detail include his role during the German invasion in the spring of 1940 and the following war years. It is an anecdotal account rather than a detailed study of the king as an administrator, yet it is worthwhile in terms of providing an understanding of the man and the modern Norwegian monarchy.

244 **The neutral ally: Norway's relations with belligerent powers in the First World War.**
Olav Riste. Oslo: Universitetsforlaget; London: George Allen & Unwin, 1965. 295p. bibliog. (Scandia Books).
This work, in three sections, deals primarily with the successful and prosperous neutral policy that Norway was able to carry out during the First World War, up to the autumn of 1916. Thereafter, Norway faced increasing difficulties particularly as a result of Germany's programme of submarine warfare.

The Second World War 1940- 1945

245 **Norway and the Second World War.**
Johannes Andenæs, Olav Riste, Magne Skodvin. Oslo: Johan Grundt Tanum Forlag, 1966. 168p. map. bibliog.
A valuable introduction to Norway's involvement in the Second World War by three of the country's foremost authorities on the subject. Discusses the diplomatic and military prelude to Norway's involvement in the war from 1939 to 1940, when both Britain and Germany became pre-occupied with Norway's increasing strategic importance; the efforts of Vidkun Quisling and German military officials to impose the 'New Order' on Norway; Norway's government-in-exile in London; the Norwegian contribution to the Allied war effort; and the post-war legal proceedings against Quisling and other collaborators.

246 **Norway 1940.**
Bernard Ash. London: Cassell, 1964. 340p. maps. bibliog.
A critical and thorough history of British military operations in Norway during the spring of 1940, which is still regarded as one of the best studies of the subject.

247 **Documents on international affairs: Norway and the war December 1939-December 1940.**
Edited by Monica Curtis. New York, London: Johnson Reprint, 1965. 154p.
An important selection of primary sources divided into three sections. Section one contains documents outlining Norway's neutral status prior to the war. Section two covers the crisis precipitated by the *Altmark* affair of February 1940, when British naval forces entered Norwegian waters to rescue prisoners of war from the German ship. The chapter also considers the mining of Norwegian territorial waters by Britain and France when Norway's neutrality seemed threatened as much by these powers as by Germany. The larger section of the work contains documents from the Norwegian government relating to Germany's invasion of Norway in 1940 and the efforts that were subsequently made to supplant the country's legal government. All non-English documents, except for one French document, have been translated into English.

248 **The campaign in Norway.**
T. K. Derry. London: HM Stationery Office, 1953. 246p. maps.
bibliog. (History of the Second World War).
This scholarly, detailed, and well-written account of British military activities in
Norway from April to June 1940 is still a basic reference work.

249 **The power of small states: diplomacy in World War II.**
Annette Baker Fox. Chicago: University of Chicago Press, 1959.
211p. bibliog.
The chapter entitled 'Norway: maritime neutral,' (p. 78-107) is an excellent, brief
introduction to Norwegian foreign policy from 1939 to 1940.

250 **The Norwegian government-in-exile, 1940-45.**
Erik J. Friis. In: *Scandinavian studies: essays presented to Henry
Goddard Leach*. Edited by Carl Bayerschmidt, Erik J. Friis.
Seattle, Washington: University of Washington Press, 1965,
p. 422-41.
Describes the impact that Trygve Lie had upon Norwegian foreign policy after
becoming Foreign Minister in late 1940. One of the few works to discuss this
aspect of the Second World War in any detail.

251 **Raeder, Hitler und Skandinavien: der Kampf für einen maritimen
Operationsplan.** (Raeder, Hitler and Scandinavia: the struggle for a
maritime operation plan.)
Carl-Axel Gemzell. Lund, Sweden: C. W. K. Gleerup, 1965.
390p. maps. bibliog. (Bibliotheca Historia Lundensis, no. 16).
Places the German naval attack on Norway of 9 April 1940 within the context of
German naval theory and the conflict within the German leadership before the
war.

252 **Norwegian resistance 1940-1945.**
Tore Gjelsvik, translated from the Norwegian by T. K. Derry.
Montreal: McGill-Queens' University Press, 1979. 224p. map.
An account of the civil resistance movement in Norway during the Second World
War, of which the author became a leader. The study is partly anecdotal in
character but also contains documents issued by both sides during the war and
makes reference to primary and secondary works which have been published
since. Originally published as *Hjemmefronten: den sivile motstand under
okkupasjonen 1940-1945* (Oslo: J. W. Cappellens Forlag, 1977).

253 **I saw it happen in Norway.**
Carl J. Hambro. London: D. Appleton-Century, 1943. 219p.
maps.
Studies the German attack on Norway of 9 April 1940 and King Haakon VII's
efforts to organize the country's resistance until his departure for England on 7

June. Hambro was then the President of the *Storting*, Norway's Parliament, and the President of the League of Nations. He provides a first-hand, often anecdotal account of the government's attempts to evade capture and regain the initiative. First published in London in 1940.

254   **Quisling: the career and political ideas of Vidkun Quisling.**
Paul M. Hayes.   Bloomington, Indiana: University of Indiana Press, 1972. 368p. bibliog.

The best work on Vidkun Quisling to date. It emphasizes his career prior to the German invasion of Norway that placed him in charge of the country's puppet government. An extensive and partially annotated bibliography enhances its value to the serious reader and the scholar.

255   **Quisling: prophet without honour.**
Ralph Hewins.   London; Toronto: Longmans, 1965; New York: John Day, 1966. 384p.

A biography exonerating Quisling's motives and conduct both before and during the German occupation in the Second World War. It de-emphasizes the similarity of his views with those of Hitler and their pre-war association and maintains that Quisling not only possessed the most honourable and wise policy for Norway before the war but also tried to maintain Norway's independence within the German Reich. This is a controversial work representing an extreme position in the post-war research and discussion on Quisling.

256   **Norway: neutral and invaded.**
Halvdan Koht.   London: Hutchinson, 1941. 224p.

Outlines Norwegian neutrality before the German invasion with the main emphasis on the invasion itself, the government's activities while still in Norway, and its reestablishment in England during the summer of 1940. The author was Norway's Foreign Minister during the crisis and this work offers interesting perspectives on the period. An appendix reprints relevant documents from the spring and summer of 1940.

257   **Hitler attacks Norway.**
Herman K. Lehmkuhl, introduction by Oscar Torp.   London: Hodder & Stoughton, 1943. 112p.

An account of Germany's invasion and conquest of Norway in 1940. Although designed to generate sympathy for Norway, it is remarkable for the degree of objectivity it possesses as a contemporary record of events. Republished in Montreal and New York by the Royal Norwegian Government Information Office in 1944.

258 **Quisling, Rosenberg, und Terboven: zur Vorgeschichte und Geschichte der nationalsozialistischen Revolution in Norwegen.**
(Quisling, Rosenberg, and Terboven: the pre-history and history of the national socialist revolution in Norway.)
Hans-Dietrich Loock.   Stuttgart, GFR: Deutsche Verlags-Anstalt, 1970. 588p. map. bibliog. (Quellen und Darstellung zur Zeitgeschichte, no. 18.).

A scholarly work describing the development of Vidkun Quisling's ideology of 'Nordic universalism' that paralleled similar lines of thought originated by Alfred Rosenberg in Germany. The author also discusses Quisling's contacts with Germany prior to the invasion of Norway, the struggle between Quisling and Josef Terboven for power from April to September 1940, and a similar conflict among Hitler's close advisors in Berlin.

259 **The Fascist economy in Norway.**
Alan S. Milward.   Oxford: Clarendon Press, 1972. 317p. bibliog.

Studies German economic policy in Norway during the Second World War, the results of their programme, and the implications of such a study on the idea of Fascism. Specific topics include a general overview of the Norwegian economy in the 1930s, German economic objectives in Norway, and their impact on Norwegian finance, aluminium industry, foreign trade, and fishing.

260 **The Norwegian campaign of 1940: a study of warfare in three dimensions.**
James Louis Moulton.   Athens, Ohio: Ohio University Press, 1968. 329p. maps. bibliog.

An analysis of the war in Norway in 1940 which was the first occasion when all three dimensions of warfare on land, air, and sea were involved. The emphasis is on the non-Norwegian combatants, the successful tactics employed by the Germans in all three dimensions, and the mistakes made by the British and French. Contains a valuable bibliography not only of Norwegian sources but also of important British secondary sources, such as regimental histories. An interesting final chapter on the Battle of Guadacanal in the Pacific during the Second World War serves as a 'yardstick' to measure the validity of the author's thesis. The work should be particularly valuable to those who require a detailed military history of the war in Norway.

261 **They came as friends.**
Tor Myklebost, translated from the Norwegian by Trygve M. Ager.   Garden City, New York: Doubleday, Doran, 1943. 297p.

An anecdotal account of the German occupation of Norway from 9 April 1940 until late 1942. The work emphasizes the resistance offered by all elements of Norwegian society to German rule and is representative of the significant amount of literature that appeared during the war echoing this theme.

262 **From day to day.**
Odd Nansen, translated from the Norwegian by Katherine
John. New York: G. P. Putnam's Sons, 1949. 485p.

A diary kept by the author, the son of Fridtjof Nansen, after his arrest by the
Germans on 13 January 1942 until 28 April 1945. The first part of his
imprisonment was spent in Norway and in October 1943 he was transferred to
Germany. An interesting portrayal of prison life during the Nazi rule of Norway.
Nansen had been a supporter of Quisling's movement for a short time during the
1930s although this is not considered in the book.

263 **Scandinavia during the Second World War.**
Edited by Henrik Nissen, translated by Thomas Munch-Petersen.
Minneapolis, Minnesota: University of Minnesota Press; Oslo:
Universitetsforlaget, 1983. 407p. maps. bibliog.

An excellent work containing eight articles by Scandinavian scholars covering the
region from the 1930s until 1949. Subjects treated include an article on the 1930s
background, Scandinavia as a disputed region among the Great Powers from 1939
to 1940, Finland's Winter War, the German invasion and occupation of Denmark
and Norway, the resistance movements, liberation in 1945, and the unsuccessful
attempts to establish a Nordic security pact after the war. Two Norwegian
historians participated in the project; Ole Kristian Grimnes contributed 'The
beginnings of the resistance movement,' (p. 182-220) and Berit Nøkleby wrote
'Adjusting to Allied victory,' (p. 279-323). A detailed and partially annotated
bibliography is particularly useful.

264 **The bitter years: the invasion and occupation of Denmark and
Norway April 1940 – May 1945.**
Richard Petrow. New York: William Morrow, 1974. 404p. maps.
bibliog.

A survey of the war years emphasizing the military aspect. Covers the invasion
and the military acts of resistance and sabotage in both countries with a
concluding chapter on German concentration camps and liberation in 1945. The
author relied mainly on English primary and secondary sources.

265 **Norway 1940-1945: the resistance movement.**
Olav Riste, Berit Nøkleby. Oslo: Johan Grundt Tanum Forlag,
1970. 93p. (Tokens of Norway).

An excellent introduction to Norway's resistance to Nazi rule. The two main
themes are the unsuccessful efforts made by Vidkun Quisling and the German
military officials to force Norway into acquiesence to German rule and the
development of the military resistance movement that sabotaged industrial and
commercial centres and maintained ties between Norway and her government-in-
exile in London.

266 **Industrial change in Norway during the Second World War:
electrification and electrical engineering.**
Olav Wicken. *Scandinavian Journal of History*, vol. 8, no. 2
(1983), p. 119-50.

Questions previous assumptions regarding the Norwegian economy during the
German occupation, and discusses other studies of the subject.

267 **Norway revolts against the Nazis.**
Jacob S. Worm-Müller. London: Lindsay Drummond, 1941.
152p. (Europe Under the Nazis).

One of the most perceptive accounts of conditions in Norway during 1940 and
1941 by a distinguished historian and a leader of Norway's Liberal Party. The
author was in Norway for most of this period and, as a party leader, was highly
aware of developments there.

268 **Norwegian diary 1940-1945.**
Myrtle Wright. London: Friends Peace Committee, 1974. 255p.

Wright was an English representative of the Friends Service Council of the
Society of Friends in Great Britain who happened to be in Oslo on 9 April 1940
and was forced to remain there until her escape to Sweden in 1944. She provides
an interesting report of daily life in Norway during the German occupation from
the standpoint of an outsider who became an insider as a result of her
experiences.

269 **The German Northern theater of operations 1940-1945.**
Earl F. Ziemke. Washington, DC: US Government Printing
Office, 1959. 342p. maps. bibliog. (Department of the Army
Pamphlet 20-271).

A narrative of German military operations in Norway and Finland during the
Second World War. Ziemke first provides a detailed description of the German
decision to invade Norway and the military operations there in 1940. He goes on
to discuss the breakdown of German-Soviet relations in 1941 and the consequent
use of German troops in Finland against the Russians. The final third of the work
studies the German presence in both countries from a common perspective until
the end of the war. One of the most detailed discussions of the Second World
War in English highlighting German activities.

Post Second World War

270 **Great Britain and the problem of bases in the Nordic areas 1945-1947.**
Knut Einar Eriksen. *Scandinavian Journal of History*, vol. 7, no. 2 (1982), p. 135-63.
A study of British diplomatic and military policy during the period with respect to three issues: revision of the treaty between Norway and Russia regarding Spitsbergen (Svalbard), the Russian occupation of Bornholm, and free Russian naval access to the Baltic. The first in particular brought them into an area where Norway clearly had different interests. The article is representative of the growing research interest in this period of Scandinavian history.

271 **America, Scandinavia and the Cold War 1945-1949.**
Geir Lundestad. New York: Columbia University Press, 1980. 434p.
A detailed narrative of US relations with the Scandinavian states from the end of the Second World War until the creation of the North Atlantic Treaty Organization (NATO). Much of the emphasis is on US policy and action and developments in Norway and Denmark, the two mainland Scandinavian states that joined Iceland in the alliance. The extensive endnotes are an important reading list on the subject.

272 **Winning the peace: vision and disappointment in Nordic security policy 1945-49.**
Karl Molin. In: *Scandinavia during the Second World War*. Edited by Henrik Nissen. Minneapolis, Minnesota: University of Minnesota Press, 1983, p. 324-82.
Briefly discusses domestic developments in the Scandinavian countries and provides a clear, detailed analysis of the military and defence policies followed by the Scandinavian states during the period. Particular emphasis is given to the discussions between Sweden, Norway, and Denmark of a neutral alliance among themselves or in conjunction with the Western powers (NATO). One of the clearest and most important studies to date of the events of this period.

273 **Norwegian attitudes to a Nordic nuclear-free zone 1958-1982.**
Rolf Tamnes. *Scandinavian Journal of History*, vol. 8, no. 4 (1983), p. 225-46.
Describes the position of the Norwegian government and its Labour Party allies towards the Nordic nuclear-free zone proposals presented by the USSR and the Finnish President Urho Kekkonen. The changes in the party's position from 1980 to 1982 are stressed.

274 **Great power politics and Norwegian foreign policy: a study of Norway's foreign relations November 1940 – February 1948.**
Nels Morten Udgaard.   Oslo: Universitetsforlaget, 1973. 319p. bibliog.

An analytical examination of Norwegian foreign policy with respect to the USA, Britain and the USSR. Udgaard traces three major developments during the period: the abandonment of pre-war neutrality by commitments made early in the war to Britain and the US for cooperation not only during the war but afterwards as well; the bridgebuilding policy begun later in the war out of concern for the reestablishment of Soviet power in the North; and the reassessment of this policy in 1947 which led later to Norway's adherence to NATO. Although modified by recent research in the field, this is an important and clear introduction to Norwegian policy, and also contains an extensive bibliography.

Historiography

275 **Snorri Sturluson.**
Marlene Ciklamini.   Boston, Massachusetts: Twayne, 1978. 188p. bibliog. (Twayne World Author's Series).

The only extensive study in English of Snorri Sturluson, (1178-1241), the great Icelandic poet and historian famous for his works of Norse mythology. Ciklamini provides a brief sketch of Sturluson's life, the major literary forces in Iceland prior to Snorri, and a lengthy discussion of the *Poetic Edda*, and the *Heimskringla*. Both works are examined chiefly from a literary point of view. The *Heimskringla*, one of the most eminent historical works of the mediaeval period, is concerned with the kings of Norway from the earliest times up to 1177.

276 **Scandinavian history in international research: some observations on Britain, France, West Germany and East Germany.**
Carl-Axel Gemzell.   *Scandinavian Journal of History*, vol. 5, no. 4 (1980), p. 239-56.

A detailed account of the research work done by historians as well as by some social scientists from these countries on Scandinavian topics.

277 **The early historians of Norway.**
William P. Ker. In: *Collected essays. Volume 2*. Edited and introduced by Charles Wibley.   London: Macmillan, 1925, p. 131-51.

Discusses historical accounts of Norway that pre-date Snorri Sturluson's *Heimskringla*. They are not only the first glimpses of Norway that we possess and the basis for Snorri's work, but they also contain incidents and a flavour not found in the great Icelandic historian's work.

278 **Sturla the historian.**
William P. Ker. In: *Collected essays.* Edited and introduced by
Charles Wibley. London: Macmillan, 1925, p. 173-95.
Provides a brief biographical sketch of Sturla Thordsson, a first cousin to Snorri
Sturluson, who left Iceland in 1204 for Norway. There he wrote *Hakonssaga*,
historically the richest and most accurate of the sagas, describing the government
and politics of King Hakon, son of King Sverre and heir to the Birkebeiner
tradition. A valuable introduction to the historian and his subject.

279 **Education of an historian.**
Halvdan Koht, translated from the Norwegian by Eric Wahlgren.
New York: Speller, 1957. 237p. (Makers of History Series).
An autobiographical account by Norway's most influential historian of the 20th
century (1873-1965) of his boyhood, education, and his career as a historian until
1920. It is worthwhile for its insights into Koht's life and views as well as for the
sketches it provides of other Norwegian historians of his time. Originally
published as *Historiker i lære* (Oslo, 1951).

280 **Driving forces in history.**
Halvdan Koht, translated from the Norwegian by Einar I. Haugen,
introduction by William L. Langer. New York: Atheneum, 1968.
217p.
A collection of essays which catch not only the ideas but also some of the flavour
and spirit of the historian. Although Koht addresses many general historical
themes, he finds many examples from Norwegian history to make his points. The
book was originally published in Norway as *Drivmakter i historie* (Oslo, 1959) and
the first edition in English appeared in 1964 (Cambridge, Massachusetts:
Harvard University Press).

281 **The strength of tradition: a historiographical analysis of research
into Norwegian agricultural history during the late Middle Ages and
the early modern period.**
Helge Salvesen. *Scandinavian Journal of History,* vol. 7, no. 2
(1982), p. 75-133.
An extensive study of a field of research that has long been an important branch
of Norwegian historical scholarship. Salvesen discusses in particular the impact of
Professor Andreas Holmsen and his students and Norwegian participation in *Det
nordiske ødegårdsprosjekt* (The Scandinavian Research Project on Deserted
Farms and Villages). The extensive footnotes form an important bibliography of
Norwegian research. For similar historiographical treatments of different periods
of agricultural and social history in the same journal, see Knut Helle's 'Norway in
the high Middle Ages: recent views on the structure of society,' vol. 6, no. 3
(1981), p. 161-89; and Kjell Haarstad's article on the 19th century, 'A
historiographical survey of *Det store hamskiftet* in Norwegian agriculture,' vol. 8,
no. 3 (1983), p. 151-70.

282 **Modern Norwegian historiography.**
Leslie F. Smith. Oslo: Norwegian Universities Press, 1962. 116p.
A survey of Norwegian historians and their work from the late 19th century until
the 1950s. While dealing briefly with the Norwegian Historical School of the 19th
century, and providing sketches of the major historians of the period, Smith deals
at length with Halvdan Koht, the most influential historian of the period. No
detailed studies of Norwegian historiography exist on a comparable scale to Ottar
Dahl's *Norsk historieforskning i 19. og 20. arhundre* (Norwegian historical
research in the 19th and 20th centuries), (Oslo: Universitetsforlaget, 1970,
originally 1959) or Nils Johan Ringdal's recent study *Statsoppfatningen hos Jens
Arup Seip* (Jens Arup Seip's concept of the state), (Oslo: Universitetsforlaget,
1981).

The voice of Norway.
See item no. 4.

Scandinavia past and present.
See item no. 10.

Mission to the North.
See item no. 37.

Historical geography in Scandinavia.
See item no. 51.

An historical geography of Scandinavia.
See item no. 57.

Norsk historisk atlas. (Norwegian historical atlas.)
See item no. 83.

Viking: hammer of the North.
See item no. 387.

The Norwegian church in its international setting.
See item no. 390.

**Rome and the Counter Reformation in Scandinavia until the establish-
ment of the *s. congregatio de propaganda fide* in 1622 based on the source
material in the Kolsrud collection.**
See item no. 393.

The fight of the Norwegian church against Nazism.
See item no. 396.

Church life in Norway 1800-1950.
See item no. 402.

Rebirth of Norway's peasantry: folk leader Hans Nielsen Hauge.
See item no. 404.

Pulpit under the sky: a life of Hans Nielsen Hauge.
See item no. 406.

History of the church and state in Norway from the tenth to the sixteenth century.
See item no. 410.

The earliest Norwegian laws: being the Gulathing and the Frostathing law.
See item no. 527.

The Eastern Greenland case in historical perspective.
See item no. 556.

Urbanization and community building in modern Norway.
See item no. 681.

The political sagas.
See item no. 700.

Sverrisaga: the saga of Sverrir of Norway.
See item no. 711.

Scandinavian Economic History Review.
See item no. 893.

Scandinavian Journal of History.
See item no. 894.

Scandinavian Studies.
See item no. 899.

Dictionary of Scandinavian history.
See item no. 906.

Bibliografi til Norges historie. (Bibliography of Norwegian history.)
See item no. 911.

Scandinavia in social science literature: an English language bibliography.
See item no. 920.

Scandinavian history 1520-1970: a list of books and articles in English.
See item no. 939.

Modern Explorers

General

283 **The book of Polar exploration.**
E. L. Elias, foreword by R. E. Priestley. London: Harrap, 1928.
302p.

An account of expeditions to the North and South Poles over the last few
centuries, thus placing Nansen's and Amundsen's exploits in their historical
context. It is perhaps too prone to hero-worship but is nevertheless a useful
introduction for the general reader.

284 **Great Norwegian expeditions.**
Thor Heyerdahl, Søren Richter, Hjalmar Reiser-Larsen. Oslo:
Dreyer Forlag, [1954]. 232p.

A useful introduction to modern Norwegian explorers. A brief introductory
chapter on the Vikings as explorers is followed by chapters by Søren Richter on
Fridtjof Nansen, Otto Sverdrup, Roald Amundsen and other late 19th- early 20th
century Norwegian explorers. Hjalmar Reiser-Larsen, a general in the Norwegian
Air Force who often accompanied Amundsen, wrote a chapter on the use of
aircraft for polar exploration, and Heyerdahl contributed a chapter on his Kon-
Tiki expedition. Published in Norwegian, *Store norske ekspedisjoner* in the same
year.

Roald Amundsen

285 **'The North West Passage': being the record of a voyage of exploration of the ship Gjøa 1903-1907 by Roald Amundsen with a supplement by First Lieutenant Hansen, vice-commander of the expedition.**
Roald Amundsen. London: Archibald Constable, 1908. 2 vols. maps.

A description of the trip, amply illustrated with photographs and sketches.

286 **Our Polar flight: the Amundsen-Ellsworth Polar flight.**
Roald Amundsen, Lincoln Ellsworth and other members of the expedition. New York: Dodd, Mead, 1926. 371p.

An account of the 1925 exploration of the Arctic in two seaplanes. The other contributors to the work were Hjalmar Reiser-Larsen, L. Dietrichson, Frederik Ramon, and Jakob Bjerkens.

287 **My life as an explorer.**
Roald Amundsen. Garden City, New York: Doubleday, Page, 1927. 282p. maps.

Amundsen's autobiography provides interesting insights into his life and journeys and has been a major source for later works on him. He does not, however, discuss his successful journey to the South Pole in 1911 in as much detail as some of his other expeditions and experiences. The book was first published in Norwegian in 1927, *Mitt liv som polarforsker* (Oslo: 1927) and thereafter translated into several languages.

288 **The South Pole: an account of the Norwegian Antarctic expedition on the *Fram* 1910-1912.**
Roald Amundsen, translated from the Norwegian by A. G. Chater, introduction by Fridtjof Nansen. London: Hurst, 1976. 2 vols. maps.

The first volume deals with Amundsen's preparations for the trip and his arrival at his winter camp and the second with his arrival at the South Pole after the 'race to the pole' that had developed with Robert Scott. Appendixes at the end of the second volume by Amundsen's colleagues provide additional scientific data secured during the trip.

289 **The last place on earth.**
Roland Huntford. New York: Atheneum, 1985. 565p. maps. bibliog.

The most recent work to concentrate on the race to the South Pole between Amundsen and Robert Scott in 1911. It was first published in 1979 as *Scott and Amundsen: the race to the South Pole.*

290 **Amundsen.**
  Bellamy Partridge.   London: Robert Hale, 1953. 206p. maps.
A biography for the general reader on Amundsen's whole career as an explorer.
For a brief article on Amundsen, see Ottar Raastad, 'Roald Amundsen: a
centennial contribution,' *Scandinavian Review*, vol. 60, no. 4 (1972), p. 392-400.

291 **Roald Amundsen, explorer.**
  Charles Turbey.   London: Methuen, 1935. 218p. maps.
This informative biography of the Norwegian explorer studies his discovery of the
South Pole on the 1910-1912 expedition and his later expeditions. The author
presents a favourable but also critical account, of interest particularly to the
general reader.

Fridtjof Nansen

292 **Farthest North.**
  Fridtjof Nansen, edited by Denys Thompson.   London: Chatto &
  Windus, 1955. 150p. maps. (The Queen's Classics).
A shortened version of Nansen's two-volume work first published in 1897
describing his Arctic voyage of 1893-1896 on the *Fram*. An interesting account for
the general reader, but those interested in the scientific data collected by Nansen
on the trip should consult the original work.

293 **Nansen: a family portrait.**
  Liv Nansen Høyer, translated from the Norwegian by Maurice
  Michael.   London: Longman, Green, 1957. 269p. maps.
A biographical account of Nansen by his daughter, discussing his explorations and
public activities. It is anecdotal in character and contains extracts from Nansen's
private correspondence with his first wife and personal recollections of the
author.

294 **Nansen the explorer.**
  Edward Shackleton.   London: H. F. & G. Witherby, 1959. 209p.
  maps.
Concentrates primarily on Nansen's two expeditions across Greenland in 1888-
1889 and to the Arctic on the *Fram* in 1893-1896, including his unsuccessful efforts
to reach the North Pole.

295   **Fridtjof Nansen: explorer-scientist-humanitarian.**
Per Vogt, Håkon Masby, Werner Werenskiold, Hjalmar Broch,
Bernh. Getz, Philip Noel-Baker, Leif Østby, Per Hokle, Johan B.
Hygen.   Oslo: Dreyer, 1961. 198p. map.
A commemorative work prepared on the 100th anniversary of Nansen's birth.
The authors present essays discussing Nansen's various scientific contributions and
three brief excerpts from Nansen's own writings are included. The longest essay is
by Vogt, 'Fridtjof Nansen: life and work', (p. 9-96). The work is illustrated by
several photographs of Nansen, drawings done by himself and, in an appendix, his
depiction by cartoonists.

296   **Fridtjof Nansen.**
Jacob S. Worm-Müller.   *Impact of Science on Society*, vol. 11
(1961), p. 223-56. bibliog.
A brief biographical sketch of Nansen's career and an assessment of his
achievements by a prominent Norwegian historian and close friend of the
explorer.

Thor Heyerdahl

297   **The Kon Tiki expedition.**
Thor Heyerdahl.   London: George Allen & Unwin, 1965. 224p.
map.
Heyerdahl's account of his voyage on the *Kon-Tiki* from Peru to Tahiti in 1947,
with many photographs from the voyage and other colour illustrations. First
published in Norwegian in 1948 as *Kon-Tiki ekspedisjon* (Oslo: Gyldendal Norsk
Forlag.) The first English translation appeared in 1950 and it has since been
reprinted several times in this language, as well as being translated into many
others.

298   **The *Ra* expeditions.**
Thor Heyerdahl, translated from the Norwegian by Patricia
Crampton and revised by the author.   New York: New American
Library, 1972. 365p. maps.
An account of Heyerdahl's two expeditions in 1968-1969 aboard *Ra* and *Ra II*
from Africa to the eastern coast of South America. Much of the book deals with
the origins of the trip and the experiences of *Ra I* with a briefer portion at the end
of the work on the more successful *Ra II*.

Modern Explorers. Thor Heyerdahl

299   **Early man and the ocean: the beginnings of navigation and seaborn civilizations.**
Thor Heyerdahl.   London: George Allen & Unwin, 1978. 392p. maps. bibliog.

A collection of Heyerdahl's scholarly reports and speeches edited to present his views on the inter-continental travel of early man. An extensive bibliography lists many references in several languages.

300   **The *Tigris* expedition: in search of our beginnings.**
Thor Heyerdahl.   London: George Allen & Unwin, 1981. 333p.

The explorer's account of the *Tigris* expedition of 1977-1978 when he and his crew sailed on a reed ship from the confluence of the Tigris and Euphrates Rivers in Iraq through the Persian Gulf and Arabian Sea to the Gulf of Aden and Djibouti.

301   **Thor Heyerdahl speaks his mind.**
Kurt Singer.   *Scandinavian Review*, vol. 68, no. 2 (1980), p. 31-41.

An interview with the famous explorer including comments on his *Kon-Tiki* and *Ra* expeditions. Photographs from these expeditions are also included.

Scandinavia and Scandinavians in the annals of the Royal Geographical Society, 1830-1914.
See item no. 56.

Thor Heyerdahl: modern Viking adventurer.
See item no. 751.

Roald Amundsen: first to the South Pole.
See item no. 753.

Fridtjof Nansen: Arctic explorer.
See item no. 754.

Population

General

302 **Population and settlement North of the Arctic Circle.**
Hallstein Myklebost. In: *Norway North of 65.* Edited by Ørnulf
Vorren. Oslo: Oslo University Press; London: George Allen &
Unwin, 1960, p. 134-46. bibliog. (Tromsø Museums Skrifter,
no. 8).

A demographic study of North Norway since the mid-19th century discussing
changes in the region's population and variations in population patterns. See also
Povl Simonsen's article, 'Settlement,' (p. 100-21), in the same book.

303 **Norway's population.**
Ørjar Øyen. In: *Norwegian society.* Edited by Natalie Rogoff
Ramsøy, translated by Susan Høivik. Oslo: Universitetsforlaget,
1974, p. 10-39.

A basic demographic study of Norway's population, examining the long-term
growth rate, its present composition, fertility and mortality rates, and migration
patterns.

Demographic studies

304 **Inn-og utvandring fra Norge 1958-1975.** (Immigration to and
    emigration from Norway 1958-1975.)
    Odd Aukrust, Knut Ø. Sørensen.   Oslo: Statistisk Sentralbyrå,
    1977. 97p. bibliog.
A statistical overview of migration to and from Norway with many tables and
charts. The text is in Norwegian but the tables and charts have English
translations and a brief English summary of the text is also provided (p. 84-86).

305 **Population and society in Norway 1735-1865.**
    Michael Drake.   Cambridge, England: Cambridge University
    Press, 1969. 256p. maps. bibliog. (Cambridge Studies in Economic
    History).
Includes discussions of such topics as the historical records available for
demographic study and their reliability, and the diet, health, and marriage
patterns of Norway's people. For a briefer study by the same author that discusses
some of these topics, see 'The growth of population in Norway, 1735-1855,'
Scandinavian Economic History Review, vol. 13, no. 2 (1965), p. 97-127.

306 **The demographic crises in Norway in the 17th and 18th centuries:**
    some data and interpretations.
    Ståle Dyrvik, Knut Mykland, Jan Oldervoll.   Bergen, Norway:
    Universitetsforlaget, 1976. 48p. maps.
The work consists of sixteen pages of text, seven maps, and eight tables. A brief
discussion of the demographic changes during the period and some of their
apparent causes is provided.

307 **The demographic history of the Northern European countries in the**
    eighteenth century.
    H. Gille.   *Population Studies*, vol. 3, no. 1 (1950), p. 3-65. bibliog.
A study of demographic conditions in Sweden, Denmark and Norway with
emphasis on the range of population movement, death-rates, marriage, and the
birth-rate. For an examination of the sources for such studies in Norway
published in the same journal see a series of three articles, 'Population statistics
and population registration in Norway.' In vol. 1, no. 2 (1947), see 'Part I: the
vital statistics of Norway: an historical overview,' by Julie E. Backer (p. 212-26),
'Part 2' by the same author in vol. 2, no. 3 (1948), p. 318-38; and 'Part 3:
population censuses' (p. 66-75), vol. 3, no. 1 (1950), by Kåre Ofstad.

308 **Trends in demographic structure in Norway 1960-2000.**
    Jon Inge Lian.   Oslo: Statistisk Sentralbyrå, 1981. 56p. bibliog.
    (Statistisk Sentralbyrå Artikler, no. 130).
A description of recent population trends in Norway and projections until 2000

AD. The article analyses demographic developments from 1960 to 1980 in terms of mortality, fertility, family formation and migration and the implications of the developments in terms of age, marital status, economic activity, and others. The last part of the work projects these developments to the year 2000.

309   **Norwegian population growth in the 19th century.**
       Sima Lieberman.   *Economy and History*, vol. 11 (1968), p. 52-66.
       bibliog.

Contains data on fertility rates, death rates, and other indices that Norway did not conform to the traditional pre-industrial population model during the period.

310   **Demographic developments and economic growth in Norway 1740-1940.**
       Thorvald Moe.   New York: Arno Press, 1977. 250p. bibliog.
       (Dissertation on European Economic History).

The publication of the author's dissertation completed at Stanford University in 1970. It is a detailed, econometric account of demographic developments and their economic consequences.

311   **Historical demography in Norway today: sources, literature and the present situation.**
       Sølvi Sogner. In: *Problèmes de mortalité: méthodes, sources et bibliographie en démographie historique. Actes du colloque international de démographie historique, Liège 18-20 avril 1963.* Edited by Paul Harris, Etienne Helen.   Liège, Belgium: Université de Liège, 1965, p. 199-216, bibliog.

The article is important for its discussion of the 17th and 18th century historical sources that are available, the list of church parish registers still existing, and the bibliography of demographic works on Norway that had been published by the early 1960s.

Genealogical study and research

312   **How to trace your ancestors in Norway.**
       Gunvald Bøe, Jan H. Olstad, Yngve Nedrebø.   Oslo: Royal Ministry of Foreign Affairs, 1984. 6th ed. 8p.

A brief pamphlet distributed without charge by the Ministry providing useful information on this subject. Included are addresses of organizations in the United States with materials helpful to the family researcher and of Norwegian archives which have relevant public documents. A brief summary is also provided of different types of Norwegian records that may be helpful. First published in 1959. For those able to read Norwegian see C. S. Schilbred, *Kjenn din slekt: Kort*

Population. Genealogical study and research

veiledning i slektsforskning (Oslo: Studentersamfundets Friundervisnings Forlag, 1974, 99p.) and Fin Michaelsen's *Slekten: innføring i ættegransking* (Oslo: Tanum-Norli, [1976]. 87p.).

313 **Standards and procedures for genealogical research in Norway.**
Salt Lake City, Utah: Genealogical Department of the Church of Jesus Christ of Latter-Day Saints, 1978. 12p. bibliog. (Series D, no. 1, 1977).

This pamphlet outlines some of the language and naming practices followed in Norway in the past that might pose problems for family researchers and the records that should be consulted in order to research the subject. Five other pamphlets are also available that discuss these subjects in more detail.

314 **So deep are my roots.**
Bent Vanberg. Minneapolis, Minnesota: Sons of Norway, 1977. 47p.

A brief guide first published in 1970 encouraging Norwegian-Americans to engage in genealogical work. It contains the names of pertinent organizations in both Norway and the United States providing useful information, addresses of research institutions in Oslo, and the *statsarkiver* (provincial archives) throughout Norway that contain public documents of interest for family history.

The travel diaries of Thomas Robert Malthus.
See item no. 38.

Nordic population mobility: comparative studies of selected parishes in the Nordic countries: a collective work of the Nordic Emigration Project.
See item no. 342.

Scandinavian Population Studies.
See item no. 897.

Minorities

General

315 **Ethnic minorities.**
Erik Allardt. In: *Nordic democracy: ideas, issues, and institutions in politics, economy, education, social and cultural affairs of Denmark, Finland, Iceland, Norway, and Sweden.* Edited by Erik Allardt, Nils Andrén, Erik J. Friis, Gylfi T. Gislason, Sten Sparre Nilson, Henry Valen, Frantz Wendt, Folmer Wisti. Copenhagen: Det Danske Selskab, 1981, p. 627-49. bibliog.

A brief survey of minority groups in the Nordic states, including the Finnish-speaking peoples of North Norway, the Lapps, Jews, gypsies, and recent immigrants, particularly from Southern Europe.

316 **'What fine people we are'.**
Gunnar Bull Gundersen, Berit Løfnes, translated from the Norwegian by Amanda Langemo. *Scandinavian Review*, vol. 66, no. 1 (1978), p. 60-65.

An article taken from the postscript of *Vi er så gode så* (What fine people we are), (Oslo: H. Aschehoug, 1975). It describes the difficulties encountered particularly by foreign workers and also contains brief excerpts from Gunderson's interviews with foreign workers.

Lapps

317 The Lapps.
Roberto Bosi. London: Thames & Hudson, 1960. 220p. maps. bibliog. (Ancient Peoples and Places).

A general study of the Lapps as a people with little reference to national borders. The volume is divided into four parts describing their origins and historical development; life and culture; religious beliefs and legends; and their identity as a people. A solid study for both general readers and scholars in the field.

318 The Lapps.
Björn Collinder. New York: Greenwood Press, 1969. 252p. maps. bibliog.

This survey of the Lapps and Lapp life was first published by Princeton University Press for the American-Scandinavian Foundation in 1949. Collinder describes the development of the Lapps in Norway, Sweden, and Finland, their culture, and livelihood. An excellent survey for both the scholar and general reader.

319 Changing Lapps: a study in culture relations in northernmost Norway.
Gutorm Gjessing. London: London School of Economics and Political Science, 1954. 70p. maps. bibliog. (Monographs on Social Anthropology, no. 13).

A scholarly study based on several lectures and papers delivered by the author in 1952. Gjessing provides a detailed discussion of Lapp development in both pre-historic and historic times and studies the characteristics of sea, land, and reindeer Lapps as they have developed in Norway, including some of the changes they have undergone in the 20th century.

320 The Laplanders: Europe's last nomads.
Per Høst. Oslo: Dreyer Forlag, 1964. 112p.

A brief photographic introduction depicting the life of the Lapps. The photographs were taken on several trips to Northern Norway and Finland by the author and others.

321 Lapps and Norsemen in olden times.
Oslo: Universitetsforlaget, 1967. 168p. (Institutet for sam-menlignende kultureforskning, Series A: forelesninger, vol. 26).

Six lectures read at a conference sponsored by the Institute for Comparative Research in Human Culture in Oslo, November 19-21, 1964. Most of the presentations centered on relations between Lapps and Scandinavians in the North Cape region in pre-historic times and are of interest to linguists, archaeologists, anthropologists, and cultural historians.

322 **Introducing the Lapps.**
Asbjørn Nesheim.   Oslo: Tanum-Norli, 1977. 56p. (Tokens of Norway).
A survey of the Lapps, first published in 1969, discussing their origin, development, social customs, religion, music, and present status.

323 **The Lappish nation: citizens of four countries.**
Karl Nickul.   Bloomington, Indiana: Indiana University Press, 1977. 134p. maps. bibliog. (Indiana University Publications: Uralic and Altaic Series).
An abridged version of *Saamelaiset kansana ja kansalaisana* published in 1970 by the Society for Finnish Literature, this work provides a study of the Lapps in Norway, Sweden, Finland and, to a lesser extent, Russia. An introduction to the Lapps living in different regions and with different forms of livelihood is followed by a more detailed study of the relationship that has existed in the past as well as the present between the Lapps and the governments that rule the region. There is a detailed bibliography; 268 plates of photographs; drawings; and maps are included as an appendix.

324 **The Lapps.**
Arthur Spencer.   New York: Crane, Russak; Newton Abbot, England: David & Charles, 1978. 160p. maps. bibliog. (This Changing World).
An introduction to the Lapps discussing their development, the importance of the reindeer to their livelihood in some areas, their culture and society, and elements of change in their present life.

325 **Lapp life and customs: a survey.**
Ørnulf Vorren, Ernst Manker, translated from the Norwegian by Kathleen McFarlane.   London: Oxford University Press, 1962. 183p. map. bibliog.
First published as *Same kulturen: en oversikt* (Lapp culture: an overview) (Oslo: Oslo University Press: 1957), this volume briefly discusses the existent evidence of Lapp development and in more detail the material culture forms of the mountain, coast, forest, and Skalt Lapps. Manker describes Lapp intellectual and cultural forms and Vorren concludes the work with a discussion of their social organization and their relationship with other groups within the Scandinavian states. For a brief survey of the Lapps by Vorren, see the article 'Lapps,' (p. 122-33) in *Norway North of 65* (q.v.).

Gypsies

326 **Gypsies.**
Erik J. Friis. *Scandinavian Review*, vol. 66, no. 1 (1978), p. 26-27.

A brief summary of the presence and status of gypsies in Scandinavia. The article is part of a special issue of *Scandinavian Review* devoted entirely to Scandinavian minorities.

327 **Norway's gypsy minority.**
Unn Jørstad. *Scandinavian Review*, vol. 58, no. 2 (1970), p. 129-37.

Discusses the difficulties associated with the reconciliation of gypsy beliefs and lifestyle with the attempts to provide assistance for them.

Jews

328 **Action or assimilation: a Jewish identity crisis.**
Morton H. Narrowe. *Scandinavian Review*, vol. 66, no. 1 (1978), p. 47-52.

A first hand account of the development of Jewish communities in each of the Scandinavian states, including those in Trondheim and Oslo. For a more detailed study in Norwegian see, Oskar Mendelsohn's *Jødernes historie i Norge gjennom 300 år* (Oslo: Universitetsforlaget, 1969, 698p.).

The Scandinavian northlands.
See item no. 64.

The North Cape and its hinterland.
See item no. 65.

The Arctic Highway: a road and its setting.
See item no. 644.

The land of the long night.
See item no. 748.

Overseas Population

General

329 **The Norwegian-Americans.**
Arlow W. Anderson, foreword by Franklin D. Scott. Boston,
Massachusetts: Twayne, 1975. 274p. bibliog.
A survey of the Norwegian-American immigration experience. Anderson
discusses the cultural and social manifestations of this phenomenon in chapters on
the immigrant press, religion, education, social and cultural organizations,
literature, and the success of Norwegian-Americans in many fields. An extensive
bibliography reflects the voluminous research that has been done on this topic.

330 **West of the Great Divide: Norwegian migration to the Pacific coast
1847-1893.**
Kenneth O. Bjork.   Northfield, Minnesota: Norwegian-American
Historical Association, 1958. 671p. maps.
An account of Norwegian migration beyond the Midwest and the Rockies during
the last half of the 19th century. Settlement in Utah, California, Oregon, and
Washington is emphasized, as are individuals such as Snowshoe Thompson, and
institutions such as the immigrant press and church.

331 **Scandinavian migration to the Canadian prairie provinces, 1893-
1914.**
Kenneth O. Bjork.   *Norwegian-American Studies*, vol. 26 (1974),
p. 3-30.
Describes the successful efforts of Canadian officials to recruit Scandinavian
settlers to the provinces of Saskatchewan, Alberta, and Manitoba. Most of the
Scandinavian settlers had first migrated to the United States and then sought a

better livelihood in Canada. For a further study on Norwegian settlement in
British Columbia by the same author, see 'The founding of Quatuno colony,'
Norwegian-American Studies, vol. 25 (1972), p. 80-164.

332 **Norwegian migration to America: the American transition.**
Theodore C. Blegen. Northfield, Minnesota: Norwegian-
American Historical Association, 1940. 655p.
A discussion of Norwegian immigration after 1860, focusing particularly on their
institutions in the New World such as the immigrant press and educational forms
during the last half of the 19th century.

333 **Land of their choice: the immigrants write home.**
Edited by Theodore C. Blegen. Minneapolis, Minnesota:
University of Minnesota Press, 1955. 463p.
A collection of letters written by Norwegian-American immigrants during the
19th century, reflecting immigrant life in some states, for example, Illinois and
Wisconsin, and illustrating basic aspects of their life, such as religion.

334 **Norwegian migration to America: 1825-1860.**
Theodore C. Blegen. New York: Arno Press and the New York
Times, 1969. 413p. maps.
First published in 1931 by the Norwegian-American Historical Association,
Blegen's work remains an important study of the entire phenomenon and of the
first wave of migration in particular. Topics discussed include the reasons for
emigration and the Norwegian government's response to it; the places in the
United States where settlement by Norwegian-Americans was greatest; and the
immigrants' songs, poems, and letters home.

335 **The Scandinavian presence in North America.**
Edited by Erik J. Friis. New York: Harper Magazine Press
[Harper & Row], 1976. 266p.
The proceedings of the Seminar on the Scandinavian Presence in America, held
in Minneapolis, Minnesota, May 2-3, 1973. The theme of the conference was the
continued Scandinavian presence in the United States through the influence of
religious, fraternal, and scholarly groups representing the Scandinavian-American
community, the teaching of Scandinavian studies within the American educational
system, and the publication of Scandinavian-American newspapers, and literary
publications.

336 **The Scandinavians in America 986-1970: a chronology and fact
book.**
Edited and compiled by Howard B. Furer. Dobbs Ferry, New
York: Oceana Publications, 1972. 154p. bibliog. (Ethnic Chron-
ology Series no. 6).
The work is divided into two sections that provide a chronological account of
Scandinavian migration to America from the 17th century until the present and
selected primary sources representing immigrant life there.

337 **The Americanization of Norwegian immigrants: a study in historical sociology.**
Stanley S. Guterman. *Sociology and Social Research*, vol. 58, no. 3 (1968), p. 252-70.
Contrasts the acculturation of Norwegian-Americans who settled in ethnically diverse urban areas with those who settled in rural areas which had a greater degree of ethnic homogeneity.

338 **Norway's organized response to emigration.**
Arne Hassing. *Norwegian-American Studies*, vol. 25 (1972), p. 54-79.
Describes the efforts of a Norwegian association that attempted from 1907 to 1914 to prevent the emigration from Norway of skilled workmen or of labourers from areas with labour shortages.

339 **The Norwegians in America 1825-1875.**
Einar I. Haugen. Oslo: Royal Ministry of Foreign Affairs, [1975]. 36p. maps. bibliog.
A brief introduction providing a summary of places of settlement, daily life, church affiliation, and cultural contributions.

340 **Norwegians in America: the last migration: bits of saga from pioneer life.**
Hjalmar Rued Holand, translated from the Norwegian by Helmer M. Blegen, edited by Evelyn Ostraat Wierenga. Sioux Falls, South Dakota: Center for Western Studies, Augustana College, 1978. 240p.
A pioneer Norwegian-American scholar, chiefly remembered for his unflagging efforts to promote the veracity of the Kensington Stone, Holand also wrote on Norwegian immigration to the United States. Blegen's translation is of Holand's work in 1930 *Den siste folkevandring: sagaastubbar fra nybyggerlivet i America*, an edited version of his 1908 study *De norske settlementers historie*. This survey of the entire immigrant experience provides vignettes of the Norwegian settlement primarily of the Upper Midwest, describing pioneer life as experienced by individuals and Norwegian communities.

341 **Scandinavian immigration and settlements in Australia before World War II.**
Olari Koivukangas. Turku, Finland: Kokkala, 1974. 333p. map. bibliog. (Migration Studies C2, Institute for Migration, Turku, Finland).
This scholarly study provides a chronological examination of Scandinavian emigration. Much of the work concentrates on the period 1870 to 1914 and attempts to treat the Scandinavian settlement of different parts of Australia separately, as well as to discuss the Scandinavian press that existed then. A separate chapter describes some of the basic demographic features of Scandin-

avian migration. For a briefer study, see Dudley Glass's 'Scandinavian builders of Australia,' *Scandinavian Review*, vol. 60, no. 1 (1972), p. 28-36.

342 **Nordic population mobility: comparative studies of selected parishes in the Nordic countries: a collective work of the Nordic Emigration Research Project.**
Bo Kronborg, Thomas Nilsson, Andres A. Svalistuen. *American Studies in Scandinavia*, vol. 9, nos. 1-2 (1977), p. 1-156. maps.

A double issue of the journal devoted to articles representing the results of the special research project by historians from all of the Nordic states. Two articles of importance with respect to Norway are Ingrid Semmingsen's 'Origin of Nordic emigration,' (p. 9-16) and Andres A. Svalestuen's 'Five local studies of Nordic emigration and migration,' (p. 17-63) in which one of the local studies is that by Elisabeth Koren, 'Utvandringen fra Ullensaker, 1867-99' (Emigration from Ullensaker, 1867-99), a Norwegian parish. The issue is important for the links it established between economic and social changes and movement within Scandinavia during the 19th century and for its work on Scandinavian migrants within the United States. It is indicative of the interest shown in this phenomenon among Scandinavian as well as American scholars. For another work of the same type, involving both American and Scandinavian scholars, see *Scando-Americana: papers on Scandinavian emigration to the United States*, edited by Ingrid Semmingsen and Per Seyersted, (Oslo: American Institute, University of Oslo, 1980, 213p.).

343 **The changing West and other essays.**
Laurence M. Larson, preface by Theodore C. Blegen. Northfield, Minnesota: Norwegian-American Historical Association, 1937. 180p.

A collection of essays by a prominent Norwegian-American scholar. Of particular importance are 'The Norwegian element in the field of American scholarship,' (p. 16-38), 'Hjalmar Hjorth Boyesen,' (p. 82-115), and '*Skandinaven*, Professor Anderson, and the Yankee school,' (p. 116-46).

344 **Makers of an American immigrant legacy: essays in honor of Kenneth O. Bjork.**
Edited by Odd S. Lovoll. Northfield, Minnesota: Norwegian-American Historical Association, 1980. 223p. bibliog.

A Festshrift to Bjork, the distinguished Norwegian-American scholar. Most of the essays discuss prominent Norwegian-Americans or related themes. The collection includes John R. Christianson's 'Literary traditions of Norwegian-American women,' (p. 92-110), Arlow W. Anderson's, 'Senator Knute Nelson: Minnesota's Grand Old Man and the Norwegian immigrant press,' (p. 29-49), and Terje I. Leiren's, 'Halvdan Koht's America,' (p. 173-85).

345 **The promise of America: a history of the Norwegian-American people.**
Odd S. Lovoll.   Minneapolis, Minnesota: University of Minnesota Press in cooperation with the Norwegian-American Historical Association, 1984. 239p. maps. bibliog.

A richly illustrated survey of the Norwegians who migrated to America from 1825 until after the First World War and their descendants in the New Land. Lovoll considers all aspects of their development in America: their settlements, customs, language, religion, education, and eventual assimilation into mainstream America. The volume is informative, easy-to-read, and provides a first-rate introduction. This work differs from other studies of the subject in its illustrations and approach, but together with *Norway to America: a history of the migration* (q.v.), it provides a solid background, based on recent research. First published in cooperation with the Norwegian-American Historical Association as *Det løfterike landet* (Oslo: Universitetsforlaget, 1983).

346 **The Scandinavians in Australia, New Zealand and the Western Pacific.**
J. Lyng.   Melbourne, Australia: Melbourne University Press, 1939. 207p.

Most of the work is devoted to a discussion of the Scandinavians in Australia with briefer studies of the other regions mentioned in the title. In all cases, an effort is made to describe the settlement in the area, and the forms of church and social life which the migrants have attempted to establish. The greater presence of Scandinavians in Australia permits an examination of their press there and of the commercial contacts with Scandinavia that have developed.

347 **Norwegian influence on the upper Midwest: proceedings of an international conference, University of Minnesota, Duluth; Duluth, Minnesota, May 22-24, 1975.**
Edited by Harald S Naess.   Duluth, Minnesota: Continuing Education and Extension, University of Minnesota, 1976. 126p.

Seventeen essays on various aspects of Norwegian-American life are included, along with studies of the contribution of Norwegian-Americans to the politics, folk art, and literature of their adopted country.

348 **Norwegian settlement in the United States.**
Carlton C. Qualey.   Northfield, Minnesota: Norwegian-American Historical Association, 1938. 285p. maps. bibliog.

A detailed and very readable study of some of the reasons for migration and an account of Norwegian settlement of each of the states of the Upper Middle West: Wisconsin, Iowa, Minnesota, South Dakota, North Dakota, and Michigan. An appendix provides census data relating to Scandinavian immigration for the period 1850 to 1900.

349 **The divided heart: Scandinavian immigrant experience through literary sources.**
Dorothy Burton Skårdal, preface by Oscar Handlin. Oslo: Universitetsforlaget; Lincoln, Nebraska: University of Nebraska Press, [1974]. 394p. bibliog. (Publications of the American Institute, University of Oslo).

This important study of Scandinavian immigrants in the United States considers the theme of success, changes in immigrant institutions, values and morals, and the cost of success, as well as 'the divided heart.' Includes an extensive bibliography of Scandinavian-American literature and an index of Scandinavian immigrant authors.

350 **Norway to America: a history of the migration.**
Ingrid Semmingsen, translated by Einar I. Haugen. Minneapolis, Minnesota: University of Minnesota Press, 1978. 213p. maps. bibliog.

A study of the entire migration experience: the periods of migration, the factors involved, individuals who contributed to the immigration process and the process of assimilation necessary for Norwegians to become Americans. Published originally in Norwegian as *Drøm og dåd* (Oslo: H. Aschehoug (W. Nygaard), 1975) on the 150th anniversary of the first organized Norwegian migration to America. Semmingsen is one of Norway's finest historians and one of the first Norwegians to promote migration studies there. For a shorter account of the subject, see her article, 'Norwegian emigration in the nineteenth century,' *Scandinavian Economic History Review*, vol. 8, no. 2 (1960), p. 150-60.

Individual accounts

351 **Cleng Peerson and the communitarian background of Norwegian immigration.**
Mario S. DePillis. *Norwegian-American Studies*, vol. 21 (1962), p. 36-57.

A study of the 'father of Norwegian immigration,' who assisted the first large-scale migration of Norwegians in America in 1825. The article discusses in particular his possible communitarian views as they may have been revealed in land purchases for members of the group in 1824 and 1826.

352 **Thorstein Veblen and his America.**
Joseph Dorfman. New York: Viking Press, 1945. 556p. bibliog.

The opening chapters of this biography of the Norwegian-American economist describe his boyhood experiences. First published in 1934.

353 **Theodore C. Blegen: a memoir.**
John T. Flanagan. Northfield, Minnesota: Norwegian-American
Historical Association, 1977. 181p. bibliog. (Authors Series, no.
4).

This biography of Blegen discusses all aspects of his life and work and should be valuable to all who are interested in history and Norwegian-American studies. Blegen was for many years a professor of history and administrator at the University of Minnesota, director of the Minnesota Historical Society, active leader of the Norwegian-American Historical Association, and scholar.

354 **Ole Edvart Rølvaag.**
Einar Haugen. Boston, Massachusetts: Twayne, 1983. 164p.
bibliog. (Twayne's United States Author Series).

A study of Rølvaag's life and particularly his literary works. Special consideration is given to his masterpiece *Giants in the earth* and to the two final works in his trilogy of Norwegian-America, *Peder victorious* and *Their father's God*.

355 **Rasmus Bjorn Anderson: pioneer scholar.**
Lloyd Hustvedt, foreword by Kenneth O. Bjork. Northfield,
Minnesota: Norwegian-American Historical Association, 1966.
381p. bibliog. (Authors Series, no. 2).

Rasmus B. Anderson was one of the first Norwegian-Americans to obtain a professorship in a large American university, the University of Wisconsin, and to promote Scandinavian studies in the United States. This biography discusses those aspects of his life and also concentrates on his editorship of a Norwegian-American newspaper, *Amerika*, in Madison, Wisconsin from 1898 to 1922.

356 **Ole Edvart Rølvaag: a biography.**
Theodore Jorgenson, Nora O. Solum. New York: Harper &
Brothers, 1939. 446p.

A detailed, sympathetic biography of the Norwegian-American writer by a colleague of Rølvaag's at St. Olaf College. It is based to a considerable extent on Rølvaag's correspondence which is quoted extensively.

357 **Moorings old and new: entries in an immigrant's log.**
Paul Knaplund, foreword by Merle Curti. Madison, Wisconsin:
State Historical Society of Wisconsin, 1963. 276p.

A distinguished American historian's memoirs of his boyhood in the Lofoten Islands of Norway, migration to the United States in 1906, and early career as a teacher and college professor.

358 **Laur. Larsen: pioneer college president.**
Karen Larsen. Northfield, Minnesota: Norwegian-American
Historical Association, 1936. 358p.

A biography of the early Norwegian-American educator by his daughter, who later distinguished herself as a scholar through her *History of Norway*. The work traces the elder Larsen's career from his childhood in Norway through his work in America as a Minnesota parish pastor, teacher at Concordia College in St. Louis, and primarily his service at Luther College from 1861 to 1902.

359 **Søren Jaabæk: Americanizer in Norway: a study in cultural exchange.**
Franklin D. Scott. *Norwegian-American Studies and Records*, vol. 17 (1952), p. 84-107.

Søren Jaabæk, a Norwegian radical peasant politician (1814-1894), and editor of the newspaper *Folketidende* reluctantly supported emigration and used the United States as a model for the social and political forms that Norway should possess. If Norway influenced America through emigration, then Jaabæk's work is an example of the reverse also being true. This article has been reprinted in the author's *Trans-atlantica: essays on Scandinavian migration and culture*, New York: Arno Press, 1979. For a further study by the author on the same theme, see 'American influence in Norway and Sweden,' *Journal of Modern History*, vol. 18, no. 1 (1946), p. 37-47, which is reprinted in *Trans-atlantica*.

Education

360 **From fjord to freeway: 100 years Augsburg College.**
Carl H. Chrislock, foreword by Oscar A. Anderson.
Minneapolis, Minnesota: Augsburg College, 1969. 262p.

A centennial history commemorating the founding of the college in 1869 after disputes between Swedish and Norwegian church leaders led to the school's separation from Augustana College in Rock Island, Illinois and its eventual location in Minneapolis. The college is representative of the colleges established in America with roots in Norwegian emigration to America.

361 **Cooperation in Scandinavian-American studies.**
John R. Christianson. *Swedish-American Historical Quarterly*, (1984), p. 374-86.

A brief summary of some of the joint ventures in the United States to promote Scandinavian-American studies. The article is particularly useful for its discussion of scholarly and popular programmes in the field during recent years.

362 **A perspective on Scandinavian studies in the United States.**
Robert B. Kvavik. *Scandinavian Studies*, vol. 54, no. (1982), p. 1-20.

One of the latest analyses of: undergraduate and graduate programmes in Scandinavian studies in the United States; problems relating to academic research in this field; and difficulties of library and archival holdings. The endnotes are particularly valuable for their reference to the relevant articles that have been published in the United States since 1911.

363 **Luther College 1861-1961.**
David T. Nelson, foreword by J. W. Ylvisaker. Decorah, Iowa: Luther College Press, 1961. 429p.

A centennial history of Luther College describing its origins, early history, increasing adaptation to the assimilation process and development as an American undergraduate institution.

364 **Cobber chronicle: an informal history of Concordia College.**
Erling Nicolas Rolfsrud, foreword by Joseph L. Knutson. Moorhead, Minnesota: Concordia College, 1966. 240p.

Part one provides a chronological narrative of the college from 1891 to the mid-1960s and part two discusses the many extra-curricular activities that developed there. Emphasis in the first section is on the roots of the college in the Norwegian Lutheran immigrants of the region and the ties that were maintained between the college, Norway, and the Norwegian-American tradition.

365 **History of St. Olaf College 1874-1974.**
Joseph M. Shaw. Northfield, Minnesota: St. Olaf College Press, 1974. 694p.

The history of the college from its founding until 1974, describing its roots in the Norwegian-American community of the Upper Midwest and its evolution into a modern American college.

366 **Through trials and triumphs: a history of Augustana College.**
Donald Sneen. Sioux Falls, South Dakota: Center for Western Studies, Augustana College, 1985. 195p.

Traces the history of the college from its founding in 1860 in Illinois as a cooperative venture with Swedish Lutherans, its 'migratory' phase as the two groups went their separate ways, its establishment in South Dakota from the Augustana Academy and the Lutheran Normal School, and the institution's modern era up to the 1980s.

Organizations

367 **The American-Scandinavian Foundation 1910-1960: a brief history.**
Erik J. Friis, introduction by Lithgow Osborne. New York:
American-Scandinavian Foundation, 1961. 135p.

Outlines the first fifty years of the organization including the development of its programme of activities. Appendixes cover the foundation's charter; lists of those who received fellowships from it during this period; and its extensive publications. For a briefer and more recent study see C. Peter Strong, 'The foundation's story,' *Scandinavian Review*, vol. 64, no. 2 (1976), p. 38-45.

368 **A folkepic: the *bygdelag* in America.**
Odd S. Lovoll. Boston, Massachusetts: Twayne for the
Norwegian-American Historical Association, 1975. 326p. maps.

An informative chronological study of the *bygdelag* associations throughout America which link Norwegian-Americans with others who have emigrated from the same region of Norway. Includes descriptions of the emigrants' origins, their period of greatest influence and popularity immediately prior to the First World War, and gradual decline thereafter. An appendix lists the various *bygdelags* that developed and, where possible, their major officers.

369 **The Norwegian-American Historical Association 1925-1975.**
Odd S. Lovoll, Kenneth O. Bjork. Northfield, Minnesota:
Norwegian-American Historical Association, 1975. 72p.

A brief description of the organization's origins, development, membership and publications.

370 **An American saga.**
C. Sverre Norborg. Minneapolis, Minnesota: Sons of Norway,
1970. 232p.

Written in honour of the 75th anniversary of the Sons of Norway fraternal organization, this is a detailed account of the organization's founding in 1895 and the spread of its local branches.

Special studies

371 **The immigrant takes his stand: the Norwegian-American press and public affairs, 1847-1872.**
Arlow W. Anderson.   Northfield, Minnesota: Norwegian-American Historical Association, 1953. 176p. bibliog.

Studies the positions taken by prominent Norwegian-American newspapers on important issues in American politics during the period, such as foreign policy, slavery, the 1860 election, the Union cause in the Civil War, and reconstruction policy.

372 **The salt of the earth: a history of Norwegian-Danish Methodism in America.**
Arlow W. Anderson.   Evanston, Illinois: Norwegian-Danish Methodist Historical Society, 1962. 338p. bibliog.

Describes the growth of Methodism among Norwegian and Danish-Americans beginning in the 1840s. The work is primarily the story of the Norwegian-Danish Conference that had responsibility for the church's work among Scandinavians until 1943.

373 **Saga in steel and concrete: Norwegian engineers in America.**
Kenneth O. Bjork.   Northfield, Minnesota: Norwegian-American Historical Association, 1947. 504p.

Studies the migration from Norway to America of men already educated as engineers who later made significant contributions in the construction industry, machinery, chemical processes, and industrial techniques.

374 **Norwegian emigrant songs and ballads.**
Edited and translated by Theodore C. Blegen, Martin B. Ruud.   New York: Arno Press, 1979. 350p. (Scandinavians in America).

This collection represents the various experiences of Norwegian emigrants. For each song the authors provide a short introduction, and the songs are in Norwegian and in an English translation. The recent reissue of this work, originally published in 1936 by the University of Minnesota Press and Oxford University Press, indicates its continued importance.

375 **Peter J. Rosendahl: Han Ola og Han Per: a Norwegian-American comic strip.**
Edited by Joan N. Buckley, Einar I. Haugen.   Oslo: Universitetsforlaget, 1984. 165p. bibliog. (Institute for Comparative Research in Human Culture, Oslo, Serie B: Skrifter 69).

From 1918 to 1935 a regular feature of the Norwegian-American newspaper *Decorah-Posten* was the comic strip 'Hans Ola og Han Per' drawn by Peter J.

95

Rosendahl, a Minnesota farmer. This work reprints the first 233 of the 599 strips that Rosendahl produced. In addition to preparing the strips for publication, there are brief essays on the humour expressed in the comic strips and the language used. The essays are in both English and Norwegian, there are English translations of the comic strip captions and Norwegian translations of the American-Norwegian expressions of the characters. A valuable work preserving important documents of Norwegian immigrant life in America.

376   **Scandinavians in America: literary life.**
      Edited by John R. Christianson.   Decorah, Iowa: Symra Literary
      Society, 1985. 342p.
Twenty-three articles by Scandinavian and American scholars on the literary interaction among Scandinavian immigrants in America. Eight of the articles deal directly with Norwegian-American literary themes and an equal number emphasize cross-Scandinavian topics.

377   **Norwegian sailors in American waters: a study in the history of**
      maritime activity on the Eastern seaboard.
      Knut Gjerset, preface by Theodore C. Blegen.   Northfield,
      Minnesota: Norwegian-American Historical Association, 1933.
      271p.
This study goes back to the Vikings but concentrates particularly on the Norwegian sailors and captains who served in the maritime occupations along the East Coast of the United States from about 1825 until the 1920s. It is a detailed and professional approach to an interesting topic. For a briefer and more recent study, see Lars Tangeraas' article of the same name in *Scandinavian Studies*, vol. 52, no. 2 (1982), p. 137-47. Gjerset's earlier work, *Norwegian sailors on the Great Lakes* (Northfield, Minnesota: Norwegian-American Historical Association, 1928), covers similar ground.

378   **Homeward to Zion: the Mormon migration from Scandinavia.**
      William Mulder, foreword by Oscar Handlin.   Minneapolis,
      Minnesota: University of Minnesota Press, 1957. 375p.
Describes the development of the Mormon Church in Scandinavia and the migration of Scandinavian Mormons from 1849 to 1905. Mulder discusses the missionary work of the Mormon Church in Scandinavia, migration experiences of Mormon converts to Utah, and their experiences there. The standard work on this aspect of Scandinavian emigration. In addition to articles by the author on the same subject, cited in the end-notes, see also Helge Seljas, 'Norwegians in "Zion" teach themselves English,' *Norwegian-American Studies*, vol. 26 (1974), p. 220-28, and Alfred Christiansen's 'Scandinavians and the New Zion in the West,' *Scandinavian Review*, vol. 60, no. 3 (1972), p. 263-71.

379   **The Lutheran Church among Norwegian-Americans: a history of
the Evangelical Lutheran Church.**
E. Clifford Nelson, Eugene L. Fevold.   Minneapolis, Minnesota:
Augsburg Publishing House, 1960. 2 vols. maps.

A detailed history of Lutheranism among Norwegian-Americans. The first volume
covers the period 1825 to 1890 and the second volume discusses events from 1890
to 1959. It is a study of the Norwegian-American assimilation process, of the
religious disputes among the Norwegian immigrants that led to schisms as often as
to consolidation, and of the significant role of the Norwegians, not only in religion
but also in such fields as higher education in America.

The Norwegian language in America: a study in bilingual behavior.
See item no. 412.

**Value systems and personality in a Western civilization: Norwegians in
Europe and America.**
See item no. 444.

**The history of Scandinavian literature: a survey of the literatures of
Norway, Sweden, Denmark, Iceland, and Finland from their origins to
the present day, including Scandinavian-American authors, and selected
bibliographies.**
See item no. 683.

The flying Norseman.
See item no. 849.

Norwegian-American Studies.
See item no. 890.

The Viking.
See item no. 901.

Religion

Pre-Christian religion

380 **The Norse myths.**
Edited by Kevin Crossley-Holland.   New York: Pantheon, 1980.
276p. bibliog.

The introduction provides a brief account of the Viking world and particularly of pre-Christian Nordic religion. The rest of the work consists of thirty-two Norse myths or legends taken from the *Elder Edda* and the *Prose Edda* of Snorri Sturluson with a short commentary on each in an appendix. The myths have been rendered into modern English by Crossley-Holland.

381 **Gods and myths of Northern Europe.**
Hilda R. Ellis Davidson.   Baltimore, Maryland: Penguin, [1964].
251p. bibliog.

A detailed description of the gods of early Scandinavia in a clear and comprehensible fashion. Special emphasis is placed on Odin and Thor although consideration is given to all the major figures and mythological concepts.

382 **The road to Hel: a study of the conception of the dead in Old Norse literature.**
Hilda R. Ellis Davidson.   New York: Greenwood Press, 1968.
208p.

Discusses Scandinavian funeral practices during the Viking Age and concepts regarding life after death, worship of the dead, and man's spirit or soul. Based on literary and archaeological sources, this is a scholarly, informative, and also very readable account, first published by Cambridge University Press in 1943.

383 **Scandinavian mythology.**
Hilda R. Ellis Davidson. London: Hamlyn, 1975. 141p. bibliog.
An uncomplicated introduction to pre-Christian Norse religious beliefs, by an acknowledged expert. First published in 1969, this profusely illustrated account is suitable for the general reader.

384 **Gods of the ancient Northmen.**
Georges Dumézil, edited by Einar I. Haugen, introduction by C. Scott Littleton, Udo Strutynski. Berkeley, California: University of California Press, 1973. 157p. bibliog. (Publications of the UCLA Center for the Study of Comparative Folklore and Mythology, no. 3).
This scholarly analysis of Scandinavian mythology presupposes some previous knowledge of the subject. The author frequently quotes saga source material and makes comparisons with ancient Greek and Hindu mythology. First published as *Les dieux des Germains* (Paris: Presses Universitaire de France, 1959).

385 **The golden horns: mythic imagination and the Nordic past.**
John L. Greenway. Athens, Georgia: University of Georgia Press, 1977. 226p. bibliog.
A scholarly discussion of ancient and modern myths.

386 **Of gods and giants: Norse mythology.**
Harald Hveberg, translated from the Norwegian by Pat Shaw Iversen. Oslo: Tanum-Norli, 1976. 86p. (Tokens of Norway).
Brief explanations of the best-known Norse myths and short descriptions of major gods and goddesses. A useful reference work for those embarking on a first reading of the myths.

387 **Viking: hammer of the North.**
Magnus Magnusson. New York: Galahad Books, 1980. 128p. maps. bibliog.
After brief chapters on pre-Viking Scandinavia, Viking expansion, and the coming of Christianity, Magnusson devotes most of the work to a discussion of Viking religion and mythology. The volume contains quotations from the *Prose Edda* and is illustrated with numerous colour photographs, chiefly of archaeological finds emphasizing Magnusson's theme. Originally published in London in 1976 by Orbis.

388 **The nine worlds: a dictionary of Norse mythology.**
Douglas A. Rossman. Baton Rouge, Louisiana: Ormsgard Press, 1983. 63p.
Brief explanations of terms and names in works of Norse mythology, which will be of assistance to the general reader encountering this subject for the first time.

Christianity and church history

389 **Four northern lights: men who shaped Scandinavian churches.**
G. Everett Arden. Minneapolis, Minnesota: Augsburg Publishing
House, 1964. 165p. bibliog.
Brief biographies of influential Scandinavian Lutherans, including a sketch of
Hans Nielsen Hauge (p. 50-76) which outlines his role as a religious reformer in
Norway at the end of the 18th century.

390 **The Norwegian church in its international setting.**
Eivind Berggrav. London: SCM Press, 1946. 31p.
The Burge Memorial Lecture emphasizing the international repercussions of the
German Nazi persecution of the Church of Norway and all other Norwegian
churches during World War II, written by the Primate of Norway and Bishop of
Oslo, who was one of the leaders of the resistance movement against the
Germans.

391 **The impact in Norway of American religious dissent.**
Nils Bloch-Hoell. In: *Contagious conflict: the impact of American
dissent on European life.* Edited by A. N. J. den Hollander.
Leiden, Netherlands: E. J. Brill, 1973. 263p.
A concise study of the history and present impact of Christian religious
denominations in Norway that originated in the United States.

392 **Catholicism in Norway.**
The Month. New series, vol. 21, no. 2 (1959), p. 69-128.
Includes articles by leading scholars on: 'Norway since the Reformation,' by
Hallvard Rieber-Mohn; 'Nicholas Breakspeare in Norway,' by David Knowles;
'The Reformation in Norway,' by Oskar Garstein; 'Sigrid Undset,' by A. H.
Winsnes; and 'Norwegian monasticism,' by John Gran.

393 **Rome and the Counter Reformation in Scandinavia until the
establishment of the *s. congregatio de propaganda fide* in 1622 based
on the source material in the Kolsrud collection.**
Oskar Garstein. Oslo: Universitetsforlaget, 1963-1980. 2 vols.
bibliog.
Emphasis is on the activities of Laurentius Norvegus, a Norwegian Jesuit, in
Sweden during the second half of the 16th century. Considerable attention is also
given, in two chapters of the second volume, to Catholicism in Denmark and
Norway during the first part of the 17th century.

394 **An embattled church.**
Frederick Hale. *Scandinavian Review*, vol. 69, no. 1 (1981), p.
52-60.
This analysis of religious trends and attitudes in Norway in the late 1970s can be
seen as a continuation of Mathiesen and Hauglin's article in *Norwegian Society*
(q.v.).

395 **Religion and power: the case of Methodism in Norway.**
Arne Hassing. Lake Junaluska, North Carolina: General Com-
mission on Archives and History, the United Methodist Church,
1980. 323p. bibliog.
A study of Methodism in Norway from 1853 to 1914. Includes a discussion of the
group as a religious movement, its relationship to the state and the Lutheran State
Church, and its impact on society and culture through its relationship with the
Norwegian Liberal Party and such organizations as the prohibition movement.

396 **The fight of the Norwegian church against Nazism.**
Bjarne Høye, Trygve Ager. New York: Macmillan, 1943. 180p.
An interesting description of the conflict between Norway's Lutheran State
Church led by Bishop Eivind Berggrav and the Nazi government from 1940 until
late 1942. An appendix contains several documents from the period.

397 **Scandinavian churches: a picture of the development and life of the**
churches of Denmark, Finland, Iceland, Norway and Sweden.
Edited by Leslie Stannard Hunter. London: Faber & Faber,
1965. 200p. bibliog.
Studies the Lutheran Church in the Scandinavian countries. Norway figures in the
discussion less than some of the other nations but is included in general chapters
such as 'Worship'. Per Junkam, who was then Bishop of Bergen, discusses
'Church and state in Norway,' (p. 75-83), and O. C. Myklebust writes on
'Ecumenical relations and missionary tasks,' in Norway (p. 166-71).

398 **History of the Scandinavian mission.**
Andrew Jenson. Salt Lake City: Deseret News Press, 1927. 570p.
A detailed account of Mormon (Church of Jesus Christ of Latter-Day Saints)
religious activity in Scandinavia from the 1850s until 1926. In addition to frequent
discussion of Norway throughout the work, the country is dealt with specifically in
sections entitled 'History of the Danish-Norwegian mission,' (p. 411-43), and
'History of the Norwegian mission, 1920-26,' (p. 501-08). The work also includes
biographical notes on Scandinavian Mormons who emigrated to America and
statistical data relating to the Mormon Church in Scandinavia.

399 **Eivind Berggrav: God's man of suspense.**
Alex Johnson, translated from the Norwegian by Kjell Jodheim,
Harriet L. Overholt. Minneapolis, Minnesota: Augsburg
Publishing House, 1960. 222p. bibliog.

An anecdotal account of Berggrav's life by a close friend, which discusses his
early life and activities as an educator, scholar, and parish pastor as well as his
experiences during the Second World War as the Bishop of Oslo and Primate of
Norway. It also contains a brief bibliography of Berggrav's literary work. First
published as *Eivind Berggrav, spenningens man* (Oslo: Land og Kirke, 1959).

400 **Hans Egede: missionary and colonizer of Greenland.**
Mads Lidegaard. *Scandinavian Review*, vol. 59, no. 3 (1971),
p. 229-44.

Describes the interesting career of Hans Egede, the Norwegian minister and
missionary who in 1721 became the first European to settle in Greenland in 200
years.

401 **Religion.**
Thomas Mathiesen, Otto Hauglin. In: *Norwegian society*. Edited
by Natalie Rogoff Ramsøy. Oslo: Universitetsforlaget, 1974, p.
226-59.

This sociological discussion of religion in Norway covers religious activity, the
number and background of (Lutheran) Church of Norway clergymen, voluntary
religious activity within the Church of Norway, non-Lutheran churches and their
membership, and common religious views.

402 **Church life in Norway 1800-1950.**
Einar Molland, translated by Harris Kaasa. Westport, Connecticut: Greenwood Press, 1978. 120p.

An abridged version of *Fra Hans Nielsen Hauge til Eivind Berggrav* (Oslo:
Gyldendal, 1951) and a reprint of the original English edition (Minneapolis,
Minnesota: Augsburg Publishing House, 1957). The work concentrates on the
theological strife that developed within the church from Hauge's time until
Berggrav emerged as bishop and war-time leader to consolidate the church's
position in the face of the German invader.

403 **Autobiographical writings of Hans Nielsen Hauge.**
Translated by Joel M. Njus. Minneapolis, Minnesota: Augsburg
Publishing House, 1954. 159p.

Selections from the writings of the leader of Norway's lay religious movement
(1771-1814), describing his life, religious experiences, and travels.

404 **Rebirth of Norway's peasantry: folk leader Hans Nielsen Hauge.**
Magnus Nodtvedt. Tacoma, Washington: Pacific Lutheran
University, 1965. 305p. bibliog.

Discusses the role of the peasantry in Norwegian society and Pietism and
Rationalism in the 18th century as factors of dissent within the Dano-Norwegian
State Church. Within this context Nodtvedt goes on to study Hauge's life and
career, and the political, economic, and social impact of his teachings, particularly
as they affected Norway's peasantry.

405 **The Norwegian Missionary Society: a short review of its work
among the Zulus.**
Stavanger, Norway: Norwegian Missionary Society, 1918. 76p.

A brief account of Norwegian missionary activity in South Africa during the 19th
century, which is an example of the intensity of the missionary work of the
Norwegian church during that period.

406 **Pulpit under the sky: a life of Hans Nielsen Hauge.**
Joseph M. Shaw, foreword by Iver Iversen. Minneapolis,
Minnesota: Augsburg Publishing House, 1955. 250p. bibliog.

This biography emphasizes in particular Hauge's active years as a preacher from
1796 to 1804 and his resultant imprisonment from 1804 to 1814. Two appendixes
reproduce Hauge's testament to his friends and provide a summary of his religious
views.

407 **History of the Baptists in Norway.**
P. Stiansen. Chicago: Blessing Press, 1933. 176p. bibliog.

Includes a lengthy discussion of the first Baptist groups in Norway during the
early 18th century and an account of the modern Baptist church in Norway as it
developed in the 19th and early 20th centuries. Emphasis is given to the church's
leaders, places of growth and organization, and relationship to the state.

408 **The popular revival movements.**
Kirsti Suolinna. In: *Nordic democracy: ideas, issues, and institu-
tions in politics, economy, education, social and cultural affairs of
Denmark, Finland, Iceland, Norway, and Sweden.* Edited by Erik
Allardt, Nils Andrén, Erik J. Friis, Gylfi T. Gislason, Sten Sparre
Nilson, Henry Valen, Frantz Wendt, Folmer Wisti. Copenhagen:
Det danske selskab, 1981, p. 589-608.

A study of the religious revival movements in Scandinavia from the late 18th
century until the early 20th century with emphasis on their economic, social, and
political repercussions. Extensive notes refer the reader to significant works on
the subject.

409 **Saga of saints.**
Sigrid Undset, translated by E. C. Ramsden. Salem, New York: Ayer, 1968. 321p. map. (Essay Index Reprint Series).

The well-known 20th century writer describes the origins and development of Christianity in Norway during the Middle Ages, St. Olav, and Oslo's patron saint, Saint Hallvard. The final sketches deal mainly with the less well-known Norwegian saints of the Middle Ages. A re-print of an earlier edition (New York: Longmans, Green, 1934).

410 **History of the church and state in Norway from the tenth to the sixteenth century.**
Thomas B. Willson. St. Clair Shores, Michigan: Scholarly Press, 1971. 382p. map.

First published in 1903, this volume remains the only extensive treatment of Christianity in Norway from Viking times until the Reformation, when a more intense Danish administration of both the church and state in Norway began.

Farms and fanes of ancient Norway: the place-names of a country discussed in their bearings on social and religious history.
See item no. 131.

Religious attitudes and arguments in the Norwegian EEC debate.
See item no. 566.

Poetic Edda.
See item no. 703.

Language

General

411 **Language conflict and language planning: the case of modern Norwegian.**
Einar I. Haugen.   Cambridge, Massachusetts: Harvard University Press, 1966. 393p. map. bibliog.

A thorough study of the linguistic controversy in Norway during the 19th century when a movement developed to establish a new national language based on peasant dialects. Haugen traces the evolution of this movement, the opposition to it, the efforts made in modern Norway to resolve the controversy, and goes on to describe the controversy in both historical and linguistic terms. An appendix provides statistics on language preferences and an extensive bibliography is also included.

412 **The Norwegian language in America: a study in bilingual behavior.**
Einar I. Haugen.   Bloomington, Indiana: Indiana University Press, 1969. 2nd ed. 2 vols. in 1. maps.

A study of the Norwegian language in America originally published in 1952. The first volume discusses how emigrants were exposed to a second language and the impact this had on both speech and writing. The second volume describes in greater detail the author's research into Norwegian dialects and particularly the process of blending and borrowing that took place.

413 **On translating from the Scandinavian.**
Einar I. Haugen. In: *Old Norse literature and mythology: a symposium.* Edited by E. C. Polome. Austin, Texas: University of Texas Press, 1969, p. 3-18.

Discusses the problems that exist in the translation of Scandinavian literature, particularly the Old Norse sagas, into English, and presents a historiographical sketch of past saga translators and the pitfalls they encountered.

414 **The Scandinavian languages: an introduction to their history.**
Einar I. Haugen. Cambridge, Massachusetts: Harvard University Press; London: Faber & Faber, 1976. 507p. maps. bibliog.

This detailed and scholarly account of the development of the Scandinavian languages includes several photographs of runic and later written texts and a translation into English as examples of linguistic development and dialects. Although unsuitable for beginners, this is a definitive work by the dean of Scandinavian linguists in the United States.

415 **The New Norse language movement.**
Lars S. Vikør. Oslo: Forlaget Novus, 1975. 133p. maps. bibliog.

Discusses the language issue in Norway from the mid-1960s to the mid-1970s from the standpoint of a Nynorsk (New Norwegian) advocate.

Dictionaries

416 **Berlitz Engelsk-norsk ordbok/Norwegian-English dictionary.**
Lausanne, Switzerland: Editions Berlitz, 1981. rev. ed. 320p.

A bilingual dictionary first published in 1974. Special sections in both languages include vocabularies for ordering food, common abbreviations, numbers, time, measures, and basic phrases.

417 **Engelsk-Norsk ordbok.** (English-Norwegian dictionary.)
Edited by Bjarne Berulfsen, Torkjell K. Berulfsen. Oslo: Kunnskapaforlaget (Aschehoug-Gyldendal), 1978. new rev. ed. 430p. (Gyldendal Blå Ordbøker).

First published in 1933, this is a valuable reference work.

418 **Cappelens store Engelsk-Norsk ordbok.** (Cappelen's large English-Norwegian dictionary.)
Edited by Bjarne Berulfsen, Herbert Svenkerud. Oslo: J. W. Cappelens Forlag, 1983. 1376p.

This detailed dictionary provides a translation of English words into Norwegian.

419 **Norwegian-English dictionary: a pronouncing and translating dictionary in modern Norwegian (Bokmål and Nynorsk) with a historical and grammatical introduction.**
Edited by Einar Haugen. Oslo: Universitetsforlaget, 1984. 3rd rev. ed. 506p. bibliog.

The most comprehensive dictionary translating both Bokmål and Nynorsk into English. The 1984 edition has revised many of the original entries, contains a new preface with comments on the present relationship of Bokmål to Nynorsk, and still contains an extensive introduction discussing the history and grammar of the language in detail. It was first published in 1964.

420 **Norsk-engelsk ordbok: stor utgave.** (Norwegian-English dictionary: large edition.)
Edited by Willy A. Kirkeby. Oslo: Kunnskapsforlaget (Aschehoug-Gyldendal), 1979. 1276p.

A detailed Norwegian-English dictionary. In addition to it, *Norsk-engelsk supplement ordbok* (Norwegian-English supplementary dictionary) (Oslo: Kunnskupsforlaget, 1983, 198p) has been published using the larger work as a base.

421 **Engelsk, amerikansk, norsk militær ordbok.** (English, American, Norwegian military dictionary.)
Edited by Ingvald Malm. Oslo: Fabritius, 1972. 276p.

A dictionary of general and military terms first in English/American to Norwegian, followed by Norwegian to English/American. The last section contains cross-translations of specific terms used in driving, topography and meteorology, in addition to conversion tables between the metric and English systems of weights and measures, computing the temperature and other differences between English and Norwegian terms that military personnel are likely to discover.

422 **Engelsk-norsk/norsk-engelsk billedordbok.**
(English-Norwegian/Norwegian-English picture dictionary.)
Edited by E. C. Parnwell. Oslo: J. W. Cappelens Forlag; Oxford: Oxford University Press, 1978. 98p. (Oxford English Picture Dictionary).

This picture dictionary containing many illustrations with Norwegian and English captions is a useful introduction to both languages for children and young adults.

423 **Min første ordbok.** (My first dictionary.)
Richard Scarry, translated from the English by Anne-Reidunn Løken. Oslo: Tanum-Norli, 1980. 63p.

A picture-book dictionary of pictures and scenes with appropriate English and Norwegian words and phrases. It is extremely useful for acquainting young children with the basics of both languages. First published in 1969.

424 **Norsk-engelsk ordbok.** (Norwegian-English dictionary.)
     Edited by Theodore Slette. Oslo: Det Norske Samlaget, 1977.
     1326p.

The most extensive Nynorsk to English dictionary available.

425 **Engelsk norsk ordbok.** (English Norwegian dictionary.)
     Edited by Hubert Svenkerud. Oslo: J. W. Cappelens Forlag,
     1975. 304p.

This helpful, brief dictionary also contains short sections on common English
abbreviations and explanations of English and American weights, measures,
monetary systems, and unusual plural forms.

Courses and grammars

426 **Snakker du norsk?** (Do you speak Norwegian?)
     Anne Arnestad, Inge-Helene Hvenekilde. Oslo: J. W. Cappelens
     Forlag, 1980. 6 vols.

This work consists of three textbooks, two accompanying workbooks, and a book
that may be used in conjunction with audio tapes. Separate transparencies and
glossary lists are worthwhile supplements. One of the most widely-used works for
beginning instruction in Norwegian at college or university level. For a brief
discussion of materials and teaching techniques, see Sidney R. Smith's 'The tools
of the Norsklærer's trade,' *Scandinavian Studies*, vol. 43, no. 3 (1971), p. 278-89.

427 **Norwegian grammar.**
     Bjarne Berulfsen. Oslo: Aschehoug, 1977. 82p.

This brief, topical discussion of the essential features of Norwegian grammar has
also been published in French as *Grammaire du norvégien* (Paris, 1970).

428 **Basic Norwegian reader.**
     Edited by Kenneth Chapman. New York: Holt, Rinehart &
     Winston, 1966. 90p.

Although designed to supplement *Spoken Norwegian* (q.v.), this work can also be
used independently. Contains selections from several prominent Norwegian
authors which provide a basic introduction to Norwegian literature. There are
also short biographical sketches of the authors.

429 **Norwegian-Nynorsk: an introduction for foreign students.**
     Peter Hallaråker. Bergen, Norway: Universitetsforlaget, 1983.
     246p. bibliog.

The only textbook for non-Norwegians with instructions in Nynorsk (New
Norwegian). Grammatical remarks are in English with a Nynorsk-English
glossary.

Language. Courses and grammars

430 **Reading Norwegian.**
Einar I. Haugen. Ithaca, New York: Spoken Language Services, 1977. 200p.

Contains a collection of stories in Norwegian for the new student and a glossary. First published in 1940 by Appleton-Century-Crofts.

431 **Spoken Norwegian.**
Einar I. Haugen, Kenneth Chapman. New York: Holt, Rinehart & Winston, 1982. 3rd ed. 450p.

One of the most-frequently used works for learning to speak Norwegian at secondary school and college level. Includes a glossary and tapes are also available. First published in 1947.

432 **Norwegian grammar: self-learning.**
Lloyd Hustvedt. Northfield, Minnesota: St. Olaf College Press, 1977. 119p.

Designed as a supplement to whatever textbook might be used, this volume concentrates on grammar only, and provides a workbook with exercises for the student.

433 **Moderne norsk litteratur.** (Modern Norwegian literature.)
Sverre Klouman, Haakon Smidt. Oslo: Universitetsforlaget, 1968. 175p.

This work, which contains excerpts from thirty-five Norwegian authors, is designed for advanced students in Norwegian. A glossary is included.

434 **Learn Norwegian.**
Sverre Klouman. Oslo: Tanum-Norli, 1981. 333p.

A practical course in spoken and written Norwegian. Explanations are in English and glossaries are included with each chapter. Contains helpful lists of common irregular verbs, alternate word forms allowed in Norwegian, and names of countries and nationalities.

435 **Så snakker vi norsk: Norwegian level one.** (Now, lets speak Norwegian.)
Ragnhild Maaso, Arne Masso. Oslo: J. W. Cappelens Forlag, 1975. 188p.

Originally published in 1970, the book is designed primarily for use by elementary school students. The explanations in the text are in English.

436 **Ny i Norge.** (New in Norway.)
Gerd. Manne. Oslo: Tiden Norsk Forlag, 1980-82. 2 vols.

This course, aimed primarily at immigrants, is therefore less concerned with grammar *per se* and more with practical applications of the basics. A teacher's edition is also available and there are glossaries translating Norwegian into English, Spanish, and Serbo-Croatian.

437 **Si det på norsk**. (Say it in Norwegian.)
Leif Nordgren, Svein Ole Satøen. [Oslo]: Friundervisningens
Forlag, 1980. 309p. 2 vols.

The work consists of a student textbook and an instructor's manual. The student
text contains short dialogues, good illustrations, and a wordlist. The lessons cover
aspects of daily life so that foreigners taking the course in Norway can adapt more
readily to life in Norway.

438 **The pronunciation of Norwegian.**
Ronald G. Popperwell. Oslo: Oslo University Press; Cambridge,
England: Cambridge University Press, 1963. 229p. bibliog.

An extensive, scholarly discussion.

439 **Norsk, nordmenn og Norge**. (Norwegian, Norwegians, and
Norway.)
Kathleen Stokker, Odd Haddal. Madison, Wisconsin; London:
University of Wisconsin Press, 1981. 617p.

A text for beginners emphasizing common vocabulary for speaking and writing as
well as grammatical concepts. The lessons also provide cultural information to
familiarize students with everyday life in Norway. The volume is designed for use
with audio tapes, a lab-manual, and an instructor's manual, all of which have
been prepared by Louis Janus.

440 **Norsk fonetikk for utlendinger**. (Norwegian phonetics for
foreigners.)
Åse-Berit Strandskogen. Oslo: Gyldendal, 1979. 196p. bibliog.

Outlines Norwegian phonetics, including intonation patterns, and exercises.

National romanticism in Norway.
See item no. 227.

Acta Philologica Scandinavica.
See item no. 877.

Scandinavian Studies.
See item 899.

A bibliography of Scandinavian language and linguistics.
See item no. 923.

A bibliography of Scandinavian dictionaries.
See item no. 924.

Society

General

441 Eilert Sundt: a pioneer in sociology and social anthropology.
Martin S. Allwood, foreword by James Mickel Williams.   Oslo:
Olaf Norlis Forlag, 1957. 112p. bibliog.

A brief biography describing the research and publications of Norway's first
sociologist in the 19th century.

442 Norway in the world community.
Johan Galtung. In: *Norwegian society*. Edited by Natalie Rogoff
Ramsøy.   Oslo: Universitetsforlaget, 1974, p. 385-427.

A sociological study of Norway and its place in the world. Through the use of
statistics and public opinion poll results, Galtung attempts to establish how
Norwegians view themselves, how they compare themselves with others, and how
Norway compares in a number of ways with other countries.

443 Elite structure and ideology: a theory with applications to Norway.
John Higley, G. Lowell Field, Knut Groholt.   Oslo:
Universitetsforlaget; New York: Columbia University Press, 1976.
367p. bibliog.

This scholarly work applies the authors' theory regarding élites to Norway. The
main data on Norway is in the second section, (p. 103-268). The volume is of use
to those interested primarily in Norway as well as to those concerned with
sociological theory. See also the earlier work by Higley and Field, *Elites in
developed societies: theoretical reflections on an initial stage in Norway* (Beverly
Hills, California: Sage Publications, 1972).

111

444 **Value systems and personality in a Western civilization: Norwegians in Europe and America.**
Christen T. Jonassen. Columbus, Ohio: Ohio State University Press, 1983. 382p.

A study of the emergence and evolution of Norwegian value systems and their role in the development of the modern welfare state. The first section explores the impact of the Vikings, Christians and Scientific Humanists on Norwegian social imperatives and social values. The author concludes with a study of abnormal behaviour, socialization, and detachment as significant characteristics of the Norwegian personality. The main emphasis is on Norway but the author also uses his research of Norwegian emigrant groups in the United States.

445 **A study of cultural change: rural-urban conflicts in Norway.**
Peter A. Munch. Oslo: H. Aschehoug (W. Nygaard), 1956. 104p. maps. bibliog. (Studia Norvegica: Vol. 3, no. 9).

Examines the reactions of a static peasant society to the advent of urban culture in the rural township of Aurdal, Norway. Munch provides a theoretical base for his work, a description of the development of peasant society in Norway, and a case study of the Norwegian town.

446 **Norwegian society.**
Edited by Natalie Rogoff Ramsøy, translated from the Norwegian by Susan Høivik. Oslo: Universitetsforlaget; London: Hurst; New York: Humanities Press, 1974. 451p. bibliog.

A translation with minor abridgement of *Det norske samfunn* (Oslo: Gyldendal Norsk Forlag, 1968). Twelve articles by noted Norwegian scholars discuss various aspects of Norwegian life such as family and marriage, the economy, education, political institutions, religion, the health system, communications media, law, leisure and recreation, and international relations within the context of society and social values. Particularly relevant to this section are Vilhelm Aubert's 'Stratification,' (p. 108-57), Erik Gronseth's 'Family, kinship, and marriage,' (p. 40-75), and Yngvar Lochen's 'The health system,' (p. 260-90).

447 **The Norwegians: a study in national culture.**
David Rodnick. Washington, DC: Public Affairs Press, 1955. 165p.

Examines the attitudes and views of many types of Norwegians, including young adults, farmers, and fishermen. It also studies family life, religious patterns, and political trends. Although it is not a complex account, the volume provides a significant understanding of Norway's people and social forms.

448 **Norway today: an introduction to modern Norwegian society.**
Arne Selbyg. Oslo: Universitetsforlaget, 1986. 240p. maps. bibliog.

An overview of current social conditions and institutions in Norway. Topics covered include voluntary organizations, health services, religion, the criminal justice system, and the arts. Each subject is discussed within the context of past developments and in comparison with either the United States or Great Britain.

Women and the family

449 **Sex roles and the socialization process.**
Sverre Brun-Gulbrandsen. In: *Changing roles of men and women.*
Edited by Edmund Dahlström. London: Gerald Duckworth,
1967, p. 59-78.
A study of sex role attitudes based on surveys of Norwegian parents and children.

450 **Norway's families: trends, problems, programs.**
Thomas D. Eliot, Arthur Hillman, Peter A. Munch, Fredrik
Barth, John C. Stephenson, Eva Nordland, John T.
Flint. Philadelphia: University of Pennsylvania Press, 1960. 485p.
Twenty-one essays on the family. The first part provides a brief sketch of Eilert Sundt and his contributions to the study of the family and culture in Norway. The second section describes different family environments by class and geographical region while the third discusses various aspects of family organization such as the status of women, child management, and the courtship and morals of youth. Section four concerns problems of family life such as divorce and alcoholism and the final section includes contributions on the church, community services, and sex education. Although some of the information is now out of date, this remains an interesting study.

451 **Women in public.**
Edited by Carol Gold, Morete Ries. *Scandinavian Review*,
vol. 65, no. 3 (1977), 128p. bibliog.
This entire issue is devoted to articles concerning women in public life and the public discussion of this growing phenomenon.

452 **Kitchen table society: a case-study of the family life and friendships of young working-class mothers in urban Norway.**
Marianne Gullestad. Oslo: Universitetsforlaget, 1984. 357p.
bibliog. (Kvinners levekår og livsløp).
A study of the everyday life of young women in Bergen with emphasis on their activities, values, and problems. Subjects considered in the work include marriage, housing, employment, and moral values.

Society. Women and the family

453 **The position of women.**
Elina Haavio-Mannila. In: *Nordic democracy: ideas, issues, and institutions in politics, economy, education, social and cultural affairs of Denmark, Finland, Iceland, Norway, and Sweden.* Edited by Erik Allardt, Nils Andrén, Erik J. Friis, Gylfi T. Gislason, Sten Sparre Nilson, Henry Valen, Frantz Wendt, Folmer Wisti. Copenhagen: Det danske selskab, 1981, p. 555-88. bibliog.
Several significant aspects regarding the role of women in the Nordic states are covered on a comparative basis. Among the general topics considered are women's economic activities, the women's movement and its organizations, political participation, and trade union activities. The women's movement is given the most extensive historical treatment while the emphasis in most of the remaining sections is on developments since the 1970s. A brief bibliography is appended as well as extensive notes of important works.

454 **Scandinavia.**
Harriet Holter. In: *Women in the modern world.* Edited, with a foreword by Raphael Patai. New York: Free Press; London: Collier-Macmillan, 1967, p. 437-62. bibliog.
The essay emphasizes the changing role of women in Scandinavia after the Second World War. Topics discussed include education, occupations, the home routine, and divorce.

455 **Patriarchy in a welfare society.**
Edited by Harriet Holter. Oslo: Universitetsforlaget, 1984. 235p. bibliog.
A collection of essays reflecting recent research in Norway on women's studies. The most common theme is the importance of gender in the distribution of wealth and power.

456 **Women in Norway: their position in family life, employment and society.**
Betty Selid, translated from the Norwegian by Dorothy Burton Skårdal. Oslo: Norwegian Joint Committee on International Social Policy in association with the Royal Ministry of Foreign Affairs, Department of Cultural Relations, 1970. 115p.
A translation of *Kvinner i yrke, hjem og samfunnet*, first published in 1968, this volume provides an overview of women in Norwegian society. The author outlines some of the main features of the women's movement in Norway during the last century before discussing the employment situation for women outside the home, the housewife, and social services available for mothers and children.

457   **Equality between the sexes: myth and reality in Norden.**
      Torild Skard, Elina Haavio-Mannila.   *Daedalus*, vol. 113, no. 1
      (1984), p. 141-67.
The article summarizes the stages in the Nordic feminist movement during the
last century and the problems that still remain in the search not only for equality
of opportunity but also for equality of results.

458   **. . . a prudent wife is from the Lord: the married peasant woman of**
      the eighteenth century in a demographic perspective.
      Sølvi Sogner.   *Scandinavian Journal of History*, vol. 9, no. 2
      (1984), p. 113-33.
A demographic study of Norwegian peasant women of the 18th century. A
number of subjects are considered, including housekeeping responsibilities,
marriage, re-marriage, fertility, and mortality. The article is part of an issue of the
journal devoted to the topic 'Women in pre-industrial Scandinavia.'

Social problems

459   **Drinking habits among Northern youth: a cross-national study of**
      male teenage drinking in the Northern capitals.
      Kettil Bruun, Ragnar Hauge, translated from the Swedish and
      Norwegian by Fred A. Fewster.   [Stockholm]: Alcohol Research
      in the Northern Countries, 1963. 97p.
A statistical and sociological study of the problem in Finland, Sweden, Norway,
and Denmark.

460   **Limits to pain.**
      Nils Christie.   Oslo: Universitetsforlaget, 1981. 122p. bibliog.
      (Institutt for Kriminologi og Straffrett Skrifter, no. 25).
A study of the punishment of crime from a sociological point of view, which
highlights the inadequacies of present systems. Includes frequent references to
conditions in Norway and the rest of Scandinavia.

461   **Suicide and Scandinavia: a psycho-analytic study of culture and**
      character.
      Harold Hendin.   New York: Doubleday, 1964. 177p.
An incisive study of suicide and national character. Hendin devotes a long chapter
to Norway, (p. 88-145), seeking in part to explain the much lower suicide rate
there than in the other Scandinavian states. The author trys to avoid the use of
complex terminology so that his results can be readily understood by the general
reader.

462 **A millennium of sexual permissiveness in the North.**
Richard F. Tomasson. *Scandinavian Review*, vol. 62, no. 4
(1974), p. 370-78.
The author views the relatively high rate of sexual permissiveness in Scandinavia
from the standpoint of its origins in pre-Christian times.

Social conditions, housing, health and welfare

463 **Housing.**
Charles Abrams. In: *Scandinavia between East and West.* Edited by
Henning Friis. Ithaca, New York; New York: Cornell University
Press, 1950, p. 169-88.
Outlines housing problems and Scandinavian solutions immediately prior to the
Second World War and in the immediate post-war years. Subjects covered include
housing cooperatives, planning and designing housing for the elderly, and land
and planning policies.

464 **Child and youth welfare in Norway 1969-1973.**
Oslo: Royal Norwegian Ministry of Social Affairs, 1973. 35p.
Describes the impact of legislative reform during the period on the care,
education, and financial support provided by the government for children.

465 **Housing in Scandinavia: urban and rural.**
John Graham, Jr. Chapel Hill, North Carolina: University of
North Carolina Press, 1940. 223p.
A comparative study of housing in Denmark, Finland, Norway, and Sweden,
which examines land, municipal housing, housing societies, and rural housing. It
reflects conditions and policy in the Scandinavian states prior to the Second World
War, provides an introduction to post-war programmes in these countries and
indicates the glaring need for a similar study of the post-war period.

466 **Health: a major issue.**
Scandinavian Review, vol. 63, no. 3 (1975), 63p. bibliog.
The entire issue is devoted to articles on health care in Scandinavia. Includes
statistical data and discussion of doctors, hospitals, consumerism, and other
related topics.

467 **Health for all by the year 2000: the Norwegian contribution to an ad hoc meeting on Health for All in Industrialized Countries, Geneva, 1-2 May 1980.**
Oslo: Helsedirektoratet, [1980]. 31p.
This pamphlet prepared for the conference is useful for the overview that is provides of Norwegian policy on health care and for the medical data it contains.

468 **Housing in Norway**
Copenhagen: [Boligdirektoratet], 1968. 43p. (Housing in the Nordic Countries).
A brief survey published by the State Housing Directorate with special emphasis on the public financing of housing and planning programmes as they affect housing.

469 **Growing old in Norway.**
Arne Kildal. *Scandinavian Review*, vol. 56, no. 2 (1968), p. 141-46.
Outlines the housing programmes being developed for the elderly in Norway during the 1960s and the cultural and other support programmes that exist.

The welfare state

470 **Rationality and irrationality of the Nordic welfare state.**
Bent Roald Andersen. *Daedalus*, vol. 113, no. 1 (1984), p. 109-39.
Describes the basic features of the welfare state in the Nordic countries and the social and economic programes generally available. The author underlines the pragmatic character of developments and the paradoxes and difficulties that are a part of the system.

471 **Medical care and family security: Norway, England, U.S.A.**
Karl Evang, D. Stark Murray, Walter J. Lear, preface by David Abrahamsen, foreword by Caldwell B. Esselltyn. Englewood Cliffs, New Jersey: Prentice-Hall, 1963. 344p. bibliog.
In this comparative work, the first part, by Evang, 'Prepaid medical care in Norway,' (p. 3-87), describes the operation of the national health insurance programme in Norway. Some of the details are now out of date but for providing a picture of the system as it was at the time, its philosophy, and general structure this is still a relevant work.

472 **Health services in Norway.**
Karl Evang. Oslo: Universitetsforlaget, 1976. 4th ed. 233p.
First published in 1957, this volume provides a comprehensive study of Norwegian health and medical care. Topics covered include the national health insurance

Society. Social conditions, housing, health and welfare

programme, nursing, programmes for several common diseases, the health
services that are available to special groups, and the administration of the national
health programme.

473 **The Scandinavian welfare state.**
Vic George. In: *Western Europe: a handbook*. Edited by John
Calmann. New York: Praeger, 1967, p. 456-63. map. bibliog.
A brief, comparative examination of the social security programmes and benefits
available in the Scandinavian states. The volume provides a statistical survey of
the population, governmental form, economy, social security system, education,
and mass media outlets in the various states. Norwegian statistics are presented
on p. 155-62.

474 **The welfare state and beyond: success and problems in Scandinavia.**
Gunnar Heckscher. Minneapolis, Minnesota: University of
Minnesota Press, 1984. 271p. bibliog. (Nordic Series, no. 11).
A well-balanced view of the roots of the Scandinavian welfare state, its ideals,
general character, and the political processes involved in governing a state based
on these principles. The author, a former leader of the Swedish Conservative
Party, also provides a critique of the imagined and real problems facing the
welfare state, particularly those created by stagflation, a new era of political
confrontation after decades of consensus, and current political issues. An
explanation, and a criticism of the welfare state by an active participant in its
construction. For a briefer discussion of some of his views, see 'Ideal of the
welfare state,' *Scandinavian Review*, vol. 70, no. 3 (1982), p. 6-16.

475 **The beginnings of the Nordic welfare states: similarities and
differences.**
Stein Kuhnle. *Acta Sociologica*, vol. 21, supplement (1978),
p. 9-35.
A comparative study of accident, sickness, old-age and unemployment insurance
programmes in Denmark, Norway, and Sweden during the last decades of the
19th century and the early 20th century. In addition to the domestic influences
that encouraged the establishment of these systems, Kuhnle also discusses the
impact of the German model. The article is part of a supplement to the journal
devoted exclusively to the Nordic Welfare State.

476 **Welfare and the quality of life.**
Stein Kuhnle. In: *Nordic democracy: ideas, issues, and institutions
in politics, economy, education, social and cultural affairs of
Denmark, Finland, Iceland, Norway, and Sweden*. Edited by Erik
Allardt, Nils Andrén, Erik J. Friis, Gylfi T. Gislason, Sten Sparre
Nilson, Henry Valen, Frantz Wendt, Folmer Wisti. Copenhagen:
Det danske selskab, 1981, p. 399-415.
Provides a brief overview of the early development of the Nordic welfare state,

118

Society. Social conditions, housing, health and welfare

the basic features of social legislation, the expenditures for social services, and the
impact that the welfare state has had on the quality of life in the Nordic countries.

477   **The National Insurance Act in Norway.**
      [Oslo]: Royal Ministry of Social Affiars, 1967. 31p.
      A basic outline of the programme when it was first introduced.

478   **The Norwegian welfare state and social mobility.**
      Natalie Rogoff Ramsøy. *Scandinavian Review*, vol. 73, no. 2
      (1985), p. 5-8.
      Describes how reforms in education and health care during the 1950s increased
      the professional work force in both areas and made them into major new avenues
      of social mobility.

Modern Norway: a study in social democracy.
See item no. 7.

**Farms and fanes of ancient Norway: the place-names of a country
discussed in their bearings on social and religious history.**
See item no. 131.

Social Scandinavia in the Viking Age.
See item no. 202.

**The old Norwegian peasant community: investigations undertaken by the
Institute for Comparative Research in Human Culture, Oslo.**
See item no. 228.

**Motive forces behind the new social policy after 1870: Norway on the
European scene.**
See item no. 236.

The dissolution of estate society in Norway.
See item no. 237.

Population and society in Norway 1735-1865.
See item no. 305.

Trends in demographic structure in Norway 1960-2000.
See item no. 308.

An everyday story: Norwegian women's fiction.
See item no. 694.

Triumph in daring.
See item no. 850.

Acta Sociologica.
See item no. 878.

Scandinavia in social science literature: an English language bibliography.
See item no. 920.

Politics

General

479 **Representative government in a bureaucratic age.**
Erik Allardt. *Daedalus*, vol. 113, no. 1 (1984), p. 169-97.
Discusses the degree of political participation and the forms of representation in Scandinavia.

480 **Scandinavia at the polls: recent political trends in Denmark, Norway, and Sweden.**
Edited by Karl H. Cerny. Washington, DC: American Enterprise Institute for Public Policy Research, 1977. 304p.
Nine essays discuss different aspects of the Scandinavian economic and political scene. The volume is divided into three sections that deal with parties and elections, social discontent and the mass media, and business and welfare in the welfare state. An article by Henry Valen and Willy Martinussen, 'Electoral trends and foreign politics in Norway: the 1973 *Storting* election and the EEC issue,' (p. 39-71) concentrates solely on Norway and most of the other articles pertain to Norway as well as to Denmark and Sweden.

481 **Political parties and public participation.**
Kjell A. Eliassen. In: *Nordic democracy: ideas, issues, and institutions in politics, economy, education, social and cultural affairs of Denmark, Finland, Iceland, Norway, and Sweden.* Edited by Erik Allardt, Nils Andrén, Erik J. Friis, Gylfi T. Gislason, Sten Sparre Nilson, Henry Valen, Frantz Wendt, Folmer Wisti. Copenhagen: Det danske selskab, 1981, p. 126-37.
A study of the degree and forms of electoral participation and political

120

involvement in the five Nordic states with emphasis on the 1960s and 1970s.

482 **The consensual democracies?: the government and politics of the Scandinavian states.**
Neil Elder, Alastair H. Thomas, David Arter.   Oxford: Martin Robertson, 1982. 244p. map. bibliog.

A study of modern politics and government in the Nordic states. The authors discuss the establishment of the 'five party' model for politics in these countries during the first half of the 20th century, the structure of government and the factors that threaten 'consensual' democracy as they define the term.

483 **Participation and democracy in Norway: the 'Distant democracy' revisited.**
William M. Lafferty.   Oslo: Universitetsforlaget, 1981. 193p. bibliog.

This study of modern Norwegian politics is a reply to Willy Martinussen's *The distant democracy* (q.v.). It analyses the sources of political participation, political equality, and political motivation and comes to conclusions on these topics that are very different from those of Martinussen.

484 **The distant democracy: social inequality, political resources and political influence in Norway.**
Willy Martinussen.   London: John Wiley & Sons, 1977. 246p. bibliog.

Martinussen proposes the existence in Norway of 'political poverty', by which he means the inequitable distribution of access to political resources that enhances the impact of some on political decisions and reduces significantly the influence others can possibly exercise on the system. A work that has provoked praise, criticism, and further research into Norway's political institutions. Originally published as *Fjerndemokratiet* (Oslo: Gyldendal Norsk Forlag, 1973).

485 **Direct democracy in national politics.**
Sten Sparre Nilson. In: *Nordic democracy: ideas, issues, and institutions in politics, economy, education, social and cultural affairs of Denmark, Finland, Iceland, Norway, and Sweden.* Edited by Erik Allardt, Nils Andrén, Erik J. Friis, Gylfi T. Gislason, Sten Sparre Nilson, Henry Valen, Frantz Wendt, Folmer Wisti.   Copenhagen: Det danske selskab, 1981, p. 138-59. bibliog.

A study of the referendum as a means by which Scandinavian voters can directly influence governmental policy. In addition to a general survey of the use of the referendum throughout Scandinavia in the 20th century, there are case studies of the Norwegian Labour Party's efforts during the 1960s to determine grass roots political opinion as an unofficial form of direct democracy and the 1972 Norwegian referendum that rejected EEC membership.

121

486 **Norway: numerical democracy and corporate pluralism.**
Stein Rokkan. In: *Political oppositions in western democracies.*
Edited by Robert A. Dahl. New Haven, Connecticut; London:
Yale University Press, 1966, p. 70-115. bibliog.

A scholarly description of Norwegian politics, which covers the development of
the Norwegian political party systems and politics, with emphasis on the period
1945 to 1965.

487 **Geography, religion, and social class: crosscutting cleavages in
Norwegian politics.**
Stein Rokkan. In: *Party systems and voter alignments: cross-
national perspectives.* Edited by Seymour M. Lipset, Stein
Rokkan. New York: Free Press; London: Collier-Macmillan,
1967, p. 367-444. (International Yearbook of Political Behavior
Research).

Examines divisions in Norwegian politics and the nature of party alignment
patterns. The study begins in 1814, but much of the article concentrates on the
period from the 1880s to the 1960s. Special attention is given to the southern and
western parts of Norway and their distinctive political features that have had a
profound effect on the nature of Norwegian politics.

488 **Citizens, elections, parties: approaches to the comparative study of
the processes of development.**
Stein Rokkan, with Angus Campbell, Per Torsvik, Henry
Valen. Oslo: Universitetsforlaget, 1970. 470p. bibliog.

A collection of fourteen essays dealing with three main themes: nation-building
and political mobilization; electoral studies; and public-opinion research.
Norwegian political conditions are discussed throughout.

489 **Regional contrasts in Norwegian politics: a review of data from
official statistics and sample surveys.**
Stein Rokkan, Henry Valen. In *Mass politics: studies in political
sociology.* Edited by Erik Allardt, Stein Rokkan, foreword by
Seymour M. Lipset. New York: Free Press; London: Collier-
Macmillan, 1970, p. 190-247.

A statistical study of political differences in the various regions of Norway, and of
aspects of the electoral research programmes developed at the University of
Bergen and the Institute for Social Research in Oslo. Studies southern and
western Norway as examples of regions that have resisted centralizing and
urbanizing forces for centuries, and northern Norway as a polarized periphery of
the country. The article was first published in *Cleavages, ideologies, and party
systems, contributions to comparative political sociology*, edited by Erik Allardt
and Y. Littunen, (Helsinki: Westermarck Society, 1964).

490   **The growth and structuring of mass politics.**
Stein Rokkan. In: *Nordic democracy: ideas, issues, and institutions in politics, economy, education, social and cultural affairs of Denmark, Finland, Iceland, Norway, and Sweden.* Edited by Erik Allardt, Nils Andrén, Erik J. Friis, Gylfi T. Gislason, Sten Sparre Nilson, Henry Valen, Frantz Wendt, Folmer Wisti. Copenhagen: Det danske selskab, 1981, p. 53-79. bibliog.

A comparative study of the political development of the Nordic countries. After providing a basic background from the 16th century, Rokkan discusses the processes of mass mobilization, cleavage structures, party systems, external political pressures, and 'policy-bargaining' structures.

491   **The distribution of political participation in Norway: alternative perspectives on a problem of democratic theory.**
Lawrence E. Rose, Ragnar Waldahl. *Scandinavian Political Studies*, new series, vol. 5, no. 4 (1982), p. 285-314. bibliog.

An important study of citizen participation in political affairs from 1965 to 1973.

Political parties

492   **The Scandinavian party system(s): a comparative study.**
Sten Berglund, Ulf Lindström. Lund, Sweden: Studentlitteratur, 1978. 203p. maps. bibliog.

A discussion of the political party systems of the Scandinavian countries and their relative conformity to the 'five party model.' Topics considered are the development of the different political parties, their relative strengths, social bases of support, and their activity within the national parliamentary bodies. The final chapter addresses the significant changes during the 1970s that occurred among these political parties. For a briefer study by Berglund on the same subject, see his essay in *Nordic democracy* (q.v.), (p. 80-125).

493   **The social democratic image of society: a study of the achievements and origins of Scandinavian social democracy in comparative perspective.**
Francis G. Castles. London; Henley, England: Boston, Massachusetts: Routledge & Kegan Paul, 1978. 162p. bibliog.

Investigates the origins of Social Democratic parties in the Scandinavian states during the 20th century, the development of the welfare state as defined by four basic criteria, and the means by which the Scandinavian Social Democratic parties have been able to achieve their results.

Politics. Political parties

494 **The Norwegian Labour Party in social democracy in a periphery of Europe.**
Knut Heidar. In: *Social Democratic parties in Western Europe.*
Edited by William E. Paterson, and Alastair H.
Thomas. London: Croom Helm, 1979, p. 292-315. bibliog.
A brief survey of the party's history with emphasis on its increasing tendency to resemble the other main parties in organization, the renewal experiences of the party while out of office, and intra-party rivalry during the mid-1970s.

495 **Norway.**
Jahn Otto Johansen. In: *Communism in Europe: continuity, change and the Sino-Soviet dispute. Volume 2.* Edited by William E.
Griffith. Oxford: Pergamon Press, 1967, p. 320-69.
Outlines the development of the Communist party in Norway during the interwar years and discusses the impact of the Sino-Soviet split on the party from 1960 to 1965.

496 **The dilemma of Social Democratic Labor parties.**
Erling Olsen. *Daedalus*, vol. 113, no. 2 (1984), p. 169-94.
An overview of the origins and development of the Social Democratic parties in the Nordic countries (the Labour Party in Norway), the threat posed by the New Left and the New Right to their domination of politics during the 1970s, and the problems they are likely to face in the near future.

497 **The Communist Party of Norway.**
Peter P. Rohde. In: *The Communist parties of Scandinavia and Finland.* Edited by Anthony F. Upton. London: Weidenfeld & Nicolson, 1973, p. 35-59. bibliog.
A brief survey of the origins and development of the party with emphasis on the interwar and immediate postwar years.

498 **Political parties in Norway: a community study.**
Henry Valen, Daniel Katz. Oslo: Universitetsforlaget, 1967.
383p. maps. bibliog.
A study of Norwegian political party organization and activity as exemplified by the city of Stavanger and the county of Rogaland during the 1957 parliamentary election.

Interest groups

499 **Organizations and pressure groups.**
Kjell A. Eliassen. In: *Nordic democracy: ideas, issues, and
institutions in politics, economy, education, social and cultural
affairs of Denmark, Finland, Iceland, Norway, and Sweden.* Edited
by Erik Allardt, Nils Andrén, Erik J. Friis, Gylfi T. Gislason, Sten
Sparre Nilson, Henry Valen, Frantz Wendt, Folmer
Wisti. Copenhagen: Det danske selskab, 1981, p. 609-26.
Studies the structure and development of the many interest groups in the Nordic
nations; the degree of structural centralization within them; and their relationship
to the state. A comparative approach is employed.

500 **Interest groups in Norwegian politics.**
Robert B. Kvavik. Oslo: Universitetsforlaget, 1976. 206p.
bibliog.
An important study of the organization and function of interest groups within the
Norwegian political process. In addition to describing these organizations, Kvavik
demonstrates the ways in which Norwegian interest groups reflect elements of
both competitive and corporatist systems of group behaviour.

Elections

501 **Norway: conflict structure and mass politics in a European
periphery.**
Henry Valen, Stein Rokkan. In: *Electoral behavior: a comparative
handbook.* Edited by Richard Rose. New York: Free Press;
London: Collier-Macmillan, 1974, p. 315-70.
In this scholarly study of Norwegian politics of the mid-1960s two of Norway's
outstanding political scientists identify seven major cleavages that can be
measured by a similar number of variables to explain Norwegian party alignment.
The election of 1965 is used as a test of these hypotheses. The nature of
Norwegian politics has changed since then but this chapter remains a cogent
explanation of politics and voting behaviour in Norway for the period discussed.

502 **Electoral research in Norway.**
Henry Valen. *Research in Norway*, (1981), p. 22-27. bibliog.
Describes the development and nature of the project in electoral research begun
by himself and the late Stein Rokkan at the Institute for Social Research in Oslo,
the Christian Michelsen Institute and the University of Bergen.

503   **The changing electoral basis of electoral parties: the case of
      Norway.**
      Henry Valen, Bernt Olav Aardal.   *Scandinavian Review*, vol. 73,
      no. 1 (1985), p. 34-42.
Outlines recent changes in electoral trends that weaken older political loyalties,
and provides four explanations of this development.

**Agrarian structure and peasant politics: a comparative study of rural
response to economic change.**
See item no. 150.

Norwegian attitudes to a Nordic nuclear-free zone 1958-1982.
See item no. 273.

The welfare state and beyond: success and problems in Scandinavia.
See item no. 474.

Norway's no to Europe.
See item no. 572.

Scandinavian Political Studies.
See item no. 896.

A selective bibliography of Scandinavian politics and policy.
See item no. 914.

**Scandinavian political institutions and political behavior 1970-1980: an
annotated bibliography.**
See item no. 915.

Scandinavia in social science literature: an English language bibliography.
See item no. 920.

**Scandinavian government and politics: a bibliography of materials in
English.**
See item no. 933.

Government and
the Constitution

General

504 **Government and politics in the Nordic countries: Denmark,
Finland, Iceland, Norway, and Sweden.**
Nils Andrén. Stockholm: Almqvist & Wiksell, 1964. 241p.
bibliog.

A survey containing brief outlines of the structure of the national government in
each of the Nordic countries and brief comparisons of various aspects of
government and politics. The information is still relevant for Norway because its
governmental structure has remained basically unchanged since the volume was
published.

505 **Political life and institutions in Norway.**
Jon G. Arntzen, Bård Bredup Knudsen. Oslo: University of
Oslo, 1980. 151p. maps. bibliog.

An excellent outline of the structure of government and the current political
issues in Norway. Although a short treatment of local and regional government is
included, the main emphasis is on the nature of the national government along
with a brief account of the way it works. Consideration is given to current foreign
policy issues and the basic differences in Norwegian politics and society.

506 **Division and cohesion in democracy: a study of Norway.**
Harry Eckstein. Princeton, New Jersey: Princeton University
Press, 1966. 293p. (Princeton Center of International Affairs).

Considers some of the reasons for disunity in Norwegian democracy but also
emphasizes a sense of community as an important cohesive force that brings
legitimacy to its political system. A general assessment of government, entitled 'A
theory of stable democracy,' is published as an appendix to the work.

507   **Norwegian democracy.**
      James A. Storing.   Boston, Massachusetts: Houghton Mifflin,
      1963. 246p. map. bibliog.
This basic introduction to the Norwegian political system concentrates primarily
on the national government, elections, political parties, and courts. However,
chapters on local government, social security, foreign policy, and the state's role
in the economy are also included. Norway's constitution in English translation is
provided as an appendix.

Constitution

508   **The Constitution of Norway and other documents of national
      importance.**
      Edited by Tønnes Andenæs.   [Oslo]: Royal Ministry of Foreign
      Affairs (Press Service), 1962. 71p.
Contains a brief sketch of Norwegian history by the editor, the Constitution of
1814 in both its present and original forms, and historical documents from 1814,
1905, and the Second World War that pertain to the Constitution and its
implementation.

509   **Norway and the Western Powers: a study of comparative
      constitutional law.**
      Frede Castberg.   Oslo: Oslo University Press; London: George
      Allen & Unwin, 1957. 24p.
A short but authoritative study of the Norwegian constitution describing its
origins, the influences on the Constitution of 1814, and some of its unique
characteristics.

510   **Norway's views on sovereignty: a report prepared for UNESCO.**
      Einar Løchen, assisted by Rolf N. Torgersen.   Bergen, Norway:
      John Griegs, 1955. 102p. bibliog. (Chr. Michelsens Institutt for
      Videnskap og Åndsfrihet, report 17:5a).
A scholarly study of the concept of sovereignty as it has been defined in the
Norwegian constitution and applied in Norwegian foreign affairs, particularly in
the United Nations. A concluding section discusses the relationship between and
application of domestic and international law as a result of foreign agreements to
which Norway is a party.

National government

511 The Nordic parliaments: a comparative analysis.
David Arter. New York: St. Martin's, 1984. 421p.
Compares the parliaments in the five Nordic nations and studies the Nordic
Council. Three basic processes of policy formulation, policy adoption, and policy
implementation are discussed from the standpoint of the 'decline of parliament'
thesis. Extensive endnotes provide information on the important literature on the
subject.

512 Top civil servants and the national budget in Norway.
John Higley, Karl Erik Brofoss, Knut Groholt. In: *The mandarins
of Western Europe: the political role of top civil servants.* Edited by
Mattei Dogan. New York: John Wiley & Sons, 1975, p. 252-74.
bibliog. (Sage Publications).
Studies the influence of Norway's top civil servants on the national budget, and
compares the group with other élites. The article is an example of the élite theory
research current in political science studies today.

**513 The intellectual civil servant: the role of the writer and the scholar
in Nordic culture.**
Lars Lönnroth. *Daedalus*, vol. 113, no. 2 (1984), p. 107-36.
Examines the development in the Nordic countries of the 'cultural worker', the
post-Second World War civil servant deeply influenced by Social Democratic
ideology and the student protest movements of the late 1960s. In a section (p.
117-20) specifically on Norway, the author explores the unique effect of
Norwegian nationalism on these developments.

514 Norway's parliament: the Storting.
Per Øisang. Oslo: Fabritius, 1962. 40p.
Outlines the functions and operations of the Storting, its leaders, and the
provisions for general elections by which its members are elected.

**515 Governing Norway: segmentation, anticipation and consensus
formation.**
Johan P. Olsen. In: *Presidents and prime ministers.* Edited by
Richard Rose, Efra N. Sulemain, foreword by Richard E.
Neustadt. Washington, DC: American Enterprise Institute for
Public Policy Research, 1981, p. 203-55.
A description of the executive branch of the Norwegian government as it
functions in the office of the Prime Minister and his Cabinet of chief ministers and
its decision-making process. Most of the examples cited are from the tenures of
Norway's prime ministers of the Labour Party: Einar Gerhardsen, Trygve
Bratteli, and Oddvar Nordli. A scholarly yet highly readable discussion.

516 **Organized democracy: political institutions in a welfare state – the case of Norway.**
Johan P. Olsen.   Bergen, Norway: Universitetsforlaget, 1983.
246p. bibliog.

A detailed, scholarly study of Norwegian governmental institutions viewed from the standpoint of citizen involvement and participation and based on organization theory.

517 **Government and central administration.**
Gustaf Petrén. In: *Nordic democracy: ideas, issues, and institutions in politics, economy, education, social and cultural affairs of Denmark, Finland, Iceland, Norway, and Sweden.* Edited by Erik Allardt, Nils Andrén, Erik J. Friis, Glyfi T. Gislason, Sten Sparre Nilson, Henry Valen, Frantz Wendt, Folmer Wisti.   Copenhagen: Det danske selskab, 1981, p. 163-81.

A comparative study of the executive and legislative bodies of the national government with secondary consideration given to their relationship with the judicial system and the civil service agencies that implement policy.

Local government

518 **Citizen participation and local government in America and Scandinavia.**
Edited by Jens Chr. Birch, Henrik Christoffersen.   Gentofte, Denmark: Erling Olsens Forlag, 1981. 219p.

Papers given at a conference on local government sponsored by the Scandinavian Seminar College and the National Association of Local Authorities in Denmark. Three of the articles relate to local government in Norway. The Norwegian Association of Local Authorities contributed an overview of local government in Norway (p. 49-56), Arne Haukvik discussed 'The system of precinct committees,' (p. 115-23), and Ingeborg Horgen described 'Municipal information activities in Norway,' (p. 175-81).

519 **Decisions, politics and change: a study of Norwegian urban budgeting.**
Andrew T. Cowart, Karl Erik Brofoss.   Oslo: Universitetsforlaget, 1979. 150p.

A study of the budget-making process of the city of Oslo with respect to pressure groups, partisan politics, and decision-making.

520 **Re-designing local government in Norway: an experiment in democracy.**
Robert Kvavik. *Scandinavian Studies*, vol. 56, no. 4 (1984), p. 333-50.
Describes and assesses the impact of local government reforms in Norway since the Second World War. Public sector growth increased the responsibilities of local government without always expanding its resources. Reforms of the system established decentralization, democratization, and rationalization as goals for its improvement.

521 **Local government.**
Krister Ståhlberg. In: *Nordic democracy: ideas, issues, and institutions in politics, economy, education, social and cultural affairs of Denmark, Finland, Iceland, Norway, and Sweden.* Edited by Erik Allardt, Nils Andrén, Erik J. Friis, Gylfi T. Gislason, Sten Sparre Nilson, Henry Valen, Frantz Wendt, Folmer Wisti. Copenhagen: Det danske selskab, 1981, p. 182-95.
A comparative analysis of local government in the Nordic countries emphasizing the different approaches and trends of the last couple of decades.

Scandinavia.
See item no. 20.

The household of the Norwegian kings in the thirteenth century.
See item no. 210.

Norges Statskalendar. (Norway's State Calendar.)
See item no. 907.

Scandinavia in social science literature: an English language bibliography.
See item no. 920.

Scandinavian government and politics: a bibliography of materials in English.
See item no. 933.

Law and the
Legal System

General

522 **Anglo-Scandinavian law dictionary of legal terms used in professional and commercial practice.**
Ralph J. B. Anderson. Oslo: Universitetsforlaget, 1977. 137p.

Separate sections define English, Norwegian, Swedish, and Danish legal terms. In each section, concise definitions are provided for each term as well as equivalent terms in the other languages where applicable. The preface presents brief sketches of the judicial systems of civil law in each country. The book was prepared under the auspices of the Royal Norwegian Ministry of Justice.

523 **Company, trade and tax law in Norway.**
Andreas Arntzen, Jens Bugge, Ulf Underland. Oslo: Den norske Creditbank, 1978, 502p.

A revised version of *Doing business in Norway* published in 1968 and 1971.

524 **Danish and Norwegian law: a general survey.**
Edited by N. V. Boeg, translated by Poul Boeg, Else Giersing, Hedevig Ring. Copenhagen: G. E. C. Gad, 1963. 251p.

Prepared by the Danish Committee on Comparative Law, much of the work describes aspects of Norwegian and Danish civil law on such matters as the family, inheritance, and property. One chapter, (p. 194-207) concerns Norwegian civil procedure and a concluding chapter discusses criminal law.

525 **The administration of justice.**
Nils Christie. In: *Norwegian society.* Edited by Natalie Rogoff
Ramsøy. Oslo: Universitetsforlaget, 1974, p. 348-84.

A sociological study of Norway's legal system, including an outline of the legal
structure, recruitment patterns of lawyers and the judiciary, and their education.
Discusses the types of offences frequently committed in Norway, provides
statistical studies of offenders, and a brief attitudinal study of prison inmates.

526 **The Scandinavian system of juvenile justice: a comparative
approach.**
Tove Stand Dahl. In: *Pursuing justice for the child.* Edited by
Margaret K. Rosenheim, foreword by Robert Maynard Hutchins.
Chicago; London: University of Chicago Press, 1976, p. 327-47.
bibliog.

Describes the Norwegian child welfare board created by laws of 1896 and 1953
with modifications in the 1960s as the 'Scandinavian model' of an administrative-
legal body which has a very different approach to child welfare and juvenile
justice problems than that of the United States.

527 **The earliest Norwegian laws: being the Gulathing and the
Frostathing law.**
Edited and translated by Laurence M. Larson.   New York:
Columbia University Press, 1935. 451p. map. bibliog. (Periods of
Civilization: Source and Study).

Provides an outline of Norwegian judicial practices during the Middle Ages and
the origins of the two law codes during the 12th and 13th centuries, along with a
translation of the codes.

528 **Norges Løver.** (Norway's Laws.)
Law Faculty of the University of Oslo.   Oslo: Grøndahl & Søn
Forlag, 1932-. annual.

A detailed presentation of Norway's laws from 1685 to the present. It is selective
in that some inoperative laws are not included. Includes a church ritual law for
both Denmark and Norway of 1685 and *Kong Christian den Femtes Norske Løv*
(King Christian V's Norwegian Law) of 1687. Law-making was sporadic until the
late 18th century and the collection really begins with the Constitution of 1814
and subsequent legislation by the *Storting* (Parliament) in the 19th century. It is
the 'bible' of Norwegian law students.

529 **Norwegian laws selected for the foreign service.**
Oslo: Royal Ministry of Foreign Affairs, 1980. 997p.

First published in 1953 for Norwegian representatives abroad, this work contains
twenty-six chapters of selected laws that deal with such subjects as nationality, the
admittance of aliens to Norway, merchant shipping, customs, marriage,
inheritance, fishing, and the offshore Continental Shelf.

530 **The growth of Scandinavian law.**
Lester Bernhardt Orfield, foreword by Benjamin F. Boyer.
Philadelphia: University of Pennsylvania Press for Temple University Publications, 1953. 363p. bibliog.

Developments in each country are treated separately in this work. The chapter on Norway (p. 128-226) outlines the history of the country, emphasizing legal and administrative developments and goes on to disuss many aspects of Norway's court system and the legal implications of post Second World War governmental policy. A useful general introduction to Norwegian law. The bibliography includes works in English on Norway (p. 336-40) and another section (p. 340-46) covers Scandinavian works that have been written primarily by Norwegians.

531 **Administration of justice in Norway: a brief summary.**
Royal Ministry of Justice in cooperation with the Royal Ministry of Foreign Affairs. Oslo: Universitetsforlaget, 1980. 2nd ed. 93p.

An overview of the administration of justice in Norway. The introduction provides a historical background to modern legal procedures; two chapters discuss court procedures for civil and criminal cases; and a brief concluding chapter deals with the status of the courts, judges, and lawyers.

Criminal law

532 **The general part of the criminal law of Norway.**
Johannes Andenæs, translated by Thomas P. Ogle. South Hackensack, New Jersey: Fred B. Rothman; London: Sweet & Maxwell, 1965. 346p. (Comparative Criminal Law Project, no. 3).

Deals with the basic principles of Norwegian criminal law. The first part discusses crime and punishment, criminality and its causes, and the purpose and methods of punishment. The second section deals with specific legal issues such as the illegal act, subjective guilt, and the limits of prosecution.

533 **Social defence in Norway.**
Arne Evensen. Oslo: Ministry of Social Affairs in collaboration with the Ministry of Justice, 1982. 94p.

An overview of the criminal justice system in Norway. Topics include criminal court procedure, legal sanctions, the detention system, programmes available to past and present offenders, and a statistical survey.

534 **Justice under fire.**
John Karevold. *Scandinavian Review*, vol. 67, no. 3 (1979), p. 37-41.

Briefly studies the Criminal Report issued by the Norwegian government in the late 1970s recommending several changes in Norway's penal and corrections programme and comments on the controversial character of this report.

535 **The Norwegian penal code.**
Translated by Harald Scholdager, Finn Backer, introduction by Johannes Andenæs. South Hackensack, New Jersey: Fred B. Rothman; London: Sweet & Maxwell, 1961. 167p. (American Series of Foreign Penal Codes, no. 3).

A translation of Norway's penal code, adopted in 1902, as it was when the book was published. The introduction provides a brief sketch of the code's origins, its later revisions and other legal statutes that relate to penal matters, and discusses the punishment and security measures that are followed.

Limits to pain.
See item no. 460.

Scandinavian Studies in Law.
See item no. 900.

A selective survey of English language studies on Scandinavian law.
See item no. 918.

Scandinavia in social science literature: an English language bibliography.
See item no. 920.

Norwegian legal publications in English, French, and German.
See item no. 925.

Norsk juridisk litteratur 1962-1966: ein bibliografi. (Norwegian legal literature 1962-1966: a bibliography.)
See item no. 926.

Scandinavian legal bibliography.
See item no. 930.

Foreign Relations and National Security

General

536 **The Nordic countries and North-South relations.**
Nils Andrén. In: *Nordic democracy: ideas, issues, and institutions in politics, economy, education, social and cultural affairs of Denmark, Finland, Iceland, Norway, and Sweden.* Edited by Erik Allardt, Nils Andrén, Erik J. Friis, Gylfi T. Gislason, Sten Sparre Nilson, Henry Valen, Frantz Wendt, Folmer Wisti. Copenhagen: Det danske selskab, 1981, p. 691-708.
An examination of Nordic reactions to five aspects of North-South confrontation: decolonization, developmental assistance, trade, security consequences, and the impact of the North-South crisis on Nordic countries in the form of immigrants to Scandinavia.

537 **New strategic factors in the North Atlantic.**
Edited by Christoph Bertram, Johan Jørgen Holst. Oslo: Universitetsforlaget; Guildford, England: IPC Science & Technology Press, 1977. 193p. maps. (Norwegian Foreign Policy Studies, no. 21).
Thirteen essays on the strategic importance of the North Atlantic. Norwegian interests and concerns are expressed in several of the essays and two deal specifically with Norway: 'The interaction of the Arctic and the North Atlantic: a Norwegian perspective,' by Finn Sollie, (p. 94-105), and Holst's, 'The strategic importance of the North Atlantic: Norway's roles and options,' (p. 178-86).

538 **Elite images and foreign policy outcomes: a study of Norway.**
Philip M. Burgess, foreword by James A. Robinson, preface by
Henry Valen. Columbus, Ohio: Ohio State University Press,
1968. 179p. bibliog. (A Publication of the Mershon Center for
Education in National Security).

A study of Norwegian foreign policy from 1940 to 1949, emphasizing the
profound change in the government's perception of Norway's position in foreign
affairs, leading to a radical change in policy. A valuable introduction to the
subject.

539 **Refugees: the Scandinavian response.**
Nadia Christensen, Neil Hollander, Harald Mertes. *Scandinavian
Review*, vol. 70, no. 1 (1982), p. 9-32.

Outlines the involvement of the Scandinavian countries, including Norway, in
aiding refugees. Particular attention is focused on the work of various
Scandinavian agencies in Hong Kong and Thailand.

540 **The Scandinavian option: opportunities and opportunity costs in
postwar Scandinavian foreign policies.**
Barbara G. Haskel, foreword by Johan Jørgen Holst. Oslo:
Universitetsforlaget, 1976. 266p. bibliog. (Norwegian Foreign
Policy Series, no. 15).

Studies three aspects of the 'Scandinavian option' of greater cooperation or
integration; namely a common defence pact in the late 1940s, economic
integration from 1947 to 1959, and cooperation in communications and the labour
movement. All are studied in terms of the 'costing' process by which each state is
shown to have evaluated the comparative advantages of the proposals.

541 **Five roads to Nordic security.**
Edited by Johan Jørgen Holst. Oslo: Universitetsforlaget, 1973.
240p. bibliog.

A collection of five articles by leading Scandinavian scholars describing the
security policy of each of the Nordic countries. Includes an essay by Holst entitled
'Norwegian security policy: options and constraints,' (p. 77-126), which discusses
the nature of Norwegian security policy in the early 1970s, attitudes towards
NATO's future course, the impact of Norway's rejection of membership in the
EEC, Norwegian defence policy, and arms control as a factor in Norwegian
foreign policy. The work also includes separate bibliographies for each of the
countries, including a section (p. 235-37) on Norway. It was originally published
as a separate issue of *Cooperation and Conflict*, vol. 7, no. 3-4, (1972).

137

542 **The pattern of Nordic security.**
Johan Jørgen Holst. *Daedalus*, vol. 113, no. 2 (1984), p. 195-225.
A concise and critical assessment of the security pattern created by the five Nordic nations. It emphasizes Norway's importance *vis-à-vis* the other states, the military and geopolitical factors involved, and discusses nuclear options. An important work by an expert in the field.

543 **International relations and world images: a study of Norwegian foreign policy elites.**
Helge Hveem. Oslo: Universitetsforlaget, 1972. 336p. bibliog. (PRIO Monographs from the International Peace Research Institute, Oslo, no. 3).
A study of foreign policy opinions and attitudes by a Norwegian élite. The first section presents the theoretical design to be followed and the main portion of the book presents the opinions measured within the group.

544 **Quest for peace: the story of the Nobel award.**
Mortimer Lipsky. South Brunswick, New Jersey; New York: A. S. Barnes; London: Thomas Yoseloff, 1966. 281p.
Discusses the creation of the Nobel Peace Prize, which is presented in Oslo, and the persons who have won it up to the middle 1960s. The treatment is often critical and provocative.

545 **Norges traktater.** (Norway's treaties.)
Oslo: Grøndahl & Søn, 1967-1970. 4 vols.
A compendium of Norway's major treaties from 1661-1967. The first three volumes contain the treaties arranged chronologically, and printed in the original language of the treaty (Norwegian, English, French, or German). Where the original is not in Norwegian, it is translated into that language. The register provides a brief overview of each treaty, an English description, and an index ordering the treaties by the country that contracted the agreement with Norway.

546 **Scandinavian security: challenge and response.**
Edited by Nils Ørvik. Kingston, Canada: Centre for International Relations, Queen's University, Kingston, 1978. 81p. (National Security Series, 2/78).
A discussion of national security issues in Denmark, Finland, and Norway. In the chapter, 'Norwegian security: deterrence and deference,' (p. 56-81), Ørvik discusses factors important to Norwegian security such as its base policy, Spitsbergen (Svalbard), and the Barents Sea.

Foreign Relations and National Security. General

547   **The foreign policy-making process in Norway: an historical perspective.**
Olav Riste.   *Forsvarsstudier*, 1982, p. 232-45.
A brief survey of the relationship between Norwegian foreign ministers from 1905 to 1945 and a special parliamentary committee on the establishment of Norway's foreign policy.

548   **Norway.**
James Stark. In: *Nordic defense: comparative decision making.* Edited by William J. Taylor, Paul M. Cole.   Lexington, Massachusetts: Lexington Books, 1985, p. 91-125.
Studies the process by which decisions on defence are made in Norway. Describes the government agencies and the unofficial bodies that are instrumental in the process and the constraints that must be considered in making defence decisions. The work concludes with two recent case studies of defence decision-making, namely Norway's decision to purchase F-16 fighter planes from the United States and the forward bases policy in North Norway.

549   **Foreign policies of Northern Europe.**
Edited by Bengt Sundelius.   Boulder, Colorado: Westview Press, 1982. 239p. bibliog.
Eight essays by leading scholars on different aspects of Nordic foreign policy. The essays are on a comparative basis and concern such subjects as the 20th century background, domestic decision-making processes, changing strategic perspectives, Nordic policy towards international organizations, the Third World, and each other as cooperating partners.

550   **Nordic cultural cooperation with the world at large.**
Folmer Wisti. In: *Nordic democracy: ideas, issues, and institutions in politics, economy, education, social and cultural affairs of Denmark, Finland, Iceland, Norway, and Sweden.* Edited by Erik Allardt, Nils Andrén, Erik J. Friis, Gylfi T. Gislason, Sten Sparre Nilson, Henry Valen, Frantz Wendt, Folmer Wisti.   Copenhagen: Det danske selskab, 1981, p. 709-42.
Discusses some of the means and purveyors of Nordic culture throughout the world. The author outlines some of the official and unofficial channels developed by each country, to provide information about itself abroad. Norway is covered on p. 713-16. Special consideration is given to universities throughout the world that provide instruction in the Nordic languages, journals that deal especially with the Nordic region, and the role of the American-Scandinavian Foundation. For an article in the same volume that discusses support by the Nordic countries for domestic cultural programmes, see Finn Jor's 'Public support for culture and the arts,' (p. 504-16).

With other Scandinavian countries

551 **The Nordic Council: a study of Scandinavian regionalism.**
Stanley V. Andersen. Seattle, Washington: University of
Washington Press, 1967. 194p.

An examination of Scandinavian regionalism as exemplified in the nature of the
Nordic Council and its results. Andersen outlines the development of cooperation
by the Nordic Interparliamentary Union after the Second World War, the
structure of the Nordic Council, the procedures followed during its sessions, and
other forms of intergovernmental cooperation. The negotiations during the 1950s
to create a Nordic common market are studied closely as an example of the limits
of integration.

552 **'Scandinavianism.'**
Scandinavian Journal of History, vol. 9, no. 3 (1984), p. 171-253.

An entire issue of the journal devoted to Scandinavianism. Articles discuss mid-
19th century Scandinavianism; the relationship between the turn-of-the-century
Nordic Inter-Parliamentary Union and the post-Second World War Nordic
Council; post-Second World War attempts to create a Nordic economic union;
and a view of conferences of Nordic historians from 1965 to 1983.

553 **The Nordic Council and Scandinavian integration.**
Erik Solem, foreword by Frantz Wendt. New York, London:
Praeger, 1977. 197p. map. bibliog. (Praeger Special Studies in
International Politics and Government).

Studies the development of the Nordic Council after the Second World War, the
areas in which the countries have developed more common policies after the
Council was established, the organizational reforms needed to create a greater
degree of integration, and the ways in which the Nordic Council conforms to
current integration theory.

554 **Nordic industry and Nordic economic co-operation: the Nordic**
industrial federations and the Nordic customs unions negotiations
1947-1959.
Bo Stråth. Stockholm: Almqvist & Wiksell, 1978. 334p. bibliog.
(Bulletin of the Department of History, University of Gothenburg,
no. 15. Research Section: Post War History: Interest Organizations
and Internationalism).

Outlines the discussions between business and governmental leaders in Denmark,
Finland, Norway, and Sweden regarding a Nordic customs union from 1947 to
1957 in the light of other options that developed for greater Western European
unity at that time. The positions of each of the national federations of industrial
firms on this question is studied, particularly in the light of the possibility of
forming the European Free Trade Area (EFTA) in 1958. A final section
summarizes the position of the federations and Nordic cooperation as demonstrated during the period.

140

555   **Managing transnationalism in Northern Europe.**
Bengt Sundelius.   Boulder, Colorado: Westview Press, 1978.
127p.

A study of the most common forms of inter-Nordic contact and communication,
and an evaluation of the means and success of the Nordic Council in managing
them. An introductory chapter discusses some of the earlier literature on the
broader subject of Scandinavian integration.

556   **The Eastern Greenland case in historical perspective.**
Oscar Svarlien.   Gainesville, Florida: University of Florida Press,
1964. 74p. (University of Florida Monographs/Social Sciences, no.
21).

The first part of the work describes the relationship of Norway and Denmark to
Greenland from the Viking Age until the early 20th century when the dispute
over possession of it developed between them. The rest of the volume is
concerned with the legal suit on this matter, which was tried before the World
Court from 1931 to 1933 and the judgement that was delivered. An important
study of a significant issue in 20th-century Norwegian foreign policy.

557   **The other European community: integration and co-operation in
Nordic Europe.**
Barry Turner with Gunilla Nordquist.   London: Weidenfeld &
Nicolson, 1982. 307p. maps. bibliog.

Contains studies of political and economic developments in Scandinavia on a
country-by-country basis and longer discussions of the efforts since 1945 for
regional economic cooperation. The summaries of Norwegian developments are
clear and useful and Norway's involvement in discussions of a Scandinavian
economic union (Nordek), EFTA, the 1972 referendum on the EEC, and the
projected Volvo-Norway agreement of the early 1980s are cogently discussed.

558   **Cooperation in the Nordic countries: achievements and obstacles.**
Frantz Wendt.   Stockholm: Almqvist & Wiksell for the Nordic
Council, 1981. 408p. bibliog.

A detailed description of the many forms of cooperation between the Nordic
countries since the Second World War and some of the impediments that have
retarded further advances in some fields, especially the unsuccessful attempts
between 1945 and 1970 to establish a Nordic Common Market (Nordek). A
revision of the author's earlier work *The Nordic Council and cooperation in
Scandinavia* (Copenhagen: Munksgaard, 1959) and many other publications on
the same subject.

With the Great Powers

559 Norway, NATO, and the forgotten Soviet challenge.
Kirsten Amundsen. Berkeley, California: Institute of International Studies, University of California, Berkeley, 1981. 50p. maps. (Policy Papers in International Affairs).

A discussion of the strategic importance of Northern Norway and Spitsbergen (Svalbard) to the North Atlantic Treaty Organization, (NATO). The author places particular emphasis on a series of incidents in 1978 in the area, provides a critical evaluation of the Norwegian government's response to them and poses possible alternative responses.

560 Europe's North Cap and the Soviet Union.
Nils Ørvik, foreword by Henry A. Kissinger. New York: AMS, 1973. 64p. maps.

Studies Soviet objectives in Northern Scandinavia, the strategy after 1945 to attain them, and the Norwegian response that restricts defence activity in Northern Norway. First published in 1963 (Cambridge, Massachusetts: Harvard University, Occasional Papers in International Affairs, no. 6). See also 'Base policy: theory and practice,' *Cooperation and Conflict*, vol. 2 (1967), p. 188-203, by the same author.

561 The Spitsbergen (Svalbard) question: United States foreign policy, 1907-1935.
Elen C. Singh. Oslo: Universitetsforlaget, 1980. 244p. maps. bibliog.

A description of US policy regarding the ownership of Spitsbergen (Svalbard) from 1907 until 1935 when Russia adhered to the Spitsbergen Treaty. Also studies the influence of the American mining companies, Arctic Coal Company and Ayer and Longyear, on the formulation of that policy.

562 The United States in Norwegian history.
Sigmund Skard. New York, London: Greenwood Press; Oslo: Universitetsforlaget, 1976. 216p. bibliog. (Contributions in American studies, vol. 26, Greenwood Press; Publications of the American Institute University of Oslo).

This abridged version of *USA i norsk historie 1000-1776-1976* (Oslo: Det Norske Samlaget, 1976), presents a study of America's image in Norway, particularly from 1815 to 1940. Includes the impressions of prominent politicians and writers and the impact of some Americans, such as Theodore Roosevelt, whom Norwegians happened to encounter in their own land.

With NATO, EFTA and the EEC

563 **Norway and Europe in the 1970's.**
Hilary Allen. Oslo: Universitetsforlaget, 1979. 289p. bibliog.
(Norwegian Foreign Policy Studies, no. 27).

A study of the events and issues involved in Norway's referendum of 1972 regarding application for membership of the European Economic Community, (EEC) and Norway's relationship with that body until 1977. Discusses Norway's initial interest in EEC membership in the 1960s; the negotiations of the late 1960s to create a Nordic economic union; and the EEC debate in Norway from 1970 to 1972. The final part deals with the post-referendum period.

564 **Norway's security and European foreign policy in the 1980's.**
European Movement in Norway. Oslo: Universitetsforlaget, 1981. 80p.

A report by the committee delegated by the organization to recommend foreign policy programmes for Norway during the 1980s. The basic suggestions of the group were the strengthening of the country's ties with the North Atlantic Treaty Organization (NATO), the EEC, and the USA.

565 **One for all or four for the fifth: standardization and the F-16 in Europe.**
Bjørn Hagelin. *Cooperation and Conflict*, vol. 13, no. 3 (1978), p. 133-46.

A critical study of the 'two-way street' policy established by the US government in the mid-1970s to develop the F-16 fighter plane in conjunction with four other NATO nations, including Norway. The author emphasizes both the benefits and the limitations of the programme.

566 **Religious attitudes and arguments in the Norwegian EEC debate.**
Thor Hall. *Scandinavian Studies*, vol. 46, no. 4 (1974), p. 370-91.

Identifies three major religious arguments that developed during the debate prior to the referendum in 1972 over Norwegian membership of the EEC. The author also discusses the impact of the religious debate on the outcome of the referendum.

567 **Norway and NATO.**
Johan Jørgen Holst. *Scandinavian Review*, vol. 72, no. 3 (1984), p. 14-18, 36-46. map.

An important assessment of Norway's participation in NATO which is based on the twin concepts of deterrence capability and reassurance to the USSR by limiting NATO access to Northern Norway and imposing restrictions on the availability of nuclear weapons.

568 **Norway and EEC.**
Ingunn Norderval Means. *Scandinavian Studies*, vol. 46, no. 4 (1974), p. 352-69.
Studies the results of the 1972 referendum that rejected membership of the EEC. Primary emphasis is given to the opposition of the young and educated people who opposed membership in far greater numbers than anticipated.

569 **The reluctant Europeans: the attitudes of the Nordic countries towards European integration.**
Toivo Miljan. Montreal: McGill-Queen's University Press, 1977. 325p. bibliog.
A study of the specific political and economic interests of Finland, Sweden, Norway, and Denmark, including their many successful attempts to cooperate with each other, and the difficulties they have had in extending this mutual cooperation as a group to wider European economic and political associations. Extensive consideration is given to the abortive efforts to create Nordek, a Nordic free trade association, the establishment of the European Free Trade Area (EFTA) and in particular the policies each established towards the EEC in the early 1970s. In addition to specific references to Norway's role and interests in these events throughout the book, the author devotes an entire chapter (p. 190-230) to Norway's rejection of membership of the EEC.

570 **From a Northern customs union to EFTA.**
Arthur Montgomery. *Scandinavian Economic History Review*, vol. 8, no. 1 (1960), p. 45-70.
Describes the deliberations of the Nordic states from 1945 to 1959 regarding economic cooperation. As a result of their desire to widen the zone of cooperation as far as possible, they rejected the option of a Nordic customs union in favour of EFTA (European Free Trade Area) in 1959.

571 **Fears and expectations: Norwegian attitudes toward European integration.**
Edited by Nils Ørvik. Oslo: Universitetsforlaget, 1972. 371p. bibliog.
Six essays discuss aspects of the debate in Norway in the 1960s on membership of the EEC. Published prior to the decisive referendum of 1972, this volume studies more thoroughly than some later works the factors that led to the referendum.

572 **Norway's no to Europe.**
Edited by Nils Ørvik. Pittsburgh, Pennsylvania: International Studies Association, University Center for International Studies, University of Pittsburgh, 1975. 79p. (International Studies, Occasional Papers, no. 5).
Three articles dealing with the EEC referendum of 1972 in Norway. Daniel Heradstveit contributed 'The red/green alliance in Norwegian politics: a strange partnership' (p. 7-17); Ørvik discussed 'The Norwegian Labor Party (NLP) and

144

the 1972 referendum' (p. 19-41); and David L. Larson's article was on 'Selected
foreign policy elites' (p. 43-70).

573 **The Scandinavian allies and the European community.**
     Edited by Nils Ørvik.   Kingston, Canada: Centre for International
     Relations, Queen's University, Kingston, 1978. 98p. (The
     European Studies Programme, 1/78).
Most of the study was written by Ørvik and his main contribution is 'Norway and
the European Community, 1972-1977,' (p. 27-64). It discusses the economic
agreement established between Norway and the EEC in 1973 and the relationship
between them afterwards as an example of the subtle changes that have occurred
in Norwegian foreign policy during the 1970s.

Scandinavia.
See item no. 20.

The Norwegian-Soviet boundary: a study in political geography.
See item no. 68.

**The decline of neutrality 1914-1941 with special reference to the United
States and the Northern neutrals.**
See item no. 149.

The Scandinavian states and the League of Nations.
See item no. 151.

**Svalbard in international politics 1871-1925: the solution of a unique
international problem.**
See item no. 152.

Svalbard in the changing Arctic.
See item no. 153.

**British views on Norwegian-Swedish problems 1880-1895: selections from
diplomatic correspondence.**
See item no. 230.

Scandinavia in great power politics 1905-1908.
See item no. 242.

**The neutral ally: Norway's relations with belligerent powers in the First
World War.**
See item no. 244.

Great Britain and the problem of bases in the Nordic areas 1945-1947.
See item no. 270.

America, Scandinavia and the Cold War 1945-1949.
See item no. 271.

Foreign Relations and National Security. With NATO, EFTA & EEC

Winning the peace: vision and disappointment in Nordic security policy 1945-49.
See item no. 272.

Norwegian attitudes to a Nordic nuclear-free zone 1958-1982.
See item no. 273.

Great power politics and Norwegian foreign policy: a study of Norway's foreign relations November 1940-February 1948.
See item no. 274.

Norway, oil, and foreign policy.
See item no. 610.

Petroleum and international relations: the case of Norway.
See item no. 620.

The political implications of North Sea oil and gas.
See item no. 623.

Bulletin of Peace Research.
See item no. 879.

Cooperation and Conflict.
See item no. 880.

Forsvarsstudier. (Defence Studies.)
See item no. 881.

Journal of Peace Research.
See item no. 882.

Scandinavia in social science literature: an English language bibliography.
See item no. 920.

Norwegian foreign policy: a bibliography 1905-1965.
See item no. 940.

Norwegian foreign policy: a bibliography 1965-1970.
See item no. 941.

Economy

General

574 Industries of Norway: technical and commercial achievements.
Edited by Olge J. Adamson, preface by Lars Evensen. [Oslo]:
Dreyer, [1952]. 391p.
A collection of short articles intended to describe virtually all facets of the
Norwegian economy and to promote Norwegian trade. Covers energy, mining,
forestry, agriculture, and fishing along with many other topics.

575 Economic Bulletin.
Oslo: Economic Intelligence Department of Norges Bank, 1925–.
quarterly.
Topical articles in English on Norwegian financial and monetary affairs, which
represent both private views and governmental policy. The bank also prepares an
annual *Report and Accounts*, an extensive survey of the Norwegian economy and
monetary conditions.

576 The Norwegian economy 1920-1980.
Fritz Hodne, introduction by Derek H. Aldcroft. London:
Croom Helm; New York: St. Martin's Press, 1983. 286p. bibliog.
(Contemporary Economic History of Europe, no. 3).
The author treats his subject chronologically, with a somewhat greater emphasis
on the decade from 1940 to 1950. Suitable for both the general reader and those
with a special interest in economic history. Also see Hodne's *An economic history
of Norway* (Trondheim, Norway: Tipir, 1975. 549p.).

577   **Industribanken: Årsberetning.** (Industry Bank: Annual Report.)
Oslo: Den norske Industribank, –. annual.

The annual report of Den norske Industribank (The Norwegian Bank for
Industry), a semi-public bank established in 1977 for the development of small
industry in Norway. Contains an English summary with statistical data.

578   **Norway at work: a survey of the principal branches of the economy.**
Ole Knudsen.   Oslo: Johan Grundt Tanum Forlag, 1972. 83p.
(Tokens of Norway).

A basic survey of the main aspects of Norway's economy. Topics covered include
farming, forestry, fishing, hydro-electric power, industry, shipping, trade, and
tourism. A useful introduction to the subject, first published in 1959.

579   **Multinational corporations in the Nordic countries.**
Olav Knudsen. In: *Nordic democracy: ideas, issues, and institutions
in politics, economy, education, social and cultural affairs of
Denmark, Finland, Iceland, Norway, and Sweden.* Edited by Erik
Allardt, Nils Andrén, Erik J. Friis, Gylfi T. Gislason, Sten Sparre
Nilson, Henry Valen, Frantz Wendt, Folmer Wisti.   Copenhagen:
Det danske selskab, 1981, p. 384-98. bibliog.

Studies the impact of multi-national corporations on the economic mechanisms of
the Nordic states and on democracy in economic life. Among the subjects
discussed are the degree of centralization in the decision-making of these
corporations and their impact on employment, sales, and specific industries.

580   **Nordic Countries Business Outlook.**
Oslo: Den norske Creditbank, –. quarterly.

A summary of Scandinavian economic and business news by banking firms in four
countries. The bank also publishes *The DNC Monthly Survey of Norwegian
Trade, Industry and Finance.*

581   **Norway: the next richest nation: a survey.**
Economist. Nov. 15, 1975. Survey. 30p. maps.

A special section outlining several aspects of Norwegian economic development
and politics. A useful brief introduction to the Norwegian economy.

582   **Norwegian American Commerce.**
New York: Norwegian-American Chamber of Commerce, –.
quarterly.

This English language magazine discusses Norwegian life, economy, and trade.
The same organization also publishes a newsletter, *Norwegian Trade Bulletin*, that
appears eight times per year, with briefer articles on Norwegian industry and
trade.

583 **Økonomisk Utsyn.** (Economic Survey.)
Oslo: Statistisk sentralbyrå, –. annual. (Norges offisielle statistikk).
Statistical survey of the Norwegian economy with an extensive summary in English and several tables labelled in English.

584 **OECD Economic Survey: Norway.**
Organisation for Economic Cooperation and Development.
Paris: Organisation for Economic Cooperation and Development, 1961-. annual.
Reports economic conditions in Norway and provides forecasts.

585 **The Norwegian economy.**
Ståle Seierstad. In: *Norwegian society*. Edited by Natalie Rogoff Ramsøy. Oslo: Universitetsforlaget, 1974, p. 76-107.
Examines the Norwegian economy in comparison with other countries, the economic implications of social welfare programmes, and major trends in economic development.

Regional studies

586 **The economic structure.**
Egil Akselsen. In: *Norway North of 65*. Edited by Ørnulf Vorren. Oslo: Oslo University Press; London: George Allen & Unwin, 1960, p. 147-58. (Tromsø Museums Skrifter, vol. 8).
Akselsen discusses the main segments of the North Norway economy based on the occupations of the population.

587 **The role of the entrepreneur in social change in Northern Norway.**
Edited by Frederik Barth. Bergen, Norway: Norwegian Universities Press, 1963. 83p. bibliog. (Acta Universitatis Bergensis Series Humaniorum Litterarum: Årsbok for Universitet i Bergen Humanistisk Serie 1963, no. 3).
Four essays discussing forms of economic, social and political activity in North Norway during the 1950s.

149

Cooperatives

588 **Cooperatives in Norway.**
O. B. Grimley. Oslo: Co-operative Union and Wholesale
Society, 1950. 178p.

An important study of the development of the cooperative movement from the
mid-19th century until the late 1940s and the agricultural, fishing, and housing
cooperatives that have been created.

589 **The cooperative movement.**
Herman Stolpe. In: *Nordic democracy: ideas, issues, and institu-*
tions in politics, economy, education, social and cultural affairs of
Denmark, Finland, Iceland, Norway, and Sweden. Edited by Erik
Allardt, Nils Andrén, Erik J. Friis, Gylfi T. Gislason, Sten Sparre
Nilson, Henry Valen, Frantz Wendt, Folmer Wisti. Copenhagen:
Det danske selskab, 1981, p. 359-83. bibliog.

Provides an outline of the cooperative activities within each of the Nordic states.
The brief section on Norway, (p. 373-77) provides a summary of the formation of
consumers' and agricultural cooperatives and their present status.

Economic policy and planning

590 **Planning in Norway.**
P. J. Bjerve. Amsterdam: North Holland Publishing Company,
1959. 383p. (Contributions to Economic Analysis, no. 16).

A detailed mathematical study of the Norwegian economy presuming both an
extensive interest in and knowledge of economics. The subjects studied include
national budgeting, production, foreign trade, consumption, investment, and
building. Bjerve was the Director of Norway's Central Bureau of Statistics when
he prepared this volume.

591 **Norway: the planned revival.**
Alice Bourneuf. Cambridge, Massachusetts: Harvard University
Press, 1958. 233p. bibliog.

Studies Norway's economic recovery from 1945 to 1952 and the government
planning policies and programmes that made it possible.

592 **State intervention and economic freedom.**
Nils Elvander. In: *Nordic democracy: ideas, issues, and institutions in politics, economy, education, social and cultural affairs of Denmark, Finland, Iceland, Norway, and Sweden.* Edited by Erik Allardt, Nils Andrén, Erik J. Friis, Gylfi T. Gislason, Sten Sparre Nilson, Henry Valen, Frantz Wendt, Folmer Wisti. Copenhagen: Det danske selskab, 1981, p. 279-307. bibliog.

Summarizes government policy in the Scandinavian countries on three major topics: industrial and employment policy; incomes and wages policy; and the issue of economic or industrial democracy, especially the creation of wage earner funds. Although the latter issue concerns Sweden much more than the other nations, Norwegian policy and experience is covered in the discussion of the first two themes.

593 **Norway twenty years after the Marshall Plan.**
Eivind Erichsen. In: *Inflation, trade and taxes: essays in honor of Alice Bourneuf.* Edited by David A. Belsley. Columbus, Ohio: Ohio State University Press, 1976, p. 163-77.

Enumerates fifteen factors affecting Norwgian economic development and change from the mid-1950s until the early 1970s. Using Alice Bourneuf's *Norway: the planned revival* (q.v.) as a basis, Erichsen emphasizes the role of governmental economic planning.

594 **Economic planning in Norway: methods and models.**
Edited by Leif Johansen, Harald Hallaråker. Oslo: Universitetsforlaget, 1970. 153p.

An explanation of the introduction and the course of economic planning models in the national governmental budgeting process in Norway in 1945 and a detailed description of the budgetary models used by the government in the late 1960s.

595 **Wages and economic control in Norway 1945-1957.**
Mark W. Leiserson, foreword by Summer H. Slichter. Cambridge, Massachusetts: Harvard University Press, 1959. 174p. (Wortheim Publications in Industrial Relations).

Examines the wages policy of the Norwegian government during the first post-war decade and the collective bargaining system.

596 **Toward income equality in Norway.**
Lee Soltow. Madison, Milwaukee, Wisconsin: University of Wisconsin Press, 1965. 155p. maps. bibliog.

A study of income distribution among different income groups in Norway. Data for the study is based primarily on the research carried out on eight Norwegian cities over a one hundred year period. The final chapter studies the effects of income redistribution in Norway in the early 1960s.

Taxation

597 **Taxes in Norway: a survey of the Norwegian tax system in 1967.**
Oslo: Royal Ministry of Finance and Customs, [1967]. 2nd. ed.
93p.

A revision of a 1965 publication intended to acquaint the English-speaking reader
with the laws as they existed at that time. Although some changes have occurred
since this work was published, it still provides a useful overview.

Norway: land, people, industries: a brief geography.
See item no. 47.

An economic geography of the Scandinavian states and Finland.
See item no. 55.

Sogn og Fjordane in the fjord economy of West Norway.
See item no. 70.

The dissolution of estate society in Norway.
See item no. 237.

The Fascist economy in Norway.
See item no. 259.

Demographic developments and economic growth in Norway 1740-1940.
See item no. 310.

Scandinavian Economic History Review.
See item no. 893.

Scandinavia in social science literature: an English language bibliography.
See item no. 920.

Finance, Banking and Investment

598 **The Norwegian monetary and credit system.**
Leif Eide, Knut Holli, Erik Bjørland. Oslo: Norges Bank, 1985.
56p. (Norges Bank Skriftserie, no. 15).

A brief explanation of Norway's financial system, emphasizing the way governmental agencies and financial institutions produce financial policy. First published by Eide in 1973 in English and Norwegian (*Det norske penge-og kreditsystem*), revised in 1980 in both languages by Eide and Holli and now issued and revised again primarily by Bjørland.

599 **The concession process and foreign capital in Norway.**
Peter Karl Kresl. Oslo: Norges Bank, 1976. 36p. bibliog. (Norges Banks Skriftserie, no. 4).

A study of the concession process, emphasizing the means of securing concessions to produce manufactured goods in Norway, and the maintenance of the license privilege.

600 **The central bank and political authorities in some industrial countries.**
Hermod Skånland. Oslo: Norges Bank, 1984. 38p. bibliog. (Norges Bank Skriftserie, no. 13).

A comparison of the role of national central banks in the determination of economic policy in a number of countries, including Norway, the USA, Canada, Australia, and Japan. To achieve this purpose, Skånland examines the relationship of the central banks to political authorities as established by law, the guidelines for monetary and credit policy, and the responsibility which these banks have in other fields.

601 **Foreign ownership in Norwegian enterprises.**
Arthur Stonehill.   Oslo: Statistisk Sentralbyrå, 1965. 213p.
(Samfunnsøkonomiske studier, no. 14).

Examines the historical development of the importation of foreign capital to
Norway from 1814 to 1864 and discusses the impact of foreign capital on Norway,
particularly its benefits for the Norwegian economy. A Norwegian summary is
included, (p. 204-13).

Trade, Industry and Shipping

602 **Industry and mining.**
  Leif Aune. In: *Norway North of 65*. Edited by Ørnulf Vorren.
  Oslo: Oslo University Press; London: George Allen & Unwin,
  1960, p. 216-36.
Describes the various timber and mining industries operating in North Norway,
their distribution within the region, and the programmes enacted by the
government during the 1950s to promote economic development in the region.

603 **A ship from Norway.**
  Edited by Einar Berggren, Finn P. Nyquist, Odd-Leif Skundberg.
  Oslo: North Sea Press/Grøndahl Production, 1974. 167p.
A richly-illustrated work that portrays a very positive image of the Norwegian
shipping industry. By no means a scholarly study, it is nevertheless useful to the
general reader as a representation of Norwegian shipping activities, ship
construction, and life aboard ship.

604 **Shipping in the Norwegian economy.**
  [Leif. F. Eide]. *Economic Bulletin: Norges Bank*, vol. 38, no. 2
  (1967), p. 66-74.
A brief survey of Norway's merchant marine from 1950 to 1967, indicating its
growth during the period and providing some predictions for the future.

605 **Norway: chemical products exports.**
  Edited by Eivind Flaatten.   Oslo: Norges Eksportsråd, 1952. 64p.
An overview of Norway's commercial chemical industry, explaining the products
manufactured in Norway and advertising them for sale abroad.

606 **Norway and the Bergen Line: a centenary publication.**
Wilhelm Keilhau. Bergen, Norway: John Griegs, 1953. 369p.

An edited translation of the author's *Norges eldste linjerederi* (Norway's oldest
shipping company), published in 1951 on the one hundredth anniversary of the
firm. The work contains a discussion of Bergen's role in Norwegian history until
1850 as well as a chronological account of the Bergen Line. A significant account
of a major Norwegian shipping firm.

607 **Iron ore production at Kirkenes, Norway.**
Trevor Lloyd. *Economic Geography*, vol. 31 (1955), p. 211-33.
maps.

Describes the development of mining at Kirkenes, the processes involved, and
shipment abroad for the production of steel.

608 **The saga of Norwegian shipping: an outline of the history, growth,
and development of a modern merchant marine.**
Oslo: Dreyers Forlag, 1955. 240p.

A historical introduction to the Norwegian shipping industry. Brief consideration
is given to the period prior to the 20th century and approximately one-half of the
book is devoted to a discussion of the Norwegian merchant marine during the
Second Word War, the problems of post-war rebuilding, and the impact of the
shipping industry on the Norwegian economy.

The Nordic countries 1850-1914.
See item no. 145.

Scandinavia 1914-1970.
See item no. 146.

**The Northern seas: shipping and commerce in Northern Europe A.D.
300-1100.**
See item no. 184.

**The Hanseatic control of Norwegian commerce during the late Middle
Ages.**
See item no. 205.

**War and trade in Northern seas: Anglo-Scandinavian economic relations
in the mid-eighteenth century.**
See item no. 220.

The industrialization of Norway 1800-1920.
See item no. 232.

The economic development of continental Europe 1780-1870.
See item no. 234.

Norwegian sailors in American waters: a study in the history of maritime activity on the Eastern seaboard.
See item no. 377.

Company, trade, and tax law in Norway.
See item no. 523.

Industriens historie: en bibliografi. (Industry's history: a bibliography.)
See item no. 928.

Energy and Natural Resources

609 **Scandinavia rejects the nuclear option.**
Dean Abrahamson, Thomas B. Johannson. *Scandinavian Review*,
vol. 70, no. 3 (1982), p. 64-71.
Discusses the interest originally shown by many of the Scandinavian countries in the non-military uses of nuclear energy and the factors that led some of them to reject this energy alternative. A worthwhile introduction to the question.

610 **Norway, oil, and foreign policy.**
John C. Ausland. Boulder, Colorado: Westview Press; Oslo: J.
W. Cappelens Forlag, 1979. 140p. maps. (Westview Special Study).
Studies Norway's development as an oil-producing nation, policy issues such as production limitations and price, the implications of oil production in the Barents Sea and Spitsbergen (Svalbard), and aspects of crisis management.

611 **Using the oil and gas revenues: the Norwegian case.**
Olav Bjerkholt, Lorents Lorentsen, Steinar Strøm. Oslo: Statistisk Sentralbyrå, 1982. 14p. bibliog. (Artikler fra Statistisk Sentralbyrå, no. 133).
A discussion of the theoretical aspects of Norwegian depletion policy and the two alternative strategies regarding the use of oil and gas revenues and their consequences. A reprint of an article originally published on p. 171-84 of *Oil or industry: energy, industrialization and economic policy in Canada, Mexico, the Netherlands, Norway and the United Kingdom* (London: Academic Press, 1981), edited by Terry Barker and Vladimir Brailovski.

158

612 **North Sea oil and gas: a geographical perspective.**
Keith Chapman. Newton Abbot, England: David & Charles,
1976. 240p. maps. (Problems in Modern Geography).

An examination in non-technical terms of the factors creating a significant
demand for oil in Europe, the discovery and development of oil resources in the
North Sea, and the policies and programmes developed by the nations concerned,
including Norway, to exploit this resource.

613 **Energy: dilemma of the decade.**
Scandinavian Review, vol. 66, no. 3 (1978), 66p.

The entire issue of the journal is devoted to the subject. Topics considered
include the nuclear power alternative, 'waste heat,' and hydroelectricity.

614 **Fact Sheet: the Norwegian Continental Shelf.**
Oslo: Royal Ministry of Petroleum and Energy, –. quarterly.

A publication in English outlining the background of Norwegian oil exploration,
the fields under production, those being considered for development, licensing
procedures, blocks awarded for development, and market conditions.

615 **Norwegian oil policies.**
Terje Lind, G. A. Mackay. Montreal: McGill-Queen's University
Press; London: Hurst, 1979. 150p. map. bibliog.

Places Norwegian oil activities in an international context and discusses
Norwegian government policy towards licensing, exploration, processing, employment considerations, Statoil (the state-owned oil company), and the use of oil
revenues.

616 **Petroleum and economic development: the cases of Mexico and
Norway.**
Ragaei El Mallakh, Øystein Noreng, Barry W. Poulson.
Lexington, Massachusetts: Lexington Books, 1984. 197p.

The impact of oil on the Norwegian economy is discussed on p. 77-140. The
authors provide a brief outline of the Norwegian economy prior to the discovery
of oil, some of the assumptions made in the early 1970s on the effect of oil on the
economy, and the problems that developed through miscalculations. An appendix
studies two of the econometric models that have been developed to study the
Norwegian economy.

617 **Second decade for Norwegian oil: second thoughts?**
Randy G. Morse. *Scandinavian Review*, vol. 65, no. 1 (1977),
p. 24-31. map.

Discusses the rapid but controlled development of Norway's oil industry and some
of the problems that have occurred.

618 **Hydro-electric power development in Norway.**
Alice F. A. Mutton. *Institute of British Geographers, Transactions and Papers*, vol. 19 (1953), p. 123-30. maps.

Outlines the use of hydroelectric power in Norway and the regional distribution of power plants.

619 **The oil industry and government strategy in the North Sea.**
Øystein Noreng, introduction by Ragaei El Mallakh. London: Croom Helm, 1980. 268p. maps. (International Research Center for Energy and Economic Development (ICEED), Boulder, Colorado).

Studies the economic aspects of North Sea energy development and the impact this has had on the development of governmental policy and regulation in Norway and the United Kingdom.

620 **Petroleum and international relations: the case of Norway.**
Cooperation and Conflict, vol. 17, no. 2 (1982), p. 86-150.

An entire issue of the journal devoted to Norway's petroleum policy and its international implications, with contributions by Øystein Noreng, Gunnar Gjerde, Helge Ole Bergesen, Willy Østreng, and Martin Sæter.

621 **Petroleum industry in Norwegian society.**
[Oslo]: Royal Norwegian Ministry of Finance, [1974]. 24p. + 103p. (Parliamentary Report, no. 25 (1973-74).)

A parliamentary report on the possibilities for securing oil from the Norwegian Continental Shelf and the North Sea and the repercussions this might have on Norwegian society and the economy.

622 **The changing pattern of Norwegian hydro-electric development.**
William Lindsay Raitt. *Economic Geography*, vol. 34 (1958), p. 127-44. maps.

A survey of Norwegian hydroelectricity undertaken in 1956, pointing out changes in the production of power through a centralization process.

623 **The political implications of North Sea oil and gas.**
Edited by Martin Saeter, Ian Smart. Oslo: Universitetsforlaget; Guildford, England: IPC Science and Technology Press, 1975. 168p. maps.

Contains seven articles on the economic and political possibilities of oil and gas development in the North Sea. Although most of the articles deal generally with all the North Sea states, Bjørn Skogstad Aamo's essay 'Norwegian oil policy: basic objectives,' (p. 81-92) and Johan Jørgen Holst's contribution, 'The strategic and security requirements of North Sea oil and gas,' (p. 131-44) are particularly relevant to Norway.

624   **The impact of North Sea oil in Norway and Scotland.**
Susan M. Squires.   *Norsk Geografisk Tidsskrift*, vol. 29 (1975),
p. 133-40. bibliog.
Outlines some of the problems connected with the oil boom in both countries in
areas such as housing, education, job disturbance, and the environment. In the
section on Norway, the emphasis is on Stavanger.

625   **Regional and structural effects of North Sea oil in Norway.**
Kjell Stenstadvold.   Bergen, Norway: Department of Geography,
Norwegian School of Economics, 1977. 55p. maps. bibliog.
(Meddelelser fra Geografisk Institutt ved Norges Handelshøyskole
og Universitet i Bergen, (Occasional Papers, no. 37).)
Emphasizes the geographical and economic aspects of Norwegian oil develop-
ment. The two main chapters discuss the regional distribution of the oil industry
in Norway and the impact of oil activities on local employment.

626   **The geography of power: its sources and transmission.**
Earl of Verulam, J. Houston Angus, S. Chaplin.   *Geographical
Journal*, vol. 118, no. 3 (1952), p. 251-66. maps.
A comparative study of hydroelectric power which includes Norwegian examples.
Places the Norwegian programme in the larger context of international
developments.

The North Sea.
See item no. 98.

Once upon a town: Susan Tyrell about Stavanger.
See item no. 107.

Care of the environment in Scandinavia.
See item no. 672.

Agriculture
and Forestry

627 **Agricultural policy in Norway.**
Paris: Organisation for Economic Co-operation and Development,
1975. 46p. (Agricultural Policy Reports).
This report provides an overview of the state of Norwegian agriculture,
supplemented by several tables and diagrams of statistical data and an explanation
of Norwegian agricultural policy.

628 **Norwegian seter-farming.**
Halvard Bjørvik. *Scandinavian Economic History Review*, vol.
11, no. 2 (1963), p. 156-66.
Consists of a review article discussing the Institutt for sammenlignende kulturforskning (Institute for Comparative Research in Human Culture) and three
articles by its director, Dr. Lars Rinton, concerning *seter* or mountain pasture
farming. The work outlines the nature and development of this form of
Norwegian agriculture.

629 **Orientation and intensity of Norwegian agriculture.**
Asbjørn Nordgård. *Norsk Geografisk Tidsskrift*, vol. 29 (1975),
p. 169-220. maps. bibliog.
Presents a detailed study of modern Norwegian agriculture, including the types of
agriculture practiced in different regions, the intensity with which these forms of
agriculture can be carried out, and some of the changes that have occurred.

630 **Types and regions of Norwegian agriculture.**
Asbjørn Nordgård. *Norsk Geografisk Tidsskrift*, vol. 31 (1977),
p. 15-26. maps. bibliog.
A scholarly study of the types and intensity of agriculture practiced.

631 **An outline of Norwegian forests, with an introduction to the Norwegian forest industry.**
Edited by Knut Skinnemoen. Oslo: Det Norske Skogselslap, 1964. 2nd ed. 124p. maps.

A survey of forestry and the timber industry, first published in 1956. Emphasis is on the latter, including felling, transport, labour conditions, and forest policy. The final chapter lists organizations, governmental bodies, and research institutions involved in the industry.

632 **The physical background of Norwegian agriculture.**
Axel Sømme. *Geography*, vol. 35 (1950), p. 141-54. maps.

A classic description of Norway's geographic and climatic features that have an impact on the nature of Norwegian agriculture. For a more specialized article in the same journal, see A. J. Savory's 'Farming in the North Trøndelag,' vol. 39, no. 4 (1954), p. 272-82.

633 **Norway's internal migration to new farms since 1920.**
Kirk H. Stone. The Hague: Martinus Nijhoff, 1971. 68p. maps. (European Demographic Monographs, no. 1).

Studies the impact of legislation passed in 1920 to encourage land reclamation and the homesteading of new farms, with particular emphasis on regions where this process has been most extensive.

634 **Reindeer.**
Ørnulf Vorren. In: *Norway North of 65*. Edited by Ørnulf Vorren. Oslo: Oslo University Press; London: George Allen & Unwin, 1960, p. 172-90. maps. bibliog.

Covers the development of reindeer-herding, its administration by the government, the slaughter and sale of reindeer, and the research and educational programmes of the industry. For an interesting article on agriculture in Northern Norway, see 'Agriculture,' by Karl Florvik and Jonas Lysso (p. 157-71) in the same volume.

635 **Private forestry in Norway: a case study in small woodland management and policy.**
John A. Zivnuska. Washington DC: Society of American Foresters, 1959. 49p. bibliog. (Forest Science Monograph no. 1).

Surveys many aspects of private forestry in Norway, including the economic and technical considerations of forest management, governmental regulation, financing operations, and marketing procedures.

Jordbrukets geografi i Norge: B: atlas. (Geography of Norwegian agriculture: B: atlas.)
See item no. 88.

Agriculture and Forestry

Farms and fanes of ancient Norway: the place-names of a country discussed in their bearings on social and religious history.
See item no. 131.

Agrarian structure and peasant politics in Scandinavia: a comparative study of rural response to economic change.
See item no. 150.

The strength of tradition: a historiographical analysis of research into Norwegian agriculture during the late Middle Ages and the early modern period.
See item no. 281.

Brewing and beer traditions in Norway: the social anthropological background of the brewing industry.
See item no. 830.

Fishing and Whaling

636 **Norway's usage and prescription in the matter of coastal fisheries.**
Christopher Meyer. Oslo: Bentzens, [1951]. 92p. map.
A discussion of the question of Norway's exclusive fishing rights in coastal waters, particularly in North Norway.

637 **The spring herring fishing and the industrial revolution in Western Norway in the nineteenth century.**
Reider Ostensjø. *Scandinavian Economic History Review*, vol. 11, no. 2 (1963), p. 135-55.
When the fishing grounds for the spring herring were centered off Western Norway from 1808 to 1870, the old subsistence economy disappeared so completely that even when this phenomenon came to an end in 1870 the older economic system did not come back.

638 **Norwegian fisheries research.**
Gunnar Rollefsen. Bergen, Norway: Directorate of Fisheries, 1966. 36p. (Fiskedirektoratets Skrifter, vol. 14, no. 1).
This history emphasizes work undertaken since 1800 with concluding comments on contemporary research.

639 **Fisheries.**
Gunnar Sætersdal. In: *Norway North of 65*. Edited by Ørnulf Vorren. Oslo: Oslo University Press; London: George Allen & Unwin, 1960, p. 191-208.
A survey of the Northern Norway fishing industry: the types of fish, number of fishermen, methods used, and the problems faced by the industry in the late 1950s. See also the article by Anton Jakobsen, 'Sealing and whaling,' in the same volume (p. 209-15).

640 **Commercial fishing in Norway.**
Lawrence M. Sommers. In: *Readings in economic geography*.
Edited by Howard G. Roepke with the assistance of Thomas J.
Maresh. New York: John Wiley & Sons, 1967, p. 71-80.

Discusses some of the changes that have taken place in Norwegian commercial
fishing during the 20th century, technological developments, and marketing and
processing innovations.

641 **The history of modern whaling.**
Johannes N. Tønnessen, Arne Odd Johnsen, translated from the
Norwegian by R. I. Christopherson. London: Hurst; Canberra:
Australian National University Press, 1982. 798p.

Originally published in Norwegian as *Den moderne hvalfangste historie: opprinelse
og utvikling*, (Oslo: H. Aschehoug & Co. (W. Nygaard), 1959-1970. 4 vols.). This
work is an abridged version. Given the importance of whaling to Norway, the
country's role in the industry is emphasized.

Transport and Communications

642   Communications.

Asbjørn Aase. In: *Norway North of 65*. Edited by Ørnulf
Vorren.   Oslo: Oslo University Press; London: George Allen &
Unwin, 1960, p. 237-47. bibliog.

Describes the different forms of communication and transport that have been
developed in Northern Norway by sea, road, railway, and air and outlines the
difficulties imposed on all forms of travel by the climate.

**643   The Scandinavian Airlines System (S.A.S.): its origin, present
organization and legal aspects.**

Henrik Bahr.   *Arkiv for Luftrett*, vol. 1 (1958-62), p. 199-253.

Studies the factors that led to the formation of the Scandinavian Airlines System,
(SAS) in 1951, the legal points of the agreement forming the airline, its
administrative apparatus, and legal issues raised by the agreement.

644   The Arctic Highway: a road and its setting.

John Douglas.   Newton Abbot, England: David & Charles;
Harrisburg, Pennsylvania: Stackpole Books, 1972. 251p. maps.

A scholarly study of the Arctic Highway that begins in Mo i Rana and extends for
over 900 miles to Kirkenes. Douglas first discusses the highway's natural setting,
its history, and development. Four chapters are devoted to a detailed description
of the highway from one end to the other and two final chapters discuss the
highway's future and its impact on the Lapps.

167

Transport and Communications

645   **Møre and Romsdal, Norway: a study of changes in the rural transport system of a coastal area.**
Margaret C. Gilpern.   *Geography*, vol. 53, no. 2 (1968),
p. 145-56. maps.

A study of the impact of post-war changes in transportation systems on the remote, rural county of Møre and Romsdal. The article traces the decline of public transportation and the increase in car travel and studies its impact on the economy of the region.

646   **Norwegian road plan II: traffic and the urban environment.**
Oslo: Universitetsforlaget, [1977]. 20p. (Norwegian Official
Reports, NOU 40 C).

An overview of the report by the Road Plan Commission regarding intra-urban transportation. It discusses some of the problems involved and the goals of the plan and includes the plans developed for the city of Haugesand as an example of the thirty-eight public transport plans created as a part of this project.

Labour Relations, the Labour Movement and Trade Unions

647 **The Norwegian trade union movement.**
Edvard Bull, preface by Konrad Nordahl. Brussels: International
Confederation of Free Trade Unions, 1956. 138p. map. bibliog.
(ICFTU Monographs on National Trade Union Movements, no.
4).

Most of the book discusses the development and growth of the trade union
movement from the very late 19th century until the immediate post-Second World
War period. The last three chapters, however, discuss various services which were
available by the 1950s to trade union members, the unions that developed during
the period and the organizational structure of the *Landsorganisasjon* (Norwegian
Federation of Trade Unions). First published in Norway as *Norsk fagbevegelse.*

648 **Trade unions-resource or regulation.**
Tom Colbjørnsen, Olav Korsnes. *Acta Sociologica*, vol. 21, no. 3
(1978), p. 197-228. bibliog.

This scholarly study of modern trade unions uses Norway's *LO* (Norwegian
Federation of Trade Unions) as an example in its discussion of the degree of
unionization and local union activity.

649 **Labor relations in Norway.**
Herbert Dorfman. Oslo: Norwegian Joint Committee on
International Social Policy, 1958. 150p.

Surveys the trade union movement and worker management relations in Norway
until the late 1950s. Dorfman describes the origins of the union movement, its
organization, and that of Norway's association of employers. Subsequent chapters
discuss relations between the two groups, the processes followed during labour
disputes, Norway's Labour Court, and working conditions in the late 1950s.

650 **Democracy at work: the report of the Norwegian industrial democracy program.**
Fred Emery, Einar Thorsrud. Leiden, Netherlands: Martinus Nijhoff Social Sciences Division, 1976. 179p. bibliog. (International Series on the Quality of the Working Life, no. 2).

A report by the Industrial Committee on Research on their work, sponsored by the Norwegian Confederation of Employers (*NAF*) and the Norwegian Confederation of Trade Unions (*LO*). The work outlines the theoretical framework established for the project, the programmes established in several industries, and the roles of trade unions and management in such programmes. For a more general and theoretical explanation of the origins of the project see *Form and content in industrial democracy from Norway and other European countries* (London: Tavistock; Assen, Netherlands: Van Gorium, 1969. 116p.), by the same authors.

651 **Labor in Norway.**
Walter Galenson, foreword by Sumner H. Schlichter.
Cambridge, Massachusetts: Harvard University Press, 1949. 373p. bibliog. (Wertheim Fellowship Publications).

Covers much the same ground as *Labor Relations in Norway* (q.v.). Despite its age, the depth and analytical nature of this work ensure its continued value.

652 **Scandinavia.**
Walter Galenson. In: *Comparative labor movements*. Edited by Walter Galenson. New York: Russell & Russell, 1968, p. 104-72.

Surveys the origins and development of the labour movements in Denmark, Norway, and Sweden and discusses union organization and structure, collective bargaining, labour ideology, and the relationship of the unions to the labour parties in these countries, until the late 1950s.

653 **Industrial democracy.**
Bjørn Gustavsen. In: *Nordic democracy: ideas, issues, and institutions in politics, economy, education, social and cultural affairs of Denmark, Finland, Iceland, Norway, and Sweden*. Edited by Erik Allardt, Nils Andrén, Erik J. Friis, Gylfi T. Gislason, Sten Sparre Nilson, Henry Valen, Frantz Wendt, Folmer Wisti.
Copenhagen: Det danske selskab, 1981, p. 324-58. bibliog.

A review of developments in the five Nordic countries of several programmes encouraging industrial democracy. Topics considered include the institutions and patterns of collective bargaining, corporation committees and work councils, redesign programmes, employee representation on boards of directors, work involvement reforms, and the revision of collective bargaining agreements. Includes a three page bibliography of works on the subject, including many in English.

Labour Relations, the Labour Movement and Trade Unions

654 **New patterns of work reform: the case of Norway.**
Bjørn Gustavsen, Gerry Hunnins, foreword by Steven Deutsch.
Oslo: Universitetsforlaget, 1981. 207p. bibliog.
Discusses many facets of industrial democracy programmes in Norway. Emphasis is placed on early work reform projects, employee representation on company boards, and the development of the 1977 Work Environment Act in Norway.

655 **Economic development and the response of labor in Scandinavia: a multi-level analysis.**
William M. Lafferty. Oslo: Universitetsforlaget, 1971. 360p. bibliog.
Part one discusses industrial development in Scandinavia during the 19th century and the second section describes the response of labour, with a historical overview of pre-19th century developments and a more detailed examination of the late 19th and 20th centuries on a country-by-country basis. The final more theoretical section discusses the determinants of party ideology. See also Lafferty's *Industrialization, community structure and socialism: an ecological analysis of Norway* (Oslo: Universitetsforlaget, 1974).

656 **Manpower policy in Norway.**
Organisation for Economic Co-operation and Development.
Paris: Organisation for Economic Co-operation and Manpower, 1972. 241p. (OECD Review of Manpower and Social Policies, no. 10).
A study discussing manpower and employment practices in Norway. It presents details of Norwegian practices and brief recommendations for changes that could be made.

657 **Industrial democracy.**
Edited by Martin Peterson, John Logue. *Scandinavian Review*, vol. 65, no. 1 (1977), 89p.
The issue is devoted to a discussion of many aspects of the topic such as worker participation on management boards, wage-earner funds, and women as a part of the labour force. Einar Thorsrud's article 'From ship deck to shop floor,' (p. 21-26) describes some of the programmes undertaken by the industrial democracy project.

658 **Corporatism and protest: organizational politics in the Norwegian trade unions.**
Don S. Schwerin. Kent, Ohio: Kent Popular Press, 1981. 80p. bibliog.
A study of the conversion of Norway's *Landsorganisasjonen* (Norwegian Confederation of Trade Unions) to the concept of a corporate incomes policy negotiated with other national interests and the criticism such a policy encountered from the rank-and-file membership, exemplified here by the members of the *Arbeidsmandsforbund* (Miners' Union).

Statistics

659   **Statistisk Årbok: Statistical Yearbook of Norway.**
Oslo: Central Bureau of Statistics, 1880-. annual.

The table of contents, most individual table headings, and the list of additional publications available from the bureau are printed in both Norwegian and English to facilitate their use by non-Norwegians. Valuable for data on virtually all subjects.

660   **Vei viser i Norsk Statistisk: Guide to Norwegian statistics.**
Oslo: Statistisk Sentralbyrå, 1980. 95p.

Parallel texts in Norwegian and English describe the different forms of statistical data collected by the bureau by subject name, the agency compiling the statistics, the scope and frequency with which the data is collected and the principal publications of the bureau in which the data is printed.

661   **Yearbook of Nordic Statistics.**
Stockholm: Norstedts, 1962-. annual.

Contains statistical data from the central statistical offices of the five Nordic nations and is published by the Office of the Presidium of the Nordic Council in Stockholm and the Nordic Statistical Secretariat in Copenhagen. The data covers a wide variety of subjects with all of the tables labelled in English and Swedish. Although less detailed than *Statistisk Årbok: Statistical Yearbook of Norway* (q.v.), this publication has the advantage of facilitating comparisons between the Scandinavian countries.

Inn-og utvandring fra Norge 1958-1975. (Immigration to and emigration from Norway 1958-1975.)
See item no. 304.

Trends in demographic structure in Norway 1960-2000.
See item no. 308.

Education

General

662 **Society, schools and progress in Scandinavia.**
[Cyril] Willis Dixon. Oxford: Pergamon Press, 1965. 193p. map.
bibliog. (Commonwealth and International Library).
A survey of the region, followed by an explanation of the educational systems of
Denmark, Sweden, and Norway (p. 115-39) as they existed in the mid-1960s and a
final comparative and analytical chapter. A valuable discussion of the subject.

663 **The system of education in Norway.**
Olav Hove. Oslo: Johan Grundt Tanum Forlag, 1976. 107p.
(Tokens of Norway).
This survey outlines the educational programmes available at different levels of
the Norwegian educational system and describes the central administrative
structure by which these programmes are carried out. The book was written when
the present educational system was being implemented so it remains a useful
introduction. For a brief discussion, see Robert E. Belding's 'New programs in
Norwegian education,' *Scandinavian Review*, vol. 59, no. 3 (1971), p. 262-67.

664 **Education in Norway.**
Tore Lindbekk. In: *Norwegian society*. Edited by Natalie Rogoff
Ramsøy. Oslo: Universitetsforlaget, 1974, p. 158-93.
An analysis of education as a social organization. Part one discusses the school as
a socializing agent and conveyor of values, in part by investigating the
backgrounds and self-perceptions of teachers. The second part deals with post-
secondary education from the standpoint of the recruitment patterns and the
differentiation processes connected with it.

Special studies

665 **Education, science and the arts.**
Asbjørn Eidnes. In: *Norway North of 65*. Edited by Ørnulf
Vorren. Oslo: Oslo University Press; London, George Allen &
Unwin, 1960, p. 248-71.
Most of the article deals with the educational system in North Norway, reflecting
both the pattern for the whole of Norway and the particular problems of the
region. Major research institutions, museums and cultural centres of North
Norway are also described briefly. Some of the material is now out of date, the
University of Tromsø was established after the article was written for example,
but it is still a valuable summary.

666 **Innovation in education: the National Council for Innovation in
Education: its structure and work.**
[Oslo]: Royal Ministry of Church and Education, [1981]. 77p.
bibliog.
This booklet describes the agency and its work, and presents a view of the general
structure of the present school systems through the upper secondary school level.
Another chapter outlines the development of this system based on recom-
mendations of the National Council and legislation enacted by the Storting
(Parliament).

667 **Adult education in the Nordic countries.**
Kim Morch Jacobsen. In: *Nordic democracy: ideas, issues, and
institutions in politics, economy, education, social and cultural
affairs of Denmark, Finland, Iceland, Norway, and Sweden.* Edited
by Erik Allardt, Nils Andrén, Erik J. Friis, Gylfi T. Gislason, Sten
Sparre Nilson, Henry Valen, Frantz Wendt, Folmer Wisti.
Copenhagen: Det danske selskab, 1981, p. 465-94. bibliog.
An examination of the different forms of adult education in the Nordic countries.
The author identifies the various programmes, outlines some of their forms and
characteristics in the different countries and makes comparisons between them.

668 **Universities and other institutions of higher education.**
Mogens Pedersen. In: *Nordic democracy: ideas, issues, and
institutions in politics, economy, education, social and cultural
affairs of Denmark, Finland, Iceland, Norway, and Sweden.* Edited
by Erik Allardt, Nils Andrén, Erik J. Friis, Gylfi T. Gislason, Sten
Sparre Nilson, Henry Valen, Frantz Wendt, Folmer Wisti.
Copenhagen: Det danske selskab, 1981, p. 444-64. bibliog.
Deals mainly with the administration of Nordic universities and the changes and
reforms that have taken place within them since the late 1960s.

669   **Réveil national et culture populaire en Scandinavie: la genèse de la højskole nordique.** (National awakening and popular culture in Scandinavia: the birth of the Nordic højskole.)
Erica Simon.   Paris: Presses Universitaire de France, 1960. 766p. maps. bibliog.

This extremely important work studies the development of the folk high school which originated in Denmark and spread throughout Scandinavia. The institution was more than a centre for popular education, it became the hotbed of both nationalism and Scandinavianism during the middle of the 19th century with all the conflicts that this entailed. An extensive section on Norway (p. 115-261) discusses both of these topics in detail.

670   **Adult education.**
Per G. Stensland. In: *Scandinavia between East and West.* Edited by Henning Friis.   Ithaca, New York; New York: Cornell University Press, 1950, p. 225-53.

Considers the origins, in the 19th century of the three Scandinavian forms of adult education, the folk high school, the public lecture programmes, and the study circle. These are linked together as products of the folk movements that have enriched so many areas of Scandinavian life during the last two centuries. The article is still valuable, despite its age.

671   **Primary education and secondary schools.**
Anne-Liisa Sysiharju. In: *Nordic democracy: ideas, issues, and institutions in politics, economy, education, social and cultural affairs of Denmark, Finland, Iceland, Norway, and Sweden.* Edited by Erik Allardt, Nils Andrén, Erik J. Friis, Gylfi T. Gislason, Sten Sparre Nilson, Henry Valen, Frantz Wendt, Folmer Wisti.
Copenhagen: Det danske selskab, 1981, p. 419-43. bibliog.

Provides a brief introduction on the development of popular education and then surveys current primary and secondary education in the Nordic states. The major theme is the development of common programmes of primary education throughout the region and more diverse programmes of secondary education.

Scandinavia in social sciences literature: an English language bibliography.
See item no. 920.

Environment, Planning, Science and Technology

672   **Care of the environment in Scandinavia.**
Edited by Joseph B. Board, Joanne Wyman.   *Scandinavian Review*, vol. 46, no. 4 (1976), 69p.

This entire issue is devoted to the theme of environmental protection. Several articles discuss basic themes common to all the Nordic countries and one article by H. Peter Krosby, 'Oil and the environment: Norway's enlightened policy,' (p. 38-44) describes the actions taken there to develop the oil industry within environmental safeguards.

673   **Environmental regulations for Svalbard.**
[Oslo]: Ministry of the Environment, 1974. 41p.

A brief introduction to Spitsbergen (Svalbard) and the environmental regulations there.

674   **Nordic research and development.**
Elisabeth Helander.   *Scandinavian Review*, vol. 72, no. 2 (1984), p. 11-15.

Discusses the difficulties impeding Nordic cooperation in research in a number of fields such as electronics and biotechnology and some factors that may lead to future success.

675   **The Norwegian wilderness: national parks and protected areas.**
Arild Holt-Jensen.   Oslo: Tanum-Norli, 1978. 78p. maps. bibliog. (Tokens of Norway).

An introduction to the protected wilderness areas of Norway and the preservation programme of the government. Covers land ownership patterns, the development of conservation thought during the mid-20th century, and descriptions of the parks established by the government in 1964. Consideration is also given to nature reserves and the programmes followed on Spitsbergen (Svalbard).

676   **Survey of Norwegian planning legislation and organization.**
Ingvar Johnsen, foreword by Thor Skrindo.   Oslo: Ministry of
Local Government and Labour, [n.d.]. 34p. maps.
Describes legislation on planning established by the Norwegian government, the means of implementing these laws and the structure of the planning organization involved.

677   **National, regional, and local planning.**
Kai Lemberg. In: *Nordic democracy: ideas, issues, and institutions in politics, economy, education, social and cultural affairs of Denmark, Finland, Iceland, Norway, and Sweden.* Edited by Erik Allardt, Nils Andrén, Erik J. Friis, Gylfi T. Gislason, Sten Sparre Nilson, Henry Valen, Frantz Wendt, Folmer Wisti.   Copenhagen: Det danske selskab, 1981, p. 239-76. bibliog.
Defines the contemporary concern in Scandinavia for physical (land-use) planning, provides an overview of the development and nature of the planning programmes in each country, and compares several features of these programmes. In the section on Norway, (p. 259-63), emphasis is given to the governmental statutes regulating physical planning and the administrative levels at which this planning takes place.

678   **Previews of national science policy: Norway.**
Organisation for Economic Co-operation and Development.
Paris: Organisation for Economic Co-operation and Development, 1970. 194p.
A survey of scientific research and development with emphasis on the coordination of such activities by governmental boards and research councils.

679   **Water management in Norway.**
J. E. Sandel.   Oslo: Ministry of Environment, [1975]. 50p. bibliog.
An account of Norwegian water resources, legislation, planning, and research with relevant statistical data.

680   **Norway: innovator in environmental planning.**
Douglas V. Smith.   Oslo: Norwegian Institute of Urban and Regional Research, 1972. 20p.
Reviews environmental problems in Norway and the measures taken to address problems such as air and water pollution.

Environment, Planning, Science and Technology

681   **Urbanization and community building in modern Norway.**
Joel S. Torstenson, Michael F. Metcalf, Tor Fr. Rasmussen.
Oslo: Urbana Press, 1985. 313p. maps.

Studies Norway's urban and regional planning policies, beginning with a chronological discussion of urban development in Norway and an outline of the general character of policies and legislation on urbanization during the 20th century. The second section examines the response of Oslo and its suburbs and satellite communities to these developments and the final portion discusses other major Norwegian cities.

Planning in Norway: literature in English.
See item no. 927.

Literature

General

682 **A history of Norwegian literature.**
Harald Beyer, edited and translated by Einar I. Haugen. New
York: New York University Press for the American-Scandinavian
Foundation, 1956. 370p. bibliog.
A translation of *Norsk litteraturhistorie* (Oslo: H. Aschehoug (W. Nygaard), 1952,
rev. ed. 1963). The work surveys Norway's literature from the Vikings to the mid
20th century. About half the book is devoted to Henrik Ibsen, Bjørnstjerne
Bjørnson, and 20th-century authors.

683 **The history of Scandinavian literatures: a survey of the literatures
of Norway, Sweden, Denmark, Iceland, and Finland, from their
origins to the present day, including Scandinavian-American
authors, and selected bibliographies.**
Edited by Frederika Blankner, based on the work of Giovanni
Bach, with additional sections by Richard Beck, Adolph Benson,
Axel Johan Uppval. New York: Dial Press, 1938. 407p.
The section on Norway (p. 11-84) covers Norway's early literary history before
concentrating on the 19th-century authors Henrik Wergeland and Henrik Ibsen,
and on the neo-romantic school at the turn of the 20th century and its chief
representative, Knut Hamsun. A brief survey of Norwegian-American literature
by Richard Beck concludes the section.

Literature. General

684 **An introduction to Scandinavian literature from the earliest time to our day.**
Elias Bredsdorff, Brita Mortensen, Ronald Popperwell.
Westport, Connecticut: Greenwood Press, 1970. 245p.
Includes sections on Norwegian literature from 1814-1870 (p. 128-44) and 1870-1950 (p. 210-37). First published in 1952.

685 **Norwegian lfe and literature: English accounts and views especially in the 19th century.**
C. B. Burchardt. Westport, Connecticut: Greenwood Press, 1974. 230p. bibliog.
Stresses the literary ties between Norway and England with special reference to the 19th century. The first section deals with English perceptions of Norway in general including: some first accounts, English attitudes towards Norway's attempted independence in 1814, English views of Norwegian life through the travel literature of the 19th century, and Norway and its people as they have appeared in English literature. The second section traces the views of English writers on Norwegian literature from Ludvig Holberg in the 18th century to Henrik Ibsen. An extensive bibliography provides valuable references on all of these subjects. First published in 1920 by Oxford University Press.

686 **Modern Norwegian literature 1860-1918.**
Brian W. Downs. Cambridge, England: Cambridge University Press, 1966. 276p. map. bibliog.
This survey of Norwegian literature focuses particularly on the work of Henrik Ibsen and Bjørnstjerne Bjørnson. Other notable authors such as Alexander Kielland, Arne Garborg, Gunnar Heiberg, and Knut Hamsun are also discussed.

687 **The writer and the public in Norway.**
Ebba Haslund. *Scandinavian Review*, vol. 63, no. 2 (1975), p. 20-26.
Discusses the efforts of the Norwegian government to provide financial assistance to writers through its purchasing programme.

688 **History of Norwegian literature.**
Theodore Jorgenson. New York: Haskell House Publishers, 1970. 559p.
Covers the period from the Viking Age to the early 20th century. Jorgenson employs a thematic approach to discuss writers of a common age and approach, although exceptions are made for Ludvig Holberg, Henrik Ibsen, and Bjørnstjerne Bjørnson.

689   **Writers and politics in modern Scandinavia.**
Janet Mawby.   London: Hodder & Stoughton, 1978. 55p. bibliog.
(Writers and Politics).

A discussion of politics and literature in Norway and Denmark during the Second World War and Sweden in the 1960s. Nordahl Grieg is discussed as an example of 'the literature of resistance;' Tarjei Vesaas' work is described as the 'images of conflict;' and Sigurd Hoel is considered as part of 'the hidden enemy.'

690   **A history of Scandinavian literature 1870-1980.**
Sven H. Rossel, translated from the German by Anne C.
Ulmer.   Minneapolis, Minnesota: University of Minnesota Press, 1982. 492p. bibliog. (Nordic Series, no. 5).

First published as *Skandinaviske literatur 1870-1970*, this work emphasizes the contributions of individual authors in the five Nordic countries rather than presenting a thematic approach. A useful introduction and reference work with an extensive bibliography of works in English.

691   **Classical tradition in Norway: an introduction with bibliography.**
Sigmund Skard.   Oslo: Universitetsforlaget, 1980. 204p. bibliog.

Discusses the period before 1850 with a detailed analysis of the High Middle Ages (1050-1350). The second part gives significant consideration to the post-1945 period.

692   **Milestones of Norwegian literature.**
Torbjørn Stoverud.   Oslo: Johan Grundt Tanum Forlag, 1967.
127p. bibliog. (Tokens of Norway).

An introductory chapter outlines the history of Norwegian literature from Petter Dass in the 17th century to the 1960s. Successive chapters deal with prominent Norwegian authors and distinctive features of their works. Those considered include Ludvig Holberg, Henrik Wergeland, Peter Christen Asbjørnsen and Jørgen Moe, Bjørnstjerne Bjørnson, Henrik Ibsen, and Tarjei Vesaas.

Anthologies

693   **Modern Scandinavian poetry: the panorama of poetry 1900-1975 in Kalatdlit-numat (Greenland), Iceland, the Faroe Islands, Denmark, Saame poetry, Norway, Sweden and Finland.**
Edited by Martin Allwood.   Oslo: Dreyer Forlag, 1982. 399p.
bibliog.

The section on Norway introduced by Eilif Straume (p. 159-229) contains many pieces of modern Norwegian poetry in translation and two contributions in the section on the Lapps (Saame) are by Norwegian Lapps (p. 151-53).

694 **An everyday story: Norwegian women's fiction.**
Edited by Katherine Hanson. Seattle, Washington: Seal Press,
1984. 249p.

A selection of thirty short stories by Norwegian women writers expressing a
variety of feminist concerns. The stories are arranged chronologically by the life
dates of their authors, ranging from Camilla Collett who wrote in the mid-19th
century to Karin Moe's very recent works. The editor provides a brief, helpful
introduction, short background information on each author, and notes on the ten
translators.

695 **20 contemporary Norwegian poets: a bilingual anthology.**
Edited by Terje Johanssen. New York: St. Martin's Press;
Oslo: Universitetsforlaget, 1984. 232p.

The editor, who also contributed three of his own poems, discusses several
aspects of contemporary Norwegian poetry, and provides a brief introduction to
most of the poets featured in the book. The poems are in the Norwegian original
with an English translation on the opposite page. Includes poems by Rolf
Jacobsen, Olav H. Hauge, and Jan Erik Vold.

696 **A pagaent of old Scandinavia.**
Edited by Henry Goddard Leach. Freeport, New York: Books
for Libraries, 1968. 350p. bibliog. (Granger Index Reprint Series).

A *smørgåsbord*, in the finest sense of the word, of Scandinavian literature from
the Middle Ages. A section, (p. 232-65) is devoted to material on Norway,
including selections from the *Heimskringla, Sverri's saga*, the *Gulating law*, and
others. Sections on religion, heroes, Iceland, and Vinland also reflect developments pertaining to Norway. A useful reference work and introduction to the
literature and sources of the period.

697 **Modern Nordic plays: Norway.**
Oslo: Universitetsforlaget, 1974. 430p. (Library of Scandinavian
Literature).

Includes translations of Johan Borgen's *The house*; Finn Havrehold's *The
injustice*; Tarjei Vesaas' *The bleaching yard*; and Alexander Kielland's *The Lord
and his servants*.

The sagas: translations and studies

698 **The saga of the Volsungs together with excerpts from the Nornagetsthátr and three chapters from the Prose Edda.**
Translated by George K. Anderson. Newark, New Jersey: University of Delaware Press, 1982. 266p. bibliog.

The saga of the Volsungs was written in Iceland but is considered to be a cornerstone of the mythology of Scandinavia. For another recent translation, see Jesse L. Byock's *The saga of the Volsungs* (Boston, Massachusetts: David R. Godine, 1986).

699 **The problem of Icelandic saga origins: a historical survey.**
Theodore M. Andersson. New Haven, Connecticut: Yale University Press, 1960. 190p. bibliog. (Yale Germanic Series, no. 1).

The work approaches the sagas chiefly as an Icelandic literary development but it is also important for its historiographical sketch of saga research, including that of the 19th century Norwegian historians, Rudolf Keyser and P. A. Munch.

700 **The political sagas.**
Melissa A. Berman. *Scandinavian Studies*, vol. 57, no. 2 (1985), p. 113-29.

Analyses three early 13th-century sagas: the saga of the Jomsvikings; the Orkneyinga saga, and the Faroe Islands saga, to point out their distinctiveness from the King's sagas. They are unique in that they all concern Viking settlements which eventually submitted to Norway, provide a geographical stage for events in their stories that involve Norway, concern not only kings but also other powerful men, and take the theme of the shift from independence to domination.

701 **The Icelandic sagas.**
Sir William Alexander Craigie. Norwood, Pennsylvania: Norwood Editions, 1976. 120p.

A general introduction to the sagas, including a chapter on the sagas which have Norway and its rulers as their chief subject. The volume was first published in 1913, but remains a useful overview.

702 **Grettir's saga.**
Translated by Denton Fox, Herman Palsson. Toronto: University of Toronto Press, 1974. 199p. maps.

This saga reflects many aspects of life during the Viking Age, particularly the frequent trips taken between Iceland and Norway by the saga's characters.

Literature. The sagas: translations and studies

703 **Poetic Edda.**
     Translated from the Icelandic and with an introduction by Lee M.
     Hollander.
     Austin, Texas: University of Texas Press, 1962. 2nd rev. ed. 343p.
A presentation of Norse mythology and heroes. Although its provenance is still
debated, it was prepared in Iceland during the 12th century and represents pre-
Christian views from Scandinavia. Other translations are available but Hollander's
is distinguished by its clarity and its useful introduction.

704 **The skalds: a selection of their poems with introduction and notes.**
     Lee M. Hollander.   Ann Arbor, Michigan: University of Michigan
     Press, 1968. 216p. bibliog.
Hollander provides a cogent introduction to the nature and development of this
form of Old Norse literature as well as explanatory notes for each of the
selections. First published by Princeton University Press in 1945 for the
American-Scandinavian Foundation.

705 **The saga of the Jómsvíkings.**
     Translated from the Old Icelandic and with an introduction by Lee
     M. Hollander.   Freeport, New York: Books for Libraries, 1971.
     116p.
Although fictional and dealing primarily with Denmark, the saga has as its high-
point the battle in AD 986 of Hjórunga Bay (Hjórungavang) between Earl Håkon
of Lade and the Danish king, Sven Forkbeard. In addition to an excellent
translation of the saga, Hollander provides a useful introduction which places the
saga in a historical context, and discusses its literary merits. A reprint of
Hollander's original work (Austin, Texas: University of Texas Press, 1955).

706 **The Old Norse sagas.**
     Halvdan Koht.   New York: Kraus Reprint, 1971. 191p. bibliog.
Studies the literary character of the sagas, their origin, the Icelandic family sagas,
and the sagas as fiction. Koht also dwells at length on the Norwegian connection
with the sagas; the Norwegian theme of most of the historical sagas, exemplified
most clearly in the work of Snorri Sturluson; and the historical value that such
works possess. The work is profound, readable, and indicative of Koht's genius as
a historian. First published in Norwegian; the first English edition was published
by W. W. Norton in 1931.

707 **Oratory in the King's sagas.**
     James E. Knirk.   Oslo: Universitetsforlaget, 1981. 247p. bibliog.
A detailed and scholarly study of oratory as it is employed as a literary device in
the *Heimskringla*.

708 **Egil's saga.**
Translated by Hermann Palsson, Paul Edwards. New York: Penguin, 1976. 254p.

The story of Egil Skallagrimsson set in 10th-century Iceland, England and Norway. One of the most highly-regarded and most often read sagas of a Viking moulded in the classic form. Authorship is sometimes attributed to Snorri Sturluson, although it has not been proven.

709 **Orkneyinga saga: the saga of the Earls of Orkney.**
Translated from the Old Icelandic and with an introduction by Hermann Palsson, Paul Edwards. London: Hogarth Press, 1978. 228p. maps.

A saga that covers about 300 years of the North Sea world, not only the Orkneys and the other Northern Islands, but also Iceland and Norway during the Viking Age.

710 **Icelandic sagas.**
Paul Schach. Boston, Massachusetts: Twayne, 1984. 220p. bibliog. (Twayne's World Authors Series).

A short history of Iceland from its discovery to the Middle Ages and a description of the major literary periods. Given the early ties between Iceland and Norway, the discussion of those connections and the origins of historical writing make the work relevant for Norway as well as Iceland. The bibliography contains an up-to-date list of the literature and the best saga translations available.

711 **Sverrisaga, the saga of Sverrir of Norway.**
Translated by John Sephton. London: Nutt, 1899. 310p. maps. (Northern Library).

Sephton's translation is the only complete presentation in English of this major account of King Sverre (ca. 1152-1202), one of the earliest of the King's sagas.

712 **The origins of Icelandic literature.**
G. Turville-Petrie. Oxford: Clarendon Press, 1953. 260p. map.

A study of the forces that helped to create and shape the development of Icelandic literature until the 'classical age' personified by Snorri Sturluson. It illustrates the ties that bound Iceland and Norway with the other parts of the North Sea world during the Viking Age. This theme is particularly evident in the chapter entitled 'Historical literature of the late twelfth century,' (p. 166-212), much of which treats the early writing of history in Norway and the development of sagas using the Norwegian kings as a theme.

Literary criticism and trends

713 **Renaissance in the North.**
W. Gore Allen. Freeport, New York: Books for Libraries, 1970.
143p.

Three Norwegians are included in these critical essays on the forces that have
shaped Scandinavia and her culture. Sigrid Undset is featured as 'The Catholic-
medieval-modern;' Knut Hamsun and Werner von Heidenstam of Sweden are
studied as 'The nationalists;' and Edvard Grieg is discussed along with Jean
Sibelius in 'The influence of music.'

714 **Eight Scandinavian novelists: criticism and reviews in English.**
Compiled by John Budd. Westport, Connecticut; London:
Greenwood Press, 1981. 179p. bibliog.

Contains annotated bibliographies and brief biographical sketches of eight
Scandinavian novelists, including Norwegians Jonas Lie, Arne Garborg, Knut
Hamsun, and Sigrid Undset. All the titles listed are in English and the volume is
divided into the author's works translated into English, and books, dissertations,
articles, and critical works about the authors.

715 **The impact of Scandinavian literature abroad.**
Delores Buttry, Dorothy S. Martin. *Scandinavian Review*, vol.
70, no. 4 (1982), p. 27-32.

A brief summary of the significant impact of several Scandinavian authors,
particularly Ibsen, Strindberg, and Hamsun, in Germany and France during the
late 19th century.

716 **Chapters in Norwegian literature, being the substance of public
lectures, given at University College, London, during the sessions
1918-1922.**
Illit Grøndahl, Ola Raknes. Freeport, New York: Books for
Libraries, 1969. 308p. bibliog. (Select Bibliographies Reprint
Series).

Originally published in 1923, this volume is still often used. It concentrates almost
exclusively on 19th and early 20th century authors with the exception of Ludvig
Holberg and Johan Herman Wessel. Includes discussions of Henrik Ibsen,
Bjørnstjerne Bjørnson, Camilla Collett, Ivar Aasen, Aasmond Vinje, Jonas Lie,
Alexander Kielland, Arne Garborg, and Knut Hamsun.

717 **Six Scandinavian novelists.**
Alrik Gustafson. New York: Princeton University Press for the
American-Scandinavian Foundation, 1940. 367p.

Includes critical essays on Norwegians Jonas Lie, Knut Hamsun, and Sigrid
Undset. The chapter on Lie is called 'Impressionistic realism,' that dealing with

Hamsun, 'Man and the soil,' and the study of Undset is entitled, 'Christian ethics in a pagan world.'

718 **Angevin Britain and Scandinavia.**
Henry Goddard Leach. Cambridge, Massachusetts: Harvard University Press; London: Oxford University Press, 1921. 432p. bibliog. (Harvard Studies in Comparative Literature, no. 6).

After a discussion of some of the agents of cultural exchange between Britain and Scandinavia during the 12th and 13th centuries, Leach devotes much of the book to tracing the transfer of British literary forms and stories to Scandinavia. Less emphasis is given to literary impulses that flowed in the opposite direction. Some of its ideas have been revised by later works but none have supplanted it in scope or purpose.

719 **Norway.**
Edited by Sverre Lyngstad. New York: Griffin House, 1983. 227p. bibliog. (Review of National Literatures, no. 12).

A collection of essays by leading scholars dealing thematically with modern Norwegian literature. Includes the editor's 'Modern Norwegian literature: an overview,' the noted Norwegian scholar, Edvard Beyer's 'Norwegian literature in the Scandinavian spectrum,' and Janet E. Rasmussen's 'Dreams and discontent: the female voice in Norwegian literature.' Of particular importance is John Hoberman's 'Bibliographical spectrum,' (p. 185-207), a critical essay discussing many works produced in English.

720 **Ibsen and the temper of Norwegian literature.**
James Walter McFarlane. London: Oxford University Press, 1960. 208p. bibliog.

A survey of Norwegian writers from Ludvig Holberg in the 18th century to Sigrid Undset in the 20th century. Extensive coverage is given to Ibsen, Henrik Wergeland, Bjørnstjerne Bjørnson, Alexander Kielland, Jonas Lie, Sigbjørn Obstfelder, and Knut Hamsun. A concluding chapter discusses *nynorsk* (New Norwegian) literature.

721 **The hero in Scandinavian literature from Peer Gynt to the present.**
Edited by John W. Weinstock, Robert T. Rovinsky. Austin, Texas; London: University of Texas Press, 1975. 226p. (Germanic Languages Symposia Series).

Two of the seven essays deal with Norwegian topics: Sverre Arestad discusses 'The Ibsen hero,' and Harald Naess writes on 'Who was Hamsun's hero?' The volume ends with a transcript of discussions by the conference participants on the main themes of the conference, and Ibsen in particular.

722 **Recent trends in Norwegian literary criticism.**
Vigdis Ystad. *Scandinavian Studies*, vol. 57, no. 1 (1985), p. 32-44.

A survey of Norwegian literary criticism since 1950, emphasizing recent trends and problems. The endnotes provide valuable current bibliographical references for further consideration of the subject.

Henrik Ibsen

723 **Ibsen: the man and his work.**
Edvard Beyer, translated from the Norwegian by Marie Wells.
London: Souvenir Press, 1978. 223p. bibliog.

A critical study of Ibsen and his literary works, with special consideration given to his best-known plays. The work is enhanced by contemporary cartoons, photographs of performances of Ibsen's works, and an extensive, partially-annotated bibliography of works on Ibsen in English. Also published in Norwegian (Oslo: J. W. Cappelens Forlag, 1978).

724 **Ibsen: a collection of critical essays.**
Edited by Rolf Fjelde. Englewood Cliffs, New Jersey: Prentice-Hall, 1965. 184p. bibliog.

A collection of fifteen essays by leading Ibsen scholars. Some deal with specific aspects of his style or themes of his plays, and others are studies of individual plays. Contributors to the work include P. F. D. Tennant, Halvdan Koht, and John Northam.

725 **Ibsen – a dissenting view: a study of the last twelve plays.**
Ronald Gray. Cambridge, England: Cambridge University Press, 1977. 231p. bibliog.

This study questions the dramatist's reputation and abilities, and serves as a counterpoise to the vast majority of works which are more favourable to Ibsen.

726 **Ibsen's drama: author to audience.**
Einar I. Haugen. Minneapolis, Minnesota: University of Minnesota Press, 1979. 185p. bibliog.

Provides an outline of Ibsen's life, discusses his major themes, his plays as theatrical productions, and the hidden message in his works.

727 **Henrik Ibsen issue.**
Scandinavian Studies, vol. 51, no. 4 (1979), p. 343-501.

A special issue of the journal in which all but one of the articles is devoted to studies of the author, his family, and his literary works. Works by him that are discussed include *An enemy of the people, Ghosts, Hedda Gabler, Brand*, and *John Gabriel Borkman.*

728 **The three Ibsens: memories of Henrik Ibsen, Suzannah Ibsen, and Sigurd Ibsen.**
Berliot Ibsen, translated by Gerik Schjelderup, foreword by
Francis Bull.   New York: American-Scandinavian Foundation,
1952. 184p.
Berliot Ibsen's memoirs emphasize the life and career of her husband, Sigurd Ibsen, and his parents, Henrik and Suzannah Ibsen. They provide a unique view of Norwegian literary life during its golden age.

729 **To the Third Empire: Ibsen's early drama.**
Brian Johnston.   Minneapolis, Minnesota: University of Min-
nesota Press, 1980. 328p. bibliog. (Nordic Series, no. 4).
A critical study of the first half of Ibsen's literary career, from *Catiline* in 1848-49 to *Emperor and Galilean* in 1873. The major theme is that of Ibsen's aesthetic and cultural development, extending his mastery or 'empire' over his public and art as he wrote. As a result, by the time of the last play studied, Ibsen, according to Johnston, had emerged as a major dramatist and poet.

730 **Life of Ibsen.**
Halvdan Koht, translated and edited by Einar I. Haugen, A. E.
Santaniello.   New York: Benjamin Blom, 1971. 507p. bibliog.
This is generally regarded as the best biography of the great writer. It is a chronological study that is also able to make the connection between the man and his literary work. First published in Norwegian in 1928-29 and revised in 1954. This translation of the revised edition includes a brief tribute by Haugen to the author.

731 **The Oxford Ibsen.**
Edited and translated by James Walter McFarlane.   London:
Oxford University Press, 1960-77. 8 vols.
The most recent and highly-regarded translation of Ibsen's works by an acknowledged expert.

732 **Ibsen: a biography.**
Michael Meyer.   Garden City, New York: Doubleday, 1971.
865p. bibliog.
An even more detailed study than *Life of Ibsen* (q.v.). Meyer emphasizes the author's works as drama, and dwells particularly on Ibsen's time in Germany from 1868 to 1884 when he produced some of his best-known works, such as *A doll's house, An enemy of the people*, and *The wild duck.*

733 **Ibsen: a critical study.**
John Northam.   Cambridge, England: Cambridge University
Press, 1973. 237p. bibliog.
Examines six of Ibsen's major works from the standpoint of his concept of
heroism. Northam concludes with a penetrating summary on 'the relevance of
Ibsen.'

Other major authors

734 **Sigrid Undset.**
Carl F. Bayerschmidt.   New York: Twayne, 1970. 176p. bibliog.
(Twayne World Authors Series, no. 107).
A biographical outline is followed by four chapters discussing Undset's literary
works in chronological order and emphasizing pertinent characteristics such as her
social novels, and those on the Middle Ages, particularly *Kristin Lavransdatter*.

735 **Ludvig Holberg.**
F. J. Billeskov Jansen.   New York: Twayne, 1974. 135p. bibliog.
(Twayne World Authors Series, no. 321).
A brief biography and discussion of Holberg and his literary work. Although
slighting Holberg's contributions to the development of Norwegian literature, this
is a useful reference work.

736 **Tarjei Vesaas.**
Kenneth G. Chapman.   New York: Twayne, 1970. 180p. bibliog.
(Twayne World Authors Series, no. 100).
In an introductory chapter Chapman identifies two major characteristics of Vesaas
and his work, namely an intuitive apprehension of reality and the use of images.
These characteristics are used as the main themes of the predominantly
chronological discussion of Vesaas and his writing that follows.

737 **Bjørnstjerne Bjørnson: a study in Norwegian nationalism.**
Harald Larson.   New York: King's Croom Press, 1944. 172p.
bibliog.
Examines Bjørnson's life and work primarily from the standpoint of his strong
sense of nationalism and the nationalistic issues in Norway during the late 19th
century. Topics covered include the language controversy, the flag issue,
Bjørnson's writing the words to Norway's national anthem, and his position on
independence.

738 **Jonas Lie.**
Sverre Lyngstad. Boston, Massachusetts: Twayne, 1977. 223p.
bibliog. (Twayne World Authors Series).

A chronological discussion of Jonas Lie's (1833-1908) major works with little
biographical information. A concluding chapter evaluates the author and his
work.

739 **Sigurd Hoel's fiction: cultural criticism and tragic vision.**
Sverre Lyngstad. Westport, Connecticut: Greenwood Press,
1984. 198p. bibliog. (Contributions to the Study of World
Literature, no. 6).

A critical study of Sigurd Hoel (1890-1960). Discusses Hoel's development as a
novelist and provides thematic studies of the novels that centre on the subjects of
childhood or the search for self-identity.

740 **Knut Hamsun.**
Harald S. Naess. Boston, Massachusetts: Twayne, 1984. 194p.
bibliog. (Twayne World Authors Series, no. 715).

The first chapter provides a biographical sketch of Hamsun (1859-1952) that
emphasizes his youth, his journeys to America, and his controversial support of
the German occupation of Norway during the Second World War. The remainder
of the study discusses Hamsun's literary works and the forces that influenced his
style.

741 **Sigbjørn Obstfelder.**
Mary Kay Norseng. Boston, Massachusetts: Twayne, 1982. 162p.
bibliog. (Twayne World Authors Series).

Obstfelder, (1866-1900) was Norway's major poet of the 1890s. A brief biography
is followed by an analysis of his poetry, prose, plays, and his novel in diary form.
See also Norseng's 'Obstfelder's prose form in general and particular,'
Scandinavian Studies, vol. 50, no. 2 (1978), p. 177-85.

742 **The Norwegian short story: Bjørg Vik.**
Carla Waal. *Scandinavian Studies*, vol. 49, no. 2 (1977),
p. 217-40.

A brief study of Vik and a translation of his short story 'They came in small
groups,' (p. 224-40). The article is part of a whole issue of the journal devoted to
the theme of the Scandinavian short story. See also Waal's translation of 'Bjørg
Vik: the widows,' *Scandinavian Review*, vol. 68, no. 4 (1980), p. 48-60.

743 **Sigrid Undset: a study in Christian realism.**
A. H. Winsnes, translated from the Norwegian by Peter G.
Foote. Westport, Connecticut: Greenwood Press, 1970. 258p.
bibliog.

This biographical and literary study portrays Undset as the representative of two
20th-century literary trends; the so-called Christian Renaissance movement; and
realism. The volume weaves Undset's experiences into an analysis of her literary
works.

The voice of Norway.
See item no. 4.

**The Norse Atlantic saga: being the Norse voyages of discovery and
settlement to Iceland, Greenland, and America.**
See item no. 180.

Fact and fancy in the Vinland sagas.
See item no. 201.

Heimskringla. (Circle of the world.)
See item no. 216.

Snorri Sturluson.
See item no. 275.

Ole Edvart Rølvaag.
See item no. 354.

Ole Edvart Rølvaag: a biography.
See item no. 356.

The Elder Edda: a selection.
See item no. 756.

Scandinavica.
See item no. 892.

Scandinavian Studies.
See item no. 899.

Forfatterlexikon omfattende Danmark, Norge og Island indtil 1814.
(Author lexicon for Denmark, Norway, and Iceland until 1814.)
See item no. 913.

Norse sagas translated into English: a bibliography.
See item no. 917.

**Norway in English: a bibliography including a survey of Norwegian
literature in English translation from 1742 to 1959.**
See item no. 921.

Norsk forfatterlexikon 1814-1880. (Norwegian author lexicon 1814-1880.)
See item no. 922.

Norwegian literary bibliography 1956-1970.
See item no. 935.

Scandinavian literature in English translation 1928-1977.
See item no. 936.

Children's Books

744 **Four sons of Norway.**
Helen Acker.   Freeport, New York: Books for Libraries, 1948.
255p. bibliog.

This work, which is suitable for older children, contains biographical sketches of Ole Bull, Henrik Ibsen, Edvard Grieg, and Fridtjof Nansen.

745 **Sea wolves: the Viking era.**
Frank Birkabaek, Charles Barren.   Gothenburg, Sweden:
Nordbok, 1975. 127p. maps. bibliog.

This elementary introduction to the Vikings, which is suitable for older children, provides a well illustrated account of Viking expansion and life during the Viking Age.

746 **With Amundsen at the North Pole.**
Gerald Bowman.   London: Frederick Muller, 1963. 144p. map.
(Adventures in Geography).

A brief biography of Amundsen describing all his explorations with emphasis on his flight in the airship *Norge* in 1926 over the North Pole. Designed for young adults but also suitable for the general reader.

747 **The Vikings.**
Brenda Ralph Lewis.   Loughborough, England: Ladybird Books,
1976. 51p. (Great Civilizations)

An introduction to the Vikings at home and abroad which is suitable for younger children.

748　The land of the long night.
Paul du Chaillu.　Detroit, Michigan: Tower Books, 1971. 266p.
Originally published in 1899, this is a book written especially for children, describing the author's winter trip to Northern Scandinavia when he travelled with the reindeer Lapps throughout the region.

749　My village in Norway.
Sonja Gidal, Tim Gidal.　New York: Pantheon Books, 1958. 78p. maps.
A description for children aged ten to twelve of life on a small fishing island off the west coast of Norway. It contains some facts and language expressions so that children might acquire a knowledge of the people and country.

750　Life in Europe: Norway.
Vincent Malmström, Ruth Malmström.　Grand Rapids, Michigan: Fideler, 1962. 160p. maps. (Life in Europe Series).
A general introduction to the country, with many black-and-white photographs. Originally published in 1955.

751　Thor Heyerdahl: modern Viking adventurer.
Julian May.　Mankato, Minnesota: Creative Educational Society, 1973. [36p.]. map.
A brief, well-illustrated biography of Thor Heyerdahl for children. Contains anecdotes from his entire life, with emphasis on his voyages.

752　How people live in Norway.
William R. Mead.　London: Ward Lock Educational, 1969. 100p. maps. (How People Live).
A general introduction to Norway, first published in 1959, for older children and young adults. Presents a view of the different regions of Norway by describing five Norwegians who live and work in different parts of the country.

753　Roald Amundsen: first to the South Pole.
Margaret J. Miller.　London: Hodder & Stoughton, 1981. 128p. maps. bibliog. (Twentieth Century People).
A biography of Amundsen for the general reader and the young adult. It discusses his entire career, as well as his journey to the South Pole.

754　Fridtjof Nansen: Arctic explorer.
Francis Noel-Baker.　London: Adam & Charles Black, 1958. 94p. (Lives to Remember).
A brief biography for young adults of Fridtjof Nansen, Arctic explorer, Norwegian statesman before and after Norwegian independence in 1905, and humanitarian representative of the League of Nations' relief and refugee programmes.

755 **The Viking Age: the Vikings in Scotland: stories from the sagas.**
Eric Simpson. Edinburgh: Chambers, 1977. 48p. maps. bibliog.
(The Way It Was).

An interesting survey appropriate for both young and more experienced readers emphasizing Viking settlement of the Orkneys and Shetland Islands. Also discusses the archaeological sources for the study of this period and region.

756 **The Elder Edda: a selection.**
Translated by Paul B. Taylor, W. H. Auden, introduction by Peter H. Salus, Paul B. Taylor. New York: Random House, 1967. 173p.

A selection from the *Elder Edda* in prose form with a brief introduction on style and Norse mythology. Notes and a glossary of terms are included at the end. It is a good introduction to Norse mythology for the new or young reader to the subject.

The two Olafs of Norway with a cross on their shields.
See item no. 171.

Viking expansion westwards.
See item no. 187.

The Laplanders: Europe's last nomads.
See item no. 320.

Norwegian folktales.
See item no. 809.

Scandinavian folk and fairy tales: tales from Norway, Sweden, Denmark, Finland, Iceland.
See item no. 810.

Scandinavian legends and folk-tales.
See item no. 815.

The Arts

General

757 **The art of Scandinavia.**
Peter Anker, Arne Andersson. London: Paul Hamlyn, 1970. 2
vols. maps. bibliog.

A study of early Scandinavian art from the pre-Viking period to the introduction
of the Gothic style during the Middle Ages. The treatment is chronological and
topical rather than geographical so Norway's contributions are discussed in
conjunction with developments in Denmark and Sweden. The exception to this is
a chapter in Volume 1 on Norwegian stave churches. Originally published as *L'art
scandinave* (Laperre-qui-Vivre: Zodiaque, 1968).

758 **Viking art.**
Ole Klindt-Jensen, David. M. Wilson. Minneapolis, Minnesota:
University of Minnesota Press, 1980. 173p. bibliog. (Nordic Series,
no. 6).

Klindt-Jensen discusses early Scandinavian art and the earliest Viking styles and
Wilson in the second half describes the five distinctive Viking art styles. A
detailed study, uncomplicated in terminology, best suited to those with a serious
interest in the subject. First published in English in 1966 (London: George Allen
& Unwin), translated from the original Danish, *Vikingetidenskunst.*

Visual arts

Painting

759 **Norwegian painting: a survey.**
Jan Askeland.   Oslo: Johan Grundt Tanum Forlag, 1971. 73p.
(Tokens of Norway).

Outlines Norwegian painting from the Middle Ages to the 1960s. Most of the work deals with the period after 1814, much of it being on recent or contemporary artists.

760 **Edvard Munch.**
Otto Benesch, translated from the German by Joan Spencer.
Garden City, New York: Phaidon, 1960. 143p. bibliog.

A critical study (p. 3-44) of Munch's life and artistic development is followed by eighty-nine annotated plates of his work.

761 **Edvard Munch.**
Frederick B. Diknatel, introduction by Johan H. Langaard.   New
York: Museum of Modern Art, 1950. 120p. bibliog.

A discussion of Munch and his artistic work, with illustrations of his paintings.

762 **Edvard Munch: paintings, sketches and studies.**
Arne Eggum, translated from the Norwegian by Ragnar
Christopherson, preface by Alf Bøe.   New York: Clarkson N.
Potter, 1984. 305p. bibliog.

A valuable chronological discussion of Munch's life and his artistic work, richly illustrated with many plates.

763 **Munch: his life and work.**
Reinhold Heller.   Chicago: University of Chicago Press; London:
John Murray Publishers, 1984. 240p.

A well-illustrated biography of Munch and discussion of his artistic works, which includes extensive quotations from Munch's correspondence. For a shorter study by the same author see, *Edvard Munch: the scream* (New York: Viking Press, 1972).

764 **Edvard Munch: masterpieces from the artist's collection in the Munch Museum, Oslo.**
Johan H. Langaard, Reider Rivold, translated from the German by Michael Bullock. New York; Toronto: McGraw- Hill, 1964. 62 plates. bibliog.
A study of Munch and his different art forms, including quotations from the artist's own writing about some of his work.

765 **Modern Norwegian painting.**
Leif Østby. Oslo: Mittet, 1949. 263p.
Discusses Norwegian art and artists from the 1920s to the 1940s. The work is richly illustrated with colour plates, (p. 40-168), representing the work of these artists. A brief section of biographical notes is included at the end of the work.

766 **Alf Rolfsen.**
Leif Østby. *Scandinavian Review*, vol. 55, no. 4 (1967), p. 371-78.
Several illustrations and photographs of Rolfsen and his work are included in this study of the mid-20th century artist.

767 **E. Munch.**
Jean Selz, translated from the French by Eileen B. Hennessy. New York: Crown Publishers, 1974. 95p. bibliog.
This useful introduction to Munch's life and work is more topical than biographical. Contains many colour illustrations of his paintings.

768 **Scandinavian art: between the past and the present.**
Thomas L. Sloan. *Scandinavian Review*, vol. 70, no. 3 (1982), p. 17-35.
A useful introduction to Scandinavian artistic trends and artists from the late 18th century to the present, with several colour photographs of works mentioned in the text.

769 **Edvard Munch: the man and the artist.**
Ragna Stang, foreword by John Boulton Smith. London: Gordon Fraser, 1979. 319p. bibliog.
An extension of *Edvard Munch* (Oslo: Johan Grundt Tanum Forlag, 1972), by the present author and her husband, N. C. Stang. This is a thorough biography of the artist and analysis of his work by an expert, richly illustrated with Munch's works, to which are appended quotations from his correspondence.

770 **Edvard Munch: close-up of a genius.**
Rolf Stenersen, edited and translated by Reidar Dittmann. Oslo: Gyldendal Norsk Forlag, 1969. 179p.
A biographical account that focuses on Munch as a person more than on his artistic work. Studies the different periods in his life and also particular topics

such as Munch as a recluse and his relationship with other prominent artists. First published in Swedish in Stockholm in 1944, and in Norwegian one year later.

771 **Northern light: realism and symbolism in Scandinavian painting 1880-1910.**
Edited by Kirk Varnedoe.   New York: Brooklyn Museum, 1982.
2nd ed. 240p. bibliog.

A series of essays and a collection of illustrations published to accompany the art exhibit of the same name that toured the United States as part of the Scandinavia Today programme. Seven essays discuss various aspects of Scandinavian art during the period and there are illustrations of works by Scandinavian artists. A worthwhile introduction to many artists who are little known outside Scandinavia.

Sculpture

772 **Norwegian Romanesque decorative sculpture 1090-1210.**
Martin Blindheim.   London: Alec Tiranti, 1965. 64p. map.
bibliog.
221 plates.

A lengthy discussion is followed by black-and-white plates illustrating the sculpture forms.

773 **Dagfin Werenskiold: a great sculptor in wood.**
Øistein Parmann.   *Scandinavian Review*, vol. 57, no. 1 (1969),
p. 12-23.

Describes the art forms and works of Werenskiold, who is best known for his work on the Rådhus (Oslo City Hall).

774 **Gustav Vigeland: the sculptor and his works.**
Ragna Stang, translated from the Norwegian by Ardis Grosjem.
Oslo: Johan Grundt Tanum Forlag, 1973. 190p. (Tokens of
Norway).

A study and critique of Vigeland and his work, describing his early years, the phases of his development and patterns in his work. One extensive chapter (p. 118-53) discusses his sculpture park, and a final chapter addresses the 'Vigeland problem,' his personality and creativity.

Graphic arts

775 **Norwegian printmakers: a hundred years of graphic arts.**
Jan Askeland, translated from the Norwegian by Pat Shaw
Iversen. Oslo: Tanum-Norli, 1978. 55p. (Tokens of Norway).
A critical survey of Norwegian graphic artists during the last century and
illustrations of their work. The study begins with Edvard Munch and also
discusses, among others, Rolf Nesch, Harald Kihle, and Sigurd Winge.

776 **Edvard Munch's graphic art.**
Bjørn Haugen. *Scandinavian Review*, vol. 55, no. 2 (1967), p.
116-35.
This critical study of Munch's graphic works discusses both his techniques and the
themes he used in this art form. Several illustrations are included.

777 **Edvard Munch: lithographs, etchings, woodcuts.**
Introduction by William S. Lieberman, notes by Ebria Feinblatt.
Los Angeles: Los Angeles County Museum of Art, 1969. 118p.
bibliog.
A brief introduction is followed by photographs of Munch's work in the three art
forms.

778 **The art of Frøydis Haavardsholm.**
Marie Lien. *Scandinavian Review*, vol. 60, no. 4 (1972), p. 348-
59.
A study of Frøydis Haavardsholm, a 20th-century artist well-known for her
stained glass works.

779 **Edvard Munch: master printmaker. An examination of the artist's
works and techniques based on the Philip and Lynn Straus
collection.**
Elizabeth Prelinger. New York, London: Norton, in association
with Busch-Reisinger Museum, Harvard University, 1983. 158p.
A detailed study of Munch's work in this field, divided according to the different
types of prints, such as intaglio prints, lithographs, and colour prints, and
illustrated with many plates of Munch's work.

Architecture

780 **Norwegian architecture throughout the ages.**
Compiled by Eyvind Alnæs, Georg Eliassen, Reidar Lund, Arne
Pedersen, Olav Platon. Oslo: H. Aschehoug & Co. (W.
Nygaard), 1950. 424p.

A survey of Norwegian architectural history, divided into chronological chapters
containing a brief narrative overview followed by photographs, with captions, and
plans of the building described.

781 **Stave churches in Norway: introduction and survey.**
Gunnar Bugge. Oslo: Dreyer Forlag, 1983. 84p. map.

An introduction to the architectural features and characteristics of stave churches
is followed by a systematic description of each of the thirty-one such churches still
in existence in Norway, noting their special features or conformity to general
characteristics. The work is well illustrated with photographs and drawings.

782 **Sverre Fehn: the thought of construction.**
Per Olaf Fjeld, introduction by Kenneth Frampton. New York:
Rizzoli International Publications, 1983. 192p. bibliog.

A discussion of the style of Norwegian architect Sverre Fehn, and some of his
best-known works. The volume is well illustrated with numerous photographs.

783 **Old art and monumental buildings in Norway restored during the
last fifty years.**
Roar Hauglid, introduction by Egil Sinding-Larsen. Oslo:
Dreyer, [1962]. 163p.

Sinding-Larsen provides a brief eighteen-page essay outlining artistic and
architectural developments in Norway from the introduction of Christianity and
the stave church in the 11th century to the 18th century. This is followed by 163
photographs of the architectural and artistic remnants of this early period that
have survived and been restored. Much of the emphasis is on religious art and
architecture until the 17th and 18th centuries when a more secular tone can be
seen.

784 **Norwegian stave churches.**
Roar Hauglid, translated from the Norwegian by R. I.
Christopherson. Oslo: Dreyer Forlag, 1970. 117p. map. bibliog.

Discusses the origin, construction and interiors of this unique architectural form.
The work contains photographic plates, plans, and construction details.

785   **Scandinavian architecture: buildings and society in Denmark, Finland, Norway, and Sweden from the Iron Age until today.**
Thomas Paulsson.   London: Leonard Hill, 1958. 256p. maps. bibliog.

A survey of Scandinavian architecture primarily from 1100 AD until the mid-20th century. A valuable study of architectural styles.

Design

786   **Norwegian arts and crafts: industrial design.**
Ferdinand Aars.   Oslo: Dreyer Forlag, 1957. 77p.

An eight page introduction discusses industrial design in general terms. The rest of the volume is illustrated with black-and-white photographs of Norwegian commercial products such as woodwork, furniture, dishes, porcelain, pewter, silver, embroidery, and tapestry.

787   **The Norwegian Design Center.**
Per Aarstad.   *Scandinavian Review*, vol. 56, no. 4 (1968), p. 357-68.

Describes the origins and work of the Norwegian Design Center, a body created in 1963 by the Export Council of Norway to promote industrial design.

788   **Scandinavian modern design 1880-1980.**
Edited by David Revere McFadden, the Cooper-Hewitt Museum.
New York: Harry N. Abrams, 1982. 287p. bibliog.

The catalogue of an exhibit of the same name displayed at the Cooper-Hewitt Museum as part of the Scandinavia Today programme. The volume treats Scandinavian design during the period in a chronological fashion, and is richly illustrated with plates.

Photography

789   **The frozen image: photography in Scandinavia.**
Anne Hoene Hoy.   *Scandinavian Review*, vol. 70, no. 3 (1982), p. 36-42.

Surveys photography in Scandinavia from the mid-19th century to the present, and includes a selection of photographs entitled 'Portfolio: a selection of photographs from The Frozen Image', (p. 42-55), chosen by the editors of *Scandinavian Review* with captions by Hoy. The 'Frozen Image' was a photographic exhibit created as part of the Scandinavia Today programme, in 1982-84.

Performing arts

Theatre

790 **The Norwegian theater: a theater in debate.**
Susan Flakes. *Scandinavian Review*, vol. 72, no. 3 (1984), p. 81-88.

An explanation of the current controversies regarding the *Nationalteatret* (The National Theatre) and *Det Norske Teatret* (The New Norwegian Theatre) in Oslo as well as local theatre developments, particularly in Bergen.

791 **The Scandinavian theatre: a short history.**
Frederick J. Marker, Lise-Lone Marker. Totowa, New Jersey: Rowman & Littlefield, 1975. 303p. bibliog. (Drama and Theatre Studies).

A study of the Scandinavian theatre from the Middle Ages. The origins of theatre in Norway are much later than in the other Scandinavian states, thus, the chapter on Norwegian drama centres on events from the 18th century to Ibsen. Subsequent developments are dealt with in chapters on Scandinavia as a whole.

792 **Johanne Dybwad: Norwegian actress.**
Carla Rae Waal, foreword by Francis Bull. Oslo: Universitetsforlaget, 1967. 354p. bibliog.

A critical study of the Norwegian actress Johanne Dybwad whose career stretched from the late 19th century until 1947. The work describes her career, discusses her acting style, and focuses particularly on her roles in Ibsen's plays.

Opera

793 **The Norwegian opera.**
Dag Simonson. *Scandinavian Review*, vol. 60, no. 2 (1972), p. 126-36.

Discusses the development of Norwegian opera and ballet companies during the 1950s and their activity until 1971.

Cinema

794 **Scandinavian film.**
Forsyth Hardy.   London: Falcon Press, 1952. 62p. (National
Cinema Series).
A discussion of early film production in Denmark, Sweden, and Norway. The
section on Norway is on p. 49-52.

795 **Norwegian film production.**
Elsa B. Marcussen.   *Scandinavian Review*, vol. 57, no. 2 (1969),
p. 149-58.
Describes the system of financial support established by the Norwegian
government in 1964 to aid film production. Films produced by this system during
the mid-to-late 1960s are also discussed.

Music

796 **Scandinavian songs and ballads: modern Swedish, Danish and
Norwegian songs.**
Edited by Martin S. Allwood.   Mullsjö, Sweden: Anglo-American
Center, 1957. 4th ed. 57p.
The music and translations into English of fifty-two Scandinavian songs. The
words of the first verse in the native language is set together with the music,
followed by the English translation of this and additional verses.

797 **Scandinavian summer music festivals.**
Sven Bernhard.   *Scandinavian Review*, vol. 63, no. 4 (1975),
p. 13-27.
Reviews several of the music festivals held annually in Scandinavia, including
Bergen's International Festival of Music.

798 **Norwegian music publication since 1800: a preliminary guide to
music publishers, printers, and dealers.**
Dan Fog, Kari Michelsen.   Copenhagen: Dan Fog Musikforlåg,
1976. 30p.
This guide to the publishing and selling of music lists known music publishers in
Norway since 1800, and provides sketches of some of Oslo's largest book
publishers who have also printed musical works.

799 **Contemporary Norwegian music.**
   Nils Grinde, translated from the Norwegian by Sandra Hamilton.
   Oslo: Universitetsforlaget, 1981. 117p. bibliog.

A survey of modern music based on the last chapters of the author's larger *Norsk musikkhistorie*. The work is divided into two chronological periods: 1920-50, and 1950-80 and provides equal coverage of each. The second section covers jazz, composers of the 1950s and 1960s and provides a brief conmmentary on the last decade.

800 **Scandinavian music: a short history.**
   John Horton.   New York: Norton, 1963. 180p. bibliog.

A survey of Scandinavian music from the Middle Ages to the 1960s. Special attention is given to the 19th and 20th centuries and, regarding Norway, to Edvard Grieg and the 20th century composer Fartein Valen.

801 **Grieg.**
   John Horton.   London: J. M. Dent & Sons, 1974. 255p. bibliog.
   (Master Musicians Series).

The first half of this volume is a chronological narrative of Grieg's life and musical development, and the second part discusses particular aspects of Grieg's work such as his relationship to Norwegian folk-music and his works for piano.

802 **Contemporary Norwegian orchestral music.**
   Bjarne Kortsen.   Bergen, Norway: [s.n.], 1969. 458p. bibliog.

A listing of composers of orchestral music and their major works, biographies of them, and a critical analysis.

803 **Contemporary Norwegian chamber music.**
   Bjarne Kortsen.   Bergen, Norway: [s.n.], 1971. rev. ed. 235p.

The author introduces the book with a short discussion of Norwegian music since Edvard Grieg and an analysis of 20th century chamber music and its composers. The works discussed are ordered by composer and each section contains a brief biographical sketch, a music score, and an evaluation of it.

804 **Grieg the writer.**
   Edited by Bjarne Kortsen.   Bergen, Norway: [s.n], 1972. 2 vols.
   bibliog.

The first volume is a collection of essays and articles written by Grieg in English, Norwegian and German on music and musicians. The second volume contains translations, by Helen M. Corlett, of Grieg's letters to his friend, Frants Beyer, with an introduction by the editor, and a list of Grieg's works.

805 **Norwegian music and musicians.**
  Bjarne Kortsen. Bergen, Norway: [s.n.], 1975. 228p.
A collection of essays and articles, a number of which were originally written for
newspapers, reviews, or journals. In addition to works on Grieg, Kortsen also
treats several Norwegian musicians who are little known outside Norway.

806 **Contemporary Norwegian piano music: a catalogue.**
  Edited by Bjarne Kortsen. Bergen, Norway: [s.n.], 1976. 3rd rev.
  ed. 54p. bibliog.
The main part of the work lists modern Norwegian composers of piano music,
provides a brief biographical outline of them, and a list of their works.

807 **Norwegian music – a survey.**
  Kristian Lange. Oslo: Johan Grundt Tanum Forlag, 1971. 120p.
  (Tokens of Norway).
A study of Norwegian music principally during the last century. The first chapter
discusses early folk music in Norway. Edvard Grieg is discussed in one chapter,
and the last portion of the work studies composers and musicians of the 20th
century. See also Lange's article, 'Modern Norwegian music,' *Scandinavian
Review*, vol. 62, no. 2 (1974), p. 151-58.

808 *Solitude, death, love and landscape:* **the music of Arne Nordheim.**
  Lorentz Reitan. *Scandinavian Review*, vol. 73, no. 2 (1985),
  p. 44-51.
Studies the musical works of Arne Nordheim, one of Norway's best-known
contemporary composers.

Norwegian emigrant songs and ballads.
See item no. 374.

**Scandinavian research theses in the history, aesthetics, sociology and
psychology of film.**
See item no. 916.

Contemporary Norwegian music: a bibliography.
See item no. 931.

**Bibliography of Norwegian art history: literature on Norwegian art
published up to the end of 1970.**
See item no. 934.

Folklore, Folk-art and Customs

Folklore

809   **Norwegian folk tales.**
Compiled by Peter Christen Asbjørnsen, Jørgen Moe, translated
by Pat Shaw, Carl Norman, illustrated by Eric Werenskiold,
Theodor Kittelsen. New York: Pantheon Books, 1982. 189p.
(Pantheon Fairy Tale and Folklore Library).
Contains fairy tales collected by Asbjørnsen and Moe in the mid-19th century and
illustrated by Werenskiold and Kittelsen later in the same century. This
combination of talents has created a worthwile collection. First published in Oslo
by Dreyer Forlag in 1960 and reprinted in 1978.

810   **Scandinavian folk and fairy tales: tales from Norway, Sweden,
Denmark, Finland, Iceland.**
Edited by Claire Booss. New York: Avenel Books, 1984. 666p.
Includes a number of Norwegian folk tales (p. 3-165), all of which were originally
collected in the 19th century by Peter Christen Asbjørnsen and Jørgen Moe
except for one by Jonas Lie. The translations used are those of the 19th-century
English translators and editors, H. L. Braekstad and Sir George Dasent. It is
interesting to compare the form and theme of the Norwegian stories with those
from other Scandinavian countries in the same volume.

811   **Phantoms and fairies from Norwegian folklore.**
Tor Åge Bringsværd. Oslo: Tanum-Norli, 1979. 124p. (Tokens of
Norway).
This introduction to Norwegian folklore discusses sixteen distinct forms of
supernatural beings. The author supplements his narrative with quotations from
folk stories. An interesting book for the general reader.

812 **Folktales of Norway.**
Reidar Th. Christiansen, translated from the Norwegian by Pat
Shaw Iversen, foreword by Richard M. Dorson. London:
Routledge & Kegan Paul; Chicago: University of Chicago Press,
1964. 984p. bibliog. (Folktales of the World).
Contains a number of legends which are not normally included in folktale
collections. The folktales are divided into sections such as historical legends,
magic and witchcraft, and spirits of the forest and mountains.

813 **The migratory legends.**
Reidar Th. Christiansen. New York: Arno Press, 1977. 221p.
(International Folklore).
The author has established a system of eight types to classify all Norwegian folk
tales, that is compatible with other general classification systems established on an
international basis. It is a complex, scholarly, and important study by an expert
on Norwegian folktales. First published with the subtitle: *A proposed list of types
with a systematic catalogue of the Norwegian variants* in 1958 in Helsinki by
Suomalainen Tiedeakatemia Academia Scientiarum Fennica. For a similar work,
see Ørnulf Hodne's *The types of Norwegian folktale* (Oslo: Universitetsforlaget,
1984).

814 **Norwegian folklore simplified.**
Zinken Hopp, translated by Toni Ramholt. Bergen, Norway:
John Griegs Forlag, 1974. 8th ed. 107p.
An introduction to Norwegian culture for the general reader, including a
discussion of folklore, runes, and peasant life.

815 **Scandinavian legends and folk-tales.**
Retold by Gwyn Jones. Oxford: Oxford University Press, 1956.
222p. (Oxford Myths and Legends).
This collection is organized by subject matter rather than by country, making it
difficult to identify the country of origin of some of the twenty-four tales, but
those familiar with Asjbørnsen and Moe will recognize some of their works in the
collection. The translation is crisp and easy to read, even for children.

816 **Folk-dancing in Norway.**
Johan Krogsæter. Oslo: Johan Grundt Tanum Forlag, 1968. 54p.
bibliog. (Tokens of Norway).
Discusses the song dance, the figure dance, the costumes, the music, and the folk
dance movement that has developed to preserve these forms of folk life. The last
section provides detailed instructions on the music and steps of four dances.
Another interesting work on the subject is Nanna Ebbing's 'Norwegian folk
dances,' *Scandinavian Review*, vol. 61, no. 2 (1973), p. 155-62.

817 **Leading folklorists of the North: biographical studies.**
Edited by Dag Strömbäck, assisted by Brynjulf Alver, Bengt
Holbek, Lea Virtanen. Oslo: Universitetsforlaget, 1971. 435p.
bibliog.

Contains brief biographies of the leading folklorists of the Nordic countries. In
the section on Norway (p. 313-405) biographies of ten to twenty pages each have
been prepared on Sophus Bugge, J. K. Qvigstad, Moltke Moe, Ingjald
Reichborn-Kjennerud, Rikard Berge, and Knut Liestøl.

Folk-art

818 **Norwegian peasant art.**
Halfdan Arneberg. Oslo: Fabritius & Sønner, 1949-51. 2 vols.

In each volume, a brief narrative introduction is followed by plates depicting
Norwegian peasant handicraft. Volume one provides examples of women's
handicraft such as weaving and embroidery. The second volume illustrates forms
of men's handicrafts such as wood, silver, and metal. The text is in English with
both English and Norwegian captions for the illustrations.

819 **Rose-painting in Norway.**
Randi Asker. Oslo: Dreyer Forlag, 1976. 2nd rev. ed. 56p.

A commentary (p. 5-16) on the origins and forms of rose-painting (*rosemåling*) is
followed by numerous plates with illustrative works by outstanding artists and
notes by Asker. First published in 1965.

820 **Norwegian porcelain.**
Alf Bøe. *Scandinavian Review*, vol. 56, no. 1 (1968), p. 6-12.

A brief history of the Porsgrund Porcelain Factory from its beginning in 1885 until
the mid-1960s, highlighting the contributions of owners and designers.

821 **Norwegian textiles.**
Helen Engelstad. Leigh-on-Sea, England: F. Lewis, 1952. 16p.
113 figures.

Contains descriptive notes of the 113 illustrations that follow.

822 **Ancient Norwegian design: pictures from the University Museum of
National Antiquities, Oslo.**
Edited by Anders Hagen, Aslak Liestøl. Oslo: J. W. Cappelens
Forlag, 1961. 88p.

Colour and black-and-white photographs of some of the artifacts housed in the
Oldsaksamlingen (University Museum of National Antiquities) in Oslo, accompanied by a commentary by two of Norway's leading archaeologists. A wide
variety of items are displayed including some from the Viking Ship Museum.

823 **Norway: a thousand years of native arts and crafts.**
Roar Hauglid. Oslo: Mittet, 1964. 124p. map.

A brief discussion of early crafts and folk-art accompanied by ninety-two plates of wood carvings, rose-paintings, weavings, and national costumes.

824 **Native art of Norway.**
Edited by Roar Hauglid, Randi Asker, Helen Engelstad, Gunvar Traetteberg. Oslo: Dreyer Forlag, 1977. 182p.

Surveys different forms of folk-art, including wood carving, rose-painting, weaving, and folk costumes. It is amply illustrated and each section is introduced by a commentary on the folk-art.

825 **Scandinavian embroidery: past and present.**
Edith Nielsen. New York: Charles Scribner's Sons, 1978. 174p. bibliog.

The first three chapters provide a brief historical outline of the development of embroidery in Norway, Sweden, and Denmark from 1700 to the mid-20th century. The remainder of the work consists of detailed instructions for individual embroidery projects that originated in these countries.

826 **Norwegian silver.**
Ada Polak. Oslo: Dreyers Forlag, 1972. 156p. bibliog.

A combination of text and illustrations, describing Norwegian silverwork from the pre-Viking period to the present. Much of the work covers the period from about 1500 to 1930. The text not only discusses the works illustrated but also the historical and social factors, such as the guild system, that had a profound effect on the work of the time.

827 **Contemporary textile art in Scandinavia.**
Charles S. Tulley. *Scandinavian Review*, vol. 70, no. 3 (1982), p. 56-63.

Outlines the history of tapestry weaving, contemporary trends, and Scandinavian characteristics within the context of international developments. The work of the Norwegian Hannah Ryggen (1894-1970) is given particular attention. The article was written in conjunction with the Scandinavian Touch, a collection of Scandinavian textile art exhibited as part of the Scandinavia Today programme in 1982-84.

Customs

828 **Christmas in Norway past and present.**
Vera Henriksen. Oslo: Johan Grundt Tanum Forlag, 1970. 63p.
(Tokens of Norway).
Describes Christmas traditions and customs from the Vikings to the present,
discusses the origins of past practices, some common Christmas customs today,
and provides recipes for a few Christmas foods still prepared in Norwegian
homes.

829 **Great day in Norway: the seventeenth of May.**
Zinken Hopp, translated from the Norwegian by Toni Ramholt.
London: Abelard-Schuman, 1962. 31p.
A children's story describing activities on May 17, Norway's Constitution Day.

830 **Brewing and beer traditions in Norway: the social anthropological
background of the brewing industry.**
Odd Nordland. Oslo: Universitetsforlaget, 1969. 320p. maps.
bibliog.
A detailed study of the traditions and customs associated with the brewing of beer
in Norway in the past. Extensive consideration is given to the utensils, the raw
materials, and procedures as well as to the implications of the practice in a rural
and peasant society.

Of Norwegian ways.
See item no. 108.

National romanticism in Norway.
See item no. 227.

Cuisine

831 Scandinavian cooking: savory dishes from the four northern sisters: Denmark, Norway, Sweden, Finland.
Compiled by Gunnevi Bonekamp.   New York: Galahad Books, 1974. 100p. (Round the World Cooking Library).
A collection of recipes of many types, as well as brief introductions highlighting unique or significant characteristics from one or more of the countries. Some of the recipes are common to all the countries and due consideration is given to Norwegian specialities.

832 Eat the Norway: traditional dishes and specialities from Norwegian cooking.
Aase Strømstad, translated by Mary Lee Nielsen.   Oslo: H. Aschehoug (W. Nygaard), 1985. 109p.
A collection of recipes for a variety of dishes most of which are distinctly Norwegian, or at least Scandinavian. Special consideration is given to fish and meat dishes, desserts, breads, and cakes.

833 Norway's delights.
Elise Sverdrup, J. Audrey Ellison.   Oslo: Tanum-Norli, 1980. 10th ed. 96p.
Recipes for many kinds of Norwegian and Scandinavian dishes, including local specialities, fish, desserts and cakes. Written in 1957 by Sverdrup and revised by Ellison.

213

Numismatics, Philately and Heraldry

834 **Norsk slektsvåpen.** (Norwegian coats-of-arms.)
     Hans A. K. T. Cappelen. Oslo: Den Norsk Våpenring, 196p.
     bibliog.

A short introduction discusses the use of coats-of-arms in Norway and the work goes on to present sketches of the coats-of-arms of Norwegian families that have been used for at least a hundred years and are still in use today. A description of the symbols and bibliographical references used for the research of a particular family is also included.

835 **Flags of Norway.**
     [Oslo]: Royal Ministry of Foreign Affairs, Office of Cultural
     Relations, 1961. 4p.

The history of Norway's flags and its coat-of-arms with illustrations of their present forms.

836 **Catalogue of Scandinavian coins: gold, silver and minor coins since
     1534 with their valuations.**
     Burton Hobson. New York: Sterling; London: Oak Tree Press,
     1970. 128p.

The section on Norway, (p. 53-70), provides illustrations of Norwegian coins from 1534 to 1964 and descriptions of their distinctive markings and estimated worth in 1964. For a more detailed study of Norway's coins see Holger Hede's *Danmarks og Norges mynter 1541-1814-1963*, (Copenhagen: Munksgaard Dansk Numismatisk Forening, 1964).

837   **Norske rederiflagg – Norwegian shipping flags.**
      Norges Rederiforbund. (The Norwegian Shipowners Association.)
      Oslo: Nautisk Forlag, 1952. 8p.
The pamphlet contains illustrations of the registered flags of Norwegian shipping firms.

838   **Norges helpost 1872-1980**. (Norway's postal stationery 1872-1980.)
      T. Soot-Ryen, Tore Haga.   Oslo: Oslo Filatelistklubb, 1981. 87p.
A catalogue of the different types of official postal stationery used in Norway during the last century with parallel Norwegian and English texts and illustrations of the stationery forms discussed.

839   **Norges mynter 1814-1982: vurderingsliste.** (Norway's coins 1814-1982: a list of their estimated worth.)
      Terje Sørensen, Tore Sørensen.   [Oslo]: Grims Trykkeri, 1983.
      56p.
A catalogue of Norway's coins since 1814 primarily to aid collectors in determining the worth of their coins. The first part of the work lists the number of each coin minted and the value of such a coin today depending upon its condition. The second part contains photographs of the coins.

840   **De norske posthorn frimerker: 100 år- Norway posthorn stamps: 100 years.**
      Carl H. Werenskiold, preface by Eilert Tommelstad.   [Oslo]:
      Postmuseet, 1972. 34p. bibliog.
A description of the posthorn stamp used in Norway. The engraving process is described and distinctive characteristics of successive groups of the stamp are noted. Text is Norwegian and English.

841   **Stamps of Denmark, Iceland, and Norway: the earlier issues.**
      Ernest H. Wise.   London: Heinemann, 1975. 214p.
In a section on Norway, (p. 116-203), the author describes the Norwegian postal system and stamps of the 19th and early 20th centuries.

Sports and
Recreation

842 **Nordic athletes in the Olympics.**
Damond Benningfield. *Scandinavian Review*, vol. 72, no. 3
(1984), p. 89-93.
Short profiles of five Nordic athletes in training at the University of Texas,
Austin for the 1984 Summer Olympic Games, including the Norwegian diver Tine
Tollan. Although about a small group of athletes, it is useful because it indicates
the frequent tendency of Nordic athletes to develop their abilities abroad.

843 **Skiing traditions in Norway.**
Olav O. Bø. Oslo: Det Norske Samlaget, 1968. 126p. map.
A history of Norwegian skiing from early times to the present. Much of the work
discusses competitive events that began in the 19th century and increased the
popularity of ski-jumping. One chapter deals with the Holmenkollen Festival,
established in 1892 as a competition for both cross-country skiing and ski-
jumping, and the final chapter discusses Norwegian skiers of the 1960s in
international competition.

844 **Norwegian cruising guide: a pilot for the Norwegian and S. W.**
Swedish coasts between Sognefjord and the Sound.
Mark Brackenbury. London: Stanford Maritime, 1978. 91p.
A guide for sailors with useful route, tide, and harbour information, and the
reference numbers of the Norwegian chart series.

845 **Nordic touring and cross country skiing: technique, equipment,**
waxing, clothing.
M. Michael Brady. Oslo: Dreyer Forlag, 1971. 80p.
The work is basically a 'how-to' book, but it also discusses Scandinavian and
Norwegian training methods, and past stars of the sport.

216

846 **Boats of the North: a history of boatbuilding in Norway.**
Arne Emil Christensen, Jr.   Oslo: Det Norske Samlaget, 1968.
94p.

A survey of Norwegian boatbuilding from pre-Viking times to the present. The emphasis is on small craft, primarily those using sails. A useful introduction to the subject.

847 **Inshore craft of Norway.**
Edited by Arne Emil Christensen, Jr., from a manuscript by
Bernhard Færøyvik, Øystein Færøyvik.   London: Conway
Maritime Press, 1979. 143p.

A description with plans of the small boats used in the different regions of Norway. A detailed work for sailors and boatbuilders.

848 **Come ski with me.**
Stein Eriksen, edited with a foreword by Martin Lurey.   London:
Frederick Muller, [ca. 1966]. 214p.

The first part the book discusses the early history of skiing in Norway, the author's boyhood, and his Olympic and World Championship experiences. The second part provides an extenstive introduction to slalom skiing.

849 **The flying Norseman.**
Leif Hovelsen, foreword by Billy Kidd.   Ishpeming, Michigan:
National Ski Hall of Fame Press, 1983. 132p. (Mather Monograph
Series, no. 2).

A biography of Carl Hovelsen written by his son. Hovelsen was a Holmenkollen ski champion who spent several years in America during the 1920s and 30s performing in the Barnum & Bailey Circus and was instrumental in the development of skiing as a sport and industry in Colorado.

850 **Triumph in daring.**
Borre Aa. Lund.   *Scandinavian Review*, vol. 69, no. 3 (1981), p.
36-44.

A report on the Beitestolen Health Sports Center in Valdres, Norway. The institution is a modern centre to rehabilitate the physically disabled and facilitate their re-adjustment to daily life.

851 **The first international medical congress on sports for the disabled,
Ustaoset Mountain Hotel, Norway, February 1-8, 1980.**
Edited by Harald Natvig.   Oslo: Royal Ministry for Church and
Education, State Office for Youth and Sports, 1980. 226p.

Proceedings of the conference that include contributions by several Norwegian scholars. Most of the articles discuss special programmes established in Norway for the disabled.

852 **Leisure and recreation.**
Odd Ramsøy. In: *Norwegian society*. Edited by Natalie Rogoff
Ramsøy. Oslo: Universitetsforlaget, 1974, p. 324-47.

A sociological study of leisure and recreation emphasizing especially the extent
and use of leisure activities. Sports and art are considered separately as two
significant examples of such activities.

853 **Second international congress on Nordic winter recreation.**
[Oslo]: Royal Ministry of Church and Education, State Office for
Youth and Sports, [1979]. 86p.

The proceedings of the conference in which all the papers dealt with winter sports
programmes in Norway, particularly cross-country skiing and participation by the
handicapped in winter activities.

854 **Sport interests of adolescents.**
Svein Stensaaven. [Oslo]: Norges Idrettshøgskole, 1978. 19p.
bibliog. (Notater og Rapporter fra Norges Idrettshøgskole, no. 52).

A report on the interest in sports of a surveyed group of Norwegian teenagers as
manifested through variables such as participation, reading about sport in
newspapers, and watching sports events on television.

855 **Angling in Norway.**
Edited by Erling Welle-Strand. Oslo: Nortrabooks (Norwegian
Tourist Board), 1981. rev. ed. 112p.

The work is divided into three sections discussing salmon, trout and freshwater
fishing, and sea fishing. Each part provides general information about the fish
sought and the rivers or other waters in each of the Norwegian counties where
they are caught, along with other pertinent information.

856 **Mountain touring holidays in Norway.**
Edited and compiled by Erling Welle-Strand. Oslo: Norwegian
Travel Board, 1983. 96p.

A guide providing information on hiking tours of the country. An introductory
chapter outlines various types of camping and housing facilities and activities such
as fishing. Two further chapters provide more detailed information on suggested
tours and facilities available in southern and northern Norway.

**Sport in Norway and where to find it together with a short account of the
vegetable productions of the country to which is added a bit of the alpine
flora of the Dovre Fjeld and of the Norwegian ferns, etc.**
See item no. 29.

Norway the Northern playground.
See item no. 43.

Bibliografi over norsk sport-og idrettslitteratur 1960-1970. . . (Bibliography of Norwegian sport and athletic literature 1960-1970 . . .)
See item no. 929.

Libraries, Archives and Museums

857 **The University Collection of National Antiquities: a short guide for foreign visitors.**
Arne Emil Christensen, Jr.   Oslo: Universitets Oldsaksamling, 1971. 37p.

Describes the display of prehistoric exhibits at the museum. Most of the exhibits are from the pre-Viking and Viking periods but there is also some material from the Middle Ages.

858 **Guide to the Viking Ship Museum.**
Arne Emil Christensen, Jr.   Oslo (Bygdøy): Universitets Oldsaksamling, 1983. 31p. map.

A discussion of the discovery and rebuilding of the Viking ships and of the artifacts found with them.

859 **The publication policies and practices of the Nordic archives.**
Harald Jørgensen.   *American Archivist*, vol. 46, no. 4 (1983), p. 400-14.

An overview of the development of archives in Denmark, Finland, Norway, and Sweden and some of the catalogues and collections published by both the central and provincial archives of the countries.

860 **Public libraries in the Nordic countries.**
Hilkka Kauppi. In: *Nordic democracy: ideas, issues, and institutions in politics, economy, education, social and cultural affairs of Denmark, Finland, Iceland, Norway, and Sweden.* Edited by Erik Allardt, Nils Andrén, Erik J. Friis, Gylfi T. Gislason, Sten Sparre Nilson, Henry Valen, Frantz Wendt, Folmer Wisti.   Copenhagen: Det danske selskab, 1981, p. 495-503.
An introduction to the origins of public libraries in the Nordic countries, the means by which they are financed, and the training of librarians.

861 **The Royal University Library in Oslo.**
Oslo: Universitetsbibliotekets hustrykkeri, 1985. 56p. bibliog.
An overview of the functions and services of Norway's oldest and largest library, which includes a discussion of the main library on Drammensveien and its branches at the university.

862 **Norway.**
Florence Janson Sheriff, Daniel T. Thomas. In: *The new guide to the diplomatic archives of Western Europe.* Edited by Daniel Thomas, Lynn M. Case.   Philadelphia: University of Pennsylvania Press, 1975, p. 243-55.
A brief outline of Norway's history, the basic organization of the *Riksarkiv* (National Archives), the *Utenriksdepartementets Arkiv* (Archives of the Royal Ministry of Foreign Affairs), and the major libraries in Oslo. Many changes have occurred in these institutions since this work was published but it is still useful to anyone preparing to use these research facilities for the first time. First published in 1959.

863 **Museums in Norway.**
Erling Welle-Strand.   Oslo: Royal Ministry of Foreign Affairs, 1974. 48p. maps.
A directory that first groups museums according to subject fields and then provides longer, more detailed descriptions of each museum, including some of its chief holdings.

The Viking Age.
See item no. 163.

The Viking ships in Oslo.
See item no. 197.

Education, science and the arts.
See item no. 665.

Mass Media

General

864 **Disorder in the orbit: the fate of NORDSAT, the Nordic television satellite.**
Hans Dahl. *Scandinavian Review*, vol. 72, no. 3 (1984), p. 25-30.
Discusses the problems that have delayed and possibly destroyed plans for a television satellite offering all Scandinavian viewers television programmes broadcast from Finland, Sweden, Norway, and Denmark.

865 **Censorship and freedom of expression in Scandinavia.**
Paul O. Frisch. *Scandinavian Review*, vol. 56, no. 1 (1968), p. 13-19.
Compares censorship regulations in the Scandinavian countries as they pertain to films and television, and press laws regarding published material.

866 **Recent research on the press in history: a survey of theories and historical studies.**
Svennik Høyer. *Scandinavian Journal of History*, vol. 7, no. 1 (1982), p. 15-30.
A general overview of research on the Norwegian press and broadcasting since about 1960, which also examines models created to study the development of the Norwegian press and recent studies of their party affiliation. The article is part of an entire issue of the journal devoted to the topic of 'Research on press history in Scandinavia.' For a related article in the same journal, see Rolf Danielson's 'The conservative press in Norway during the nineteen twenties,' vol. 4, no. 2 (1979), p. 105-22.

867 **Public debate: how the Scandinavians do it.**
Michael E. Metcalf. *Scandinavian Review*, vol. 70, no. 3 (1982),
p. 72-76.
A commentary on the extent and nature of the cultural and political debate in
Scandinavian newspapers. Most examples are from Sweden but there are also
references to situations which are common to the whole of Scandinavia.

868 **Politics and the development of mass communications.**
Niels Thomsen. In: *Nordic democracy: ideas, issues, and institu-
tions in politics, economy, education, social and cultural affairs of
Denmark, Finland, Iceland, Norway, and Sweden.* Edited by Erik
Allardt, Nils Andrén, Erik J. Friis, Gylfi T. Gislason, Sten Sparre
Nilson, Henry Valen, Frantz Wendt, Folmer Wisti. Copenhagen:
Det danske selskab, 1981, p. 517-51.
A wide-ranging discussion of the mass media, primarily in Norway, Sweden, and
Denmark, and its relationship to politics and government. The author provides a
brief outline of the development of the press and its early difficulties with
censorship. He also discusses the origins of radio and television, the administra-
tion of the latter by public agencies, the question of controls associated with it,
and recent changes experienced by newspapers.

869 **The mass media and communication.**
Per Torsvik. In : *Norwegian society.* Edited by Natalie Rogoff
Ramsøy. Oslo: Universitetsforlaget, 1974, p. 291-323.
A sociological investigation of newspapers and magazines and to a lesser extent of
television and radio. Discusses the availability, ownership, readers, and content of
newspapers affiliated with political parties.

870 **The Norwegian press: black on white and read all over.**
Donna Vear. *The Norseman*, vol. 25, no. 4 (1985), p. 14-16.
Outlines the history of the Norwegian press from its origins in the 1760s, and
provides an entertaining sketch of the main Oslo newspapers today.

Newspapers

871 **Aftenposten.** (Evening News.)
Oslo: Chr. Schibsteds Forlag, 1860-. twice daily.
This newspaper is Norway's equivalent to the London or New York *Times*: solid,
informative, and respected. It is the country's second-largest newspaper, with a
circulation of about 230,000, and is generally considered to be the spokesman of
Norway's Conservative Party. In summer it usually has a brief English summary
on an inside page of both morning and evening editions. In common with all other
Norwegian newspapers, it does not print a Sunday edition.

872 **Arbeiderbladet.** (Worker's Paper.)
Oslo: Arbeiderbladet, 1886-. daily.

The spokesman of the Labour Party and therefore takes a left of centre position on most issues. It was called *Social-Demokraten* from 1886 to 1923 and was banned from 1940 to 1945 by the Germans. It has a daily circulation of about 52,000.

873 **Bergens Tidende.** (Bergen Times.)
Bergen, Norway: Bergens Tidende, 1968-. daily.

The main newspaper for Western Norway with a circulation of about 94,000. The paper is politically independent.

874 **Trondheim Addresseavisen.** (Trondheim Address Paper.)
Trondheim, Norway: Addresseavisen, 1767-. daily.

Norway's oldest newspaper and the main paper of the Trøndelag region. Its circulation is approximately 83,000 and it is affiliated with the Conservative Party.

875 **Verdens Gang.** (World's Turn.)
Oslo: Verdens Gang, 1945-. daily.

This newspaper's circulation has increased dramatically during the last decade so that it has become the largest daily, with a circulation of about 260,000. It is politically independent and has a reputation for sensationalism.

Professional
Periodicals

876   **Acta Archaeologica.**
Copenhagen: Munksgaard, 1930-. annual.
A scholarly journal containing articles in English and other major languages,
written mostly by Scandinavian archaeologists.

877   **Acta Philologica Scandinavica: Tidsskrift for Nordisk
Sprogforskning. (Acta Philologica Scandinavica: Journal of
Scandinavian Philology.)**
Copenhagen: Gyldendal, 1926/27-. quarterly.
A scholarly journal, including studies of all the Scandinavian languages by an
international group of authors. Many of the articles are in English but there are
also some in the Scandinavian languages, and in French and German. Each issue
contains a bibliography of recently published works on Scandinavian philology.

878   **Acta Sociologica: the Journal of the Scandinavian Sociological
Association.**
Oslo: Universitetsforlaget, 1955-. quarterly.
One of the founding organizations of this research journal was the Norwegian
Sociological Society. The articles are in English and most deal with research
carried out in Scandinavia. In addition to articles, the journal also contains
research notes, review essays, and book reviews.

879   **Bulletin of Peace Research.**
Oslo: Universitetsforlaget, 1970-. quarterly.
The journal is edited at the International Peace Research Institute in Oslo under
the auspices of the International Peace Research Association, the World Policy
Institute, and the Berghof Foundation for Conflict Research. It contains articles,
documents, and short papers dealing with peace and international security. The

225

subject matter and contributors are international although the journal has provided a significant forum for Scandinavian peace researchers in particular to present their views.

880 Cooperation and Conflict: Journal of International Politics.
Oslo: Universitetsforlaget, 1965-. quarterly.

The journal is published by the Nordic Cooperation Committee for International Politics. The articles, which are in English, cover foreign policy, disarmament, and international security, and the journal also contains research notes and book reviews. Many of the articles are by Scandinavian scholars and concern Scandinavian topics. The journal's contents up to 1976 are included in Janet Kvamme's *Index Nordicus* (q.v.).

881 Forsvarsstudier: Årbok for Forsvarshistorisk Forskningssenter, Forsvarets Høgskole. (Defence Studies: Yearbook for the Military History Research Centre, Military Academy.)
Oslo: Tanum Norli, 1981-. annual.

Papers on military affairs and foreign relations on Scandinavia in general and Norway in particular during and after the Second World War. Many of the articles are written in English by leading scholars in these fields, or include an English summary. The papers are first published by the research centre as part of their FHFS *NOTAT* series and are compiled at the end of the year as *Forsvarsstudier*.

882 Journal of Peace Research.
Oslo: Universitetsforlaget, 1964-. quarterly.

A scholarly, interdisciplinary journal edited by the International Peace Research Institute, with articles in English on peace research. The journal is international in its contributors and subject content and Scandinavians are frequent participants.

883 News of Norway.
Washington, DC: Royal Ministry of Foreign Affairs, 1941-. irregular.

The newsletter contains articles on current affairs in Norway, and brief notices of events, book reviews and other information. Although its publication varies, twelve or thirteen issues usually appear each year.

884 The Nordic Bulletin: a Monthly Calendar of Nordic Events.
Minneapolis, Minnesota: University of Minnesota Center for Northwest European Language and Area Studies, 1980-. 10 issues per year.

A newsletter describing cultural and academic events throughout the United States regarding Scandinavian studies, exchanges, fellowships, recently published books, and other information of interest.

226

Professional Periodicals

885 **Nordic Journal of Botany.**
Copenhagen: Council for Nordic Publications in Botany, 1981-. bi-monthly.

The journal has an editorial board of botanists from the universities of Denmark, Finland, Norway, and Sweden. Its sections comprise holarctic and general taxonomy, geobotany, structural botany, mycology, lichenology, and phycology. Articles are devoted to Scandinavian botany but also to relevant topics in other countries. From 1971 until 1980 the journal had the title *Norwegian Journal of Botany*; it was merged with other Scandinavian botanical journals in 1981 under the present title.

886 **The Norseman.**
Oslo: Nordmanns Forbundet, 1948-. bi-monthly.

The magazine of the *Nordmanns Forbundet* (The Norsemen's Federation). It contains brief articles in English and Norwegian on current events.

887 **Norsk Geografisk Tidsskrift.** (Norwegian Journal of Geography.)
Oslo: Universitetsforlaget, 1926-. quarterly.

Articles, notes and reviews primarily in English but also in the Scandinavian languages and French. An important journal that considers a wide variety of subjects with a geographical orientation.

888 **Norsk Geologisk Tidsskrift.** (Norwegian Journal of Geology.)
Trondheim, Norway: Norsk Geologisk Forening, 1905-. quarterly.

A scholarly journal with articles and occasionally brief notes on minor subjects. Most of the articles are in English with occasional contributions in another major language, usually German. A cumulative index covering vols. 1-42 (1905-1962) has been published.

889 **Norway Information.**
Oslo: Royal Norwegian Ministry of Foreign Affairs.

The ministry publishes an extensive series of fact sheets on a wide range of topics, including the royal family, the government, the constitution, and policy statements on economic, diplomatic, and social policy.

890 **Norwegian-American Studies.**
Northfield, Minnesota: Norwegian-American Historical Association, 1926-. irregular.

A scholarly publication dealing chiefly with Norwegian immigration to the United States and the history and culture of Norwegian-Americans. Normally a bibliography is included of recent works published on the subject and on American immigration in general. For a cumulative index of vols. 1-29 (1926-1983) see vol. 29 (1983), p. 380-401. The journal was originally entitled *Norwegian-American Studies and Records* until 1962.

891 **Norwegian Archaeological Review.**
Oslo: Universitetsforlaget, 1968-. quarterly.
Contains articles in English by Norwegian archaeologists on Norwegian topics, and is an importance resource.

892 **Scandinavica: an International Journal of Scandinavian Studies.**
Norwich, England: University of East Anglia, 1961-. quarterly.
Concentrates primarily on studies of Scandinavian literature and language by international specialists, although there are some articles on other topics. It also includes book reviews of scholarly works in all fields and a selective bibliography of Scandinavian literary journals and of books on Scandinavia in non-Scandinavian languages. An index to the journal for vols. 1-10 appeared in vol. 10 (1971) and for vols. 11-20 in vol. 20 (1981). The journal is indexed in *Index Nordicus* (q.v.).

893 **Scandinavian Economic History Review.**
Oslo: Universitetsforlaget, 1953-. quarterly.
Produced by the Scandinavian Society for Economic and Social History and Historical Geography, this is a scholarly English-language journal dealing in a very broad sense with Scandinavian economic and social history. Review articles and book reviews are also regularly included. An index for vols. 1-20 (1953-1972) was published in 1972 and the journal is catalogued in Janet Kvamme's *Index Nordicus* (q.v.).

894 **Scandinavian Journal of History.**
Stockholm: Almqvist & Wiksell, 1976-. quarterly.
Contains articles in English by Scandinavian scholars, mostly on Scandinavian subjects. From 1985 the journal includes book reviews and has assumed the bibliographic functions previously exercised by *Excerpta Historica Nordica* from 1955 until 1985 as a bibliography of historical materials published in the Scandinavian languages.

895 **Scandinavian Journal of Psychology.**
Stockholm: Almqvist & Wiksell, 1960-. quarterly.
This scholarly English language journal of the Psychological Associations of Denmark, Finland, Norway, and Sweden, contains empirical reports and theoretical and methodological papers. It also reviews Scandinavian books and dissertations.

896 **Scandinavian Political Studies.**
Oslo: Universitetsforlaget, 1966-. quarterly.
The journal of the Nordic Political Science Association containing articles in English on Scandinavian law, government, and politics. Volumes 1-12 were issued from 1966-1977. The numbering system for the journal was revised in 1978, so that the numbers issued that year began again from volume 1 new series. Notes and book reviews are also included and a bibliography of Nordic political science appears regularly. The journal was indexed up to 1976 in *Index Nordicus* (q.v.).

897 **Scandinavian Population Studies.**
Helsinki: Scandinavian Demographic Society, 1969-. irregular.
Proceedings of the symposia held by the Scandinavian Demographic Society. It publishes the papers presented at symposium seminars, most of which are by Scandinavian scholars and treat specific studies in Scandinavian demographics.

898 **Scandinavian Review.**
New York: American-Scandinavian Foundation, 1913-. quarterly.
The official publication of the American-Scandinavian Foundation, containing articles, short stories, poetry, and photographic essays. Written in English, the journal often contains works that were originally published in a Scandinavian language. Many issues include notes on current events, book reviews, and notices of books, films, and records on Scandinavia. Members also receive a newsletter, *Scan*, that provides information on the activities of the foundation's independent chapters throughout the Unites States, scholarship and exchange programmes with Scandinavia, and other information. The journal was entitled *American Scandinavian Review* until 1974. For a cumulative index of the journal until 1976 see Janet Kvamme's *Index Nordicus* (q.v.).

899 **Scandinavian Studies.**
Urbana, Illinois: University of Illinois Press, 1911-. quarterly.
The journal of the Society for the Advancement of Scandinavian Study, the chief professional organization of Scandinavian scholars in the United States. It publishes articles in English on a range of subjects including Scandinavian literature, linguistics, history and political science. Regularly contains book reviews and book notes. The newsletter of the society, *News and Notes*, provides information on conferences, grants, programmes, and exchanges. Originally entitled *Publications of the Society for the Advancement of Scandinavian Study*, the journal became *Scandinavian News and Notes* with vol. 4 in 1917 and assumed its present title with vol. 16 in 1941. For several years the society sponsored an annual bibliography of works on Scandinavia that appeared in the final number of each volume or as a special supplement. It was issued as a separate publication by the Center for Northwestern European Studies, University of Minnesota in 1975, and discontinued thereafter. The journal was indexed until 1976, in *Index Nordicus* (q.v.).

900 **Scandinavian Studies in Law.**
Stockholm: Almqvist & Wiksell, 1957-. annual.
The journal publishes articles in English on virtually all facets of law, including aspects of Norwegian law, and Norwegian scholars are frequent contributors.

901 **The Viking.**
Minneapolis, Minnesota: Sons of Norway, 1904-. monthly.
The official publication of the Sons of Norway. It contains news of the organization's activities and programmes and articles on Norwegian and Norwegian-American culture and personalities. First published in Norwegian as *Sønner af Norge*, it was given a magazine format in 1913, was published in English from 1942, and its title was changed to *The Viking* in 1962.

Reference Books, Directories and Biographical Dictionaries

902 **They came from Norway: portraits of ten men who made history.**
Edited by Lorentz Eckhoff. Oslo: Alb. Cammermeyers, 1956.
124p.

A collection of biographical sketches on ten distinguished Norwegians of the last two centuries: Niels Henrik Abel, Ole Bull, Henrik Ibsen, Bjørnstjerne Bjørnson, Edvard Grieg, Armauer Hansen, Fridtjof Nansen, Roald Amundsen, Edvard Munch, and Gustav Vigeland.

903 **Hvem er Hvem.** (Who's Who.)
Oslo: Kunnskapsforlaget (Aschehoug-Gyldendal), 1912-. irregular.

Published intermittently about every four or five years. The latest edition, published in 1984, contains 4,300 entries, 1,200 of which are new.

904 **Hvem, Hva, Hvor.** (Who, What, When.)
Oslo: Chr. Schibsteds, 1934-. annual.

An almanac containing a wealth of information and data, much of which relates directly to Norway. It includes statistics, and summaries of the most important national and international events of the preceding year. A frequently used reference guide.

905 **Dictionary of Scandinavian biography: with a memoir on the work of the Nordic Council by G. F. D. Dawson and with a full text of the Treaty of Cooperation between Denmark, Finland, Iceland, Norway, and Sweden.**
Edited by Ernest Kay. Cambridge, England: International Centre, 1976. 2nd ed. 497p.

Biographies in English of living Scandinavians. Eminent Norwegians are well-represented in the work by short, but useful, sketches.

906 **Dictionary of Scandinavian history.**
Edited by Byron Nordstrom. Westport, Connecticut: Greenwood
Press, 1986. 1300p. bibliog.
Over 400 entries on the outstanding individuals and events in Scandinavian
history. Although some coverage is given to prehistoric and Viking times, most
of the entries are on topics from the Middle Ages to the present. Short
bibliographies follow each entry and a larger one by the editor lists the major
historical works on Scandinavia in English.

907 **Norges Statskalendar.** (Norway's State Calendar.)
Oslo: H. Aschehoug (W. Nygaard), annual.
An annual government publication, listing every governmental department, with
a short description of its responsibilities, and the names of its employees.

908 **Norsk biografisk leksikon.** (Norwegian biographical dictionary.)
Oslo: H. Aschehoug (W. Nygaard), 1923-1983. 19 vols.
Biographical portraits by leading scholars of famous Norwegians, often with
extensive bibliographic references.

909 **Scandinavia: a chronology and fact book.**
Edited by Robert T. Vexler.   Dobbs Ferry, New York: Oceana
Publications, 1977. 185p.
The work is divided into chronologies of key dates in Scandinavian history and
those of the three countries including Norway, (p. 34-60). This is followed by a
series of important public documents including Norway's Constitution of 1814 and
the text by which Norway's *Storting* dissolved the country's union with Sweden in
1905.

910 **World of Learning.**
London: Europa, 1947-. annual.
Entries on Norway, include membership of Norwegian learned honorary
organizations, the addresses and officers of learned societies, research institutes,
libraries, archives, museums, art galleries, and the addresses, administrative
officers and professors of Norway's universities and advanced training institutions.
A valuable reference work, particularly for anyone planning to do research in
Norway.

Norsk historisk atlas. (Norwegian historical atlas.)
See item no. 83.

The Scandinavians in America 986-1970: a chronology and fact book.
See item no. 336.

Bibliographies

911 **Bibliografi til Norges Historie.** (Bibliography of Norway's History.) Oslo: Den norsk historiske forening, 1916-. irregular.

Issued by Norway's Historical Association, originally as part of *Historisk Tidsskrift* (Historical Journal), and, later, as a supplement to it. The bibliographies are prepared by the *Universitetsbiblioteket i Oslo* (University of Oslo Library) and bibliographies covering literature up to 1977 have been issued so far. They have been bound into volumes for the years 1916-25, 1926-35, 1936-45, 1946-55, 1956-65, and 1966-75 with registers for each. The bibliographies cover a wide variety of subjects.

912 **Bibliographies des sciences préhistoriques en Norvège 1900-1935.** (Bibliography of prehistory in Norway 1900-1935.) Compiled by Anathon Bjørn. Oslo: Universitets Oldsaksamling, 1936. 51p.

A brief introduction in French is followed by an unannotated listing of works. An important work, despite its age, because of the research carried out at that time by A. W. Brøgger and Haakon Shetelig.

913 **Forfatterlexikon, omfattende Danmark, Norge og Island indtil 1814.** (Author lexicon for Denmark, Norway and Iceland until 1914.) Compiled by H. Ehrencron-Müller. Copenhagen: H. Aschehoug, 1824-1835. 12 vols.

This massive work contains biographical sketches and a list of published works for each author included. The last three volumes deal exclusively with Ludvig Holberg.

914 **A selective bibliography of Scandinavian politics and policy.**
Compiled by Eric S. Einhorn, John Logue. Amherst,
Massachusetts: International Area Studies Programs, University of
Massachusetts at Amherst, 1984. 17p. (Program in West European
Studies, Occasional Papers, no. 1).

A brief unannotated bibliography, containing entries relevant not only to politics
and government but also to economics, industrial relations, and sociology.

915 **Scandinavian political institutions and political behavior 1970-1980:**
an annotated bibliography.
Compiled by Kjell A. Eliassen, Mogens N. Pedersen. Odense,
Denmark: Odense University Press, 1985. 168p.

Contains entries that deal with political institutions and behaviour in Denmark,
Norway, and Sweden. Both Scandinavian and non-Scandinavian works are
considered with an English translation of all important entries and an English
summary.

916 **Scandinavian research theses in the history, aesthetics, sociology**
and psychology of film.
Compiled by Margerite Engbert. *Historical Journal of Film,*
Radio and Television, vol. 3, no. 1 (1983), p. 67-70.

A brief bibliography of Scandinavian theses on these subjects. The works are
listed with titles in both the native language where applicable and in English.

917 **Norse sagas translated into English: a bibliography.**
Compiled by Donald K. Fry. New York: AMS Press, 1980. 139p.

A bibliography of Old Norse sagas available in English translation by 1979.
Entries are arranged alphabetically by saga and subdivided by the various
translations that have been made.

918 **A selective survey of English language studies on Scandinavian law.**
Ruth Bader Ginsburg. South Hackensack, New Jersey: Frederick
B. Rothman, 1970. 53p.

A partially annotated bibliography of legal studies pertaining to Scandinavia as a
whole and the individual countries.

919 **Current Norwegian serials.**
Compiled by Ger Svein Gjønnes, foreword by Gerhard Munthe.
Oslo: Universitetsbiblioteket i Oslo, 1970. 64p.

A representative selection of Norwegian periodicals from many fields. It is not
complete but does include what might be regarded as the most important
publications. No single publication has since been published to update this list but
subsequent annual editions of *Norsk Bokfortegnelse* (q.v.) list journals begun
during that year.

Bibliographies

920 **Scandinavia in social science literature: an English language bibliography.**
Compiled by Sven Groennings. Bloomington, Indiana: Indiana University Press, [1970]. 284p.
An excellent, detailed, unannotated bibliography covering economics, education, geography, history, international relations, law, political science, and sociology. Entries are for Scandinavia as a whole and for each of the five Nordic nations.

921 **Norway in English: a bibliography including a survey of Norwegian literature in English translation from 1742 to 1959.**
Compiled by Erling Grönland. Oslo: Norwegian Universities Press, 1961. 152p. (Norsk Bibliografisk Bibliotek, vol. 19).
A thorough, unannotated bibliography, providing excellent coverage of the literature on Norway published prior to 1960.

922 **Norsk forfatter-lexikon 1814-1880.** (Norwegian author lexicon 1814-1880.)
Compiled by J. B. Halvorsen. Oslo: Den Norske Forlagsforening, 1885-1908. 6 vols.
The bibliography is organized according to the same format used by Ehrencron-Müller for the period prior to 1814 and was designed to supplement it for Norway during the 19th century.

923 **A bibliography of Scandinavian language and linguistics.**
Compiled by Einar I. Haugen. Oslo: Universitetsforlaget, 1974. 527p.
A bibliography arranged alphabetically by author with keys to indicate the language and subject of each entry.

924 **A bibliography of Scandinavian dictionaries.**
Compiled by Eva L. Haugen, introduction by Einar I. Haugen. White Plains, New York: Kraus International Publications, 1984. 387p.
Covers dictionaries published in Scandinavia from 1510 to 1980. It is arranged topically and alphabetically with brief annotations on the publishing history and content of each entry. The introduction provides a survey of the publishing of dictionaries in Scandinavia during the period.

925 **Norwegian legal publications in English, French, and German.**
Compiled by Kaare Haukaas. Oslo: Universitetsforlaget, 1967. 106p.
A comprehensive bibliography of publications on Norwegian law published in English, French, and German. The work is divided into categories such as private law, public law, public international law and within these sections entries are arranged alphabetically by author. A substantial number of the entries are in English and offer an excellent resource for the study of the subject.

926   **Norsk juridisk litteratur 1962-1966: ein bibliografi.** (Norwegian
      legal literature, 1962-1966: a bibliography.)
      Compiled by Kaare Haukaas.   Oslo: Universitetsforlaget, 1968.
      (Norsk bibliografisk bibliotek, no. 37).
A bibliography of materials on Norwegian law and other legal subjects.

927   **Planning in Norway: literature in English.**
      Compiled by Anne Roed Helgesen, Inger Helene Andresen.
      Oslo: Norwegian Institute for Urban and Regional Research, 1980.
      4th rev. ed. 31p. (NIBR-note 1980:112).
Items include those in a general section on planning and those pertaining to
particular economic and social topics such as housing, leisure, the environment,
and natural resources. The bibliography is not annotated. Includes a supplement
of recently published works.

928   **Industriens historie: Norge: en bibliografi.** (Industry's history:
      Norway: a bibliography.)
      Compiled by Tom Arbo Hoeg, Gunnar Christie Wasberg.   Oslo:
      Norges Industriforbund, 1972. 172p.
Deals with industry in Norway from 1814 to 1870. An index lists works cited in
the bibliography written in English, French, and German.

929   **Bibliografi over norsk sport-og idrettslitteratur 1960-1970: tillegg
      norske klubbaviser og sportstidsskrifter, idrettsfilmer.** (Biblio-
      graphy of Norwegian sports and recreation literature 1960-1970: a
      supplement on Norwegian sports club newspapers, magazines, and
      sports films.)
      Compiled by Tone Høst.   Oslo: Norges Idrettshøgskole, 1970.
      119p.
Few of the entries are in English but this work is nevertheless a good
introduction.

930   **Scandinavian legal bibliography.**
      Compiled by Stig Iuul.   Stockholm: Almqvist & Wiksell, [1961].
      196p.
A short summary of the basic works on Norwegian law by Kaare Haukaas (p. 12-
18) is one of several such expositions on the Scandinavian countries. The
remainder of the work consists of the bibliography, which is organized by topic.
Almost all the works are in the Scandinavian languages but English translations of
the titles are provided.

235

Bibliographies

931 **Contemporary Norwegian music: a bibliography and discography.**
Compiled by Bjarne Kortsen. Bergen, Norway: [s.n.], 1980. 47p.
The bibliography is divided into sections which cover a single artist or composer.
A brief biographical sketch is provided for each individual, along with a list of his
works, and those by others discussing his work.

932 **Index Nordicus: a cumulative index to English periodicals on
Scandinavian studies.**
Compiled by Janet Kvamme. Boston, Massachusetts: G. K. Hall,
1980.
An extensive bibliography of the contents of six major scholarly English journals
on Scandinavia from their origins until 1976. The journals indexed are
*Cooperation and Conflict, Scandinavian Economic History Review, Scandinavian
Political Studies, Scandinavian Review, Scandinavian Studies*, and *Scandinavica*.
Entries are by subject, title, author's name, or book reviewer.

933 **Scandinavian government and politics: a bibliography of materials
in English.**
Compiled by Robert B. Kvavik. Minneapolis, Minnesota:
University of Minnesota, 1984. 21p. (Minnesota Papers in Political
Science).
A listing of recent books and articles published on Scandinavian politics. The
main categories covered include general resources, social democracy, political
institutions, political behaviour, political organization, and public policy.

934 **Bibliography of Norwegian art history: literature on Norwegian art
published up to the end of 1970.**
Compiled by Anne M. Langballe, Gunnar Danbolt. Oslo:
Universitetsforlaget, 1976. 390p. (Norsk Bibliografisk Bibliotek,
no. 51).
Covers all forms of art, including crafts and industrial art, such as commercial
design and utensils. Most of the works are in Norwegian or another Scandinavian
language and were published during this century. The table of contents is in both
English and Norwegian.

935 **Norwegian literary bibliography 1956-1970.**
Compiled by Harald S. Naess. Oslo: Universitetsforlaget, 1975.
128p. (Norsk Bibliografisk Bibliotek, no. 50).
A bibliography of Norwegian literature including many English titles. It is divided
into entries on general works, and the 18th, 19th, and 20th centuries. It is
intended as a continuation of and addition to Reidar Øksnevad's *Norsk
litteraturhistorisk bibliografi 1946-1955* and the bibliographical work included in
Harald and Edvard Beyer's *Norsk litteraturhistorie* (1970).

236

936 **Scandinavian literature in English translation 1928-1977.**
Compiled by Maria Ng, Michael S. Batts. Vancouver, Canada:
Canadian Association of University Teachers of German, 1978.
95p.

The bibliography is divided into a general section on Scandinavia and separate
units for each of the component nations. Norway is covered on p. 41-56.
Publishing information is provided for each work and entries included in
anthologies edited by others are cross-referenced.

937 **Norske aviser 1763-1970: en bibliografi.** (Norwegian newspapers
1963-1970: a bibliography.)
Oslo: Universitetsbiblioteket, 1973. 2 vols.

A bibliography listing all Norwegian newspapers of the period, their dates of
existence, editors, and changes in title that may have occurred.

938 **Norsk Bokfortegnelse.** (The Norwegian National Bibliography.)
Oslo: Den Norske Bokhandlerforening, 1921-. annual.

Prepared by the *Norske Avdeling* (Norwegian Division) of the *Universitetsbiblioteket i Oslo* (University of Oslo Library), this is a catalogue of all works published
in Norway and on Norway printed abroad. It has been collated for 5-year
intervals from 1921 to 1976. (The 1971-1976 volume is to be published soon.)
Material published since 1976 is covered by annual catalogues.

939 **Scandinavian history 1520-1970: a list of books and articles in
English.**
Compiled by Stewart P. Oakley. London: Historical Association,
1984. 232p. (Helps for Students of History, no. 91).

A very useful partially annotated bibliography of works published from 1880 to
1980 on Scandinavian history. The work is divided into six chronological periods
which are further sub-divided into sections for works on Scandinavia and on each
of the five Nordic countries.

940 **Norwegian foreign policy: a bibliography 1905-1965.**
Edited by Nils Ørvik. Oslo: Universitetsforlaget, 1968. 104p.
(Norsk Bibliografisk Bibliotek, no. 34).

A short introduction on Norwegian foreign policy is followed by the bibliography,
which is arranged by topic with English title translations in brackets where
applicable.

941 **Norwegian foreign policy: a bibliography 1965-1970.**
Compiled by Nils Ørvik. Oslo: Universitetsforlaget, 1973. 74p.

The work is divided into two sections: one for books and short publications and
another for periodical articles. Most of the articles are in Norwegian, but
translations of the titles are given in English, as are section headings.

942 **Itineraria Norvegica: a bibliography of foreigners' travels in Norway until 1900.**
Eiler H. Schiøtz. Oslo: Universitetsforlaget, 1970. 589p. (Norsk Bibliografisk Bibliotek, no. 44).

An annotated bibliography, arranged alphabetically, with a brief addendum of additional titles at the end. It lists translations and reprints as well as original works. An author index is provided as well as indexes identifying works by the specific locations and regions that they discuss and by the nationality of the author. Annotations are in Norwegian but references to chapters or subjects are cited in their original language.

Index

The index is a single alphabetical sequence of authors (personal and corporate), titles of publications and subjects. Index entries refer both to the main items and to other works mentioned in the notes to each item. Title entries are in italics. Numeration refers to the items as numbered.

Banks and banking *contd.*
  Canada 600
  influence on economic policy 600
  Japan 600
  monetary policy 600
  statistics 577
  USA 600
Baptist Church
  history 407
Barents Sea 546
  oil production 610
Barker, T. 611
Barnard, M. R. 29
Barnum & Bailey Circus 849
Barren, C. 745
Barth, F. 450, 587
Barton, H. A. 142
Basic Norwegian reader 428
Battles
  Guadacanal 260
  Viking 167, 170, 192
Batts, M. S. 936
Bayerschmidt, C. 250
Bayerschmidt, C. F. 734
Bears, Polar 119
Beck, R. 683
Beitestolen Health Sports Center 850
Belding, R. E. 663
Belsley, D. A. 593
Benesch, O. 760
Benningfield, D. 842
Benson, A. 683
Berge, R. 817
Bergen 18
  archaeology 128
  control by Hanseatic League 205
  history 156, 606
  International Festival of Music 797
  maps 86, 100
  newspapers 873
  theatre 790
  travel guides 100, 112
  travellers' accounts 36, 44
  women 452
Bergen Guide: English Edition 100
Bergen Line
  history 606
Bergen University
  electoral research programmes 489,
    502
Bergendal, K. 239
Bergens Tidende 873

Bergesen, H. O. 620
Berggrav, Eivind 30, 390, 399, 402
  role in World War II 396, 399, 402
Berggren, E. 603
Berghof Foundation for Conflict
    Research 879
Berglund, S. 492
Berlin 258
*Berlitz Engelsk-norsk
    ordbok/Norwegian-English
    dictionary* 416
Berman, M. A. 700
Bernadotte, Jean Baptiste Jules 225
Bernhard, S. 797
Bertram, C. 537
Berulfsen, B. 417-418, 427
Berulfsen, T. K. 417
Beskow, A. 22
Beyer, E. 719, 723, 935
Beyer, F. 804
Beyer, H. 682, 935
*Bibliografi over norsk sport-og
    idrettslitteratur 1960-1970: tillegg
    norske klubbaviser og
    sportstidsskrifter, idrettsfilmer* 929
Bibliografi til Norges Historie 911
Bibliographies 8, 908, 911-942
  American immigration 890
  demography 311
  dictionaries 924
  economics 914, 920
  education 920
  English language works on Norway
    921
  environment 927
  foreign policy 940-941
  foreign relations 541, 920
  geography 46, 52, 57, 920
  government 914, 933
  historiography 281
  history 146, 179, 189, 195, 201, 204,
    207, 234, 894, 906, 911-912, 920,
    939
  housing 927
  industrial development 928
  labour relations 635, 914
  language 411, 923
  law 530, 918, 920, 925-926, 930
  literary figures 913, 922
  literature 685, 690-691, 714, 719,
    722-723, 935-936
  music 931

243

247

260

278

Study 899
Publishing
  music 798
Pugh, D. C. 223
*Pulpit under the sky: a life of Hans
  Nielsen Hauge* 406
Punishment 460, 532
Pursuing justice for the child 526

Q

Qualey, C. C. 348
Quaternary 90
Quaternary system 90
Quest for America 161
*Quest for peace: the story of the Nobel
  award* 544
*Quisling: the career and political ideas
  of Vidkun Quisling* 254
Quisling: prophet without honour 255
*Quisling, Rosenberg und Terboven: zur
  vorgeschichte und geschichte der
  nationalsozialistischen Revolution
  in Norwegen* 258
Quisling, Vidkun, 241, 245, 254-255
  role in World War II 254-255
  theory of Nordic universalism 258
  trial 245
Qvigstad, J. K. 817

R

Ra expeditions 298, 301
Ra expeditions 298
Ra (vessel) 298
Ra II (vessel) 298
Raastad, O. 290
Radio 868-869
Radio Norway 2
Raeder, E. 251
*Raeder, Hitler und Skandinavien: der
  Kamf für einen maritimen
  Operationsplan* 251
Railway
  Northern Norway 642
Raitt, W. L. 622
Raknes, O. 716
Ramholt, T. 138, 814, 829
Ramon, F. 286
Ramsden, E. C. 409
Ramsøy, N. Rogoff 303, 401, 442, 446,
  478, 525, 585, 664, 852, 869

Ramsøy, O. 852
Rands, R. L. 198
Rankama, K. 90
*Rasmus Bjorn Anderson: pioneer
  scholar* 355
Rasmussen, J. 719
Rasmussen, T. Fr. 681
Reading Norwegian 430
Readings in economic geography 640
*Rebirth of Norway's peasantry: folk
  leader Hans Nielsen Hauge* 404
Redmond, J. R. 193
Rees, G. 98
Referendums 485
  EEC issue 485, 541, 557, 563, 566,
  568-569, 571-572
Reformation 392
Refugees
  Scandinavian aid 539
Regional geography 46, 49, 52, 63-70
*Regional and structural effects of North
  Sea oil in Norway* 625
Reichborn-Kjennerud, I. 817
Reindeer 324
  herding 634
Reise i Norge 35
Reiser-Larsen, H. 284, 286
Reitan, L. 808
Religion 36, 401, 446-488
  Baptist Church 407
  Counter Reformation 393
  development of Christianity 172,
    387, 409-410
  experiences of Hauge 405
  gods and goddesses 381, 386
  Greek mythology 384
  Hindu mythology 384
  history 144, 147, 167, 170, 172,
    380-393, 395-400, 402-410
  impact of USA 391
  Lapps 317, 322
  Lutheran Church 389, 395-397,
    401-406
  Methodist Church 372, 395
  missions and missionaries 400, 405
  modern mythology 385
  Mormon Church 378, 398
  Norse mythology 164, 168, 172, 192,
    275, 380-388
  Norwegian-Americans 329-330, 333,
    339, 345
  persecution in World War II 390, 396

282

Nordek discussions 557-558, 563, 569-570
Nordic Council 21, 511, 551-553, 555, 905
Scandinavian Journal 38
Scandinavian Journal of History 894
Scandinavian Journal of Psychology 895
Scandinavian lands 59
Scandinavian languages: an introduction to their history 414
Scandinavian legal bibliography 930
Scandinavian legends and folk-tales 815
Scandinavian literature in English translation 1928-1977 936
Scandinavian modern design 1800-1980 788
Scandinavian music: a short history 800
Scandinavian mythology 383
Scandinavian News and Notes 899
Scandinavian northlands 64
Scandinavian option: opportunities and opportunity costs in postwar Scandinavian foreign policies 540
Scandinavian party system(s): a comparative study 492
Scandinavian political institutions and political behavior 1970-1980: an annotated bibliography 915
Scandinavian Political Studies 896, 932
Scandinavian Population Studies 897
Scandinavian presence in North America 335
Scandinavian Review 898, 932
Scandinavian Research Project on Deserted Farms and Villages 207, 281
Scandinavian roundabout 19
Scandinavian security: challenge and response 546
Scandinavian Seminar College 518
Scandinavian Society for Economic and Social History and Historical Geography 893
Scandinavian Sociological Association 878
Scandinavian songs and ballads: modern Swedish, Danish and Norwegian songs 796
Scandinavian states and the League of Nations 151
Scandinavian studies 362

bibliographies 899
periodicals 892, 899
Scandinavian Studies 899, 932
Scandinavian studies: essays presented to Henry Goddard Leach 250
Scandinavian Studies in Law 900
Scandinavian theatre: a short history 791
'Scandinavian Touch' 827
Scandinavian world 61
Scandinavianism 227, 229
Scandinavians 11
Scandinavians in America: literary life 376
Scandinavians in America 986-1970: a chronology and fact book 336
Scandinavians in Australia, New Zealand and the Western Pacific 346
Scandinavica 932
Scandinavica: an International Journal of Scandinavian Studies 892
Scando-Americana: papers on Scandinavian emigration to the United States 342
Scarry, R. 423
Schach, P. 710
Schetelig, J. 93
Schilbred, C. S. 312
Schiøtz, E. H. 32, 942
Schjelderup, G. 728
Schlichter, S. H. 651
Scholdager, H. 535
Schwerin, D. 658
Science 26, 295
research and development 674, 678
Scotland
impact of North Sea oil 624
Viking settlement 165
Scott and Amundsen: the race to the South Pole 289
Scott, F. D. 20, 329, 359
Scott, P. 119
Scott, Robert 288-289
Sculpture 772-774
Romanesque 772
Sea transport 642
Sea wolves: the Viking era 745
Sealing 639
Second international congress on Nordic winter recreation 853
Secondary education 671

287

Davy, Sir Humphrey 32
Denmark 40, 45
Finland 34
fjords 36
for children 748
Gladstone, William 32
Hauge, Hans Nielsen 403
Lapland 31, 34
Malthus, Thomas 32, 38
Northern Norway 31, 33, 44
Oslo 31, 35
Sognefjord 44
Stavanger 44
Sweden 34-35, 40, 45
Trondheim 31, 35-36, 44
Wollstonecraft, Mary 32, 45
*Travellers discovering Norway in the
    last century: an anthology* 32
*Travels in various countries of Europe,
    Asia and Africa. Part the third:
    Scandinavia* 35
*Travels through Norway during the
    years 1806, 1807, and 1808* 31, 35
Treaties 545
    Integrity Treaty 242
    Spitsbergen (1920) 67
    Treaty of Kiel 225
Treaty of Kiel 225
*Trends in demographic structure in
    Norway 1960-2000* 308
Trial of Vidkun Quisling 245
Tromsø University 665
Trondheim 18
    history 155
    Jewish community 328
    maps 86
    newspapers 874
    travel guides 112
    travellers' accounts 31, 35-36, 44
Trondheim Addresseavisen 874
Tulley, C. S. 827
Turbey, C. 291
Turner, B. 557
Turville-Petrie, G. 712
*20 contemporary Norwegian poets: a
    bilingual anthology* 695
*Two Olafs of Norway with a cross on
    their shields* 171
*2,500 miles on the Norwegian coastal
    steamer* 110
Types of Norwegian folktale 813
Tyrell, S. 44, 107

U

Udgaard, N. M. 274
Ulmer, A. C. 690
Underland, U. 523
Undset, Sigrid 392, 409, 713-714, 717,
    720, 734, 743
Union with Sweden 221, 225-237
    dissolution (1905) 233, 909
    problems 229-230, 233
    security issue (1814) 223
United Nations 510
United States in Norwegian history 562
United States and Scandinavia 20
Universitetsbiblioteket 911
Universities
    Bergen 489, 502
    directories 910
    Minnesota 353, 899
    Nordic students 218
    Scandinavia 885
    Texas 842
    Tromsø 665
    Wales 235
    Wisconsin 355
University Collection of National
    Antiquities 163, 822, 857
*University Collection of National
    Antiquities: a short guide for
    foreign visitors* 857
University of Minnesota 353
University of Wales 235
*Unprotected females in Norway; or the
    pleasantest way of travelling there,
    passing through Denmark and
    Sweden with Scandinavian sketches
    from nature* 40
Uppval, A. J. 683
Upton, A. F. 497
Urban budgeting 519
Urban planning
    development 681
    Oslo 681
    policies and legislation 681
Urbanization 445
*Urbanization and community building
    in modern Norway* 681
USA 4, 16, 740
    banks 600
    economic exploitation of Spitsbergen
        152
    foreign policy 561

289

Weapons
  Viking 196
Weaving 818, 823-824
Weinstock, J. W. 721
Welfare state 11-12, 30, 444, 470-478,
  480, 493
  health system 446, 448, 466-467, 471-
  478
  impact on social mobility 478
  National Insurance Act 477
  origins and development 475-476
  Scandinavia 470, 473-476
*Welfare state and beyond: success and
  problems in Scandinavia* 474
Welle-Strand, E. 28, 110-112,
  855-856, 863
Wells, M. 723
Wendt, F. 9, 315, 408, 453, 476, 481,
  485, 490, 499, 517, 521, 536, 550,
  553, 558, 579, 589, 592, 653,
  667-668, 671, 677, 860, 868
Werenskiold, D. 773
Werenskiold, E. 809
Werenskiold, C. H. 840
Werenskiold, W. 62, 295
Wergeland, H. 683, 692, 720
Wergeland, W. 4
Wessel, J. H. 716
Wessel, Peter 217
West Norway
  history 156
  politics 489
*West Norway and its fjords: a history of
  Bergen and its provinces* 156
*West of the Great Divide: Norwegian
  migration to the Pacific coast
  1847-1893* 330
Westergaard, H. 239
Western Europe
  Viking presence 160
Western Europe: a handbook 473
Western Pacific
  Scandinavian migration 346
*Westviking: the ancient Norse in
  Greenland and North America* 190
*Westward to Vinland: the discovery of
  pre-Columbian house-sites in
  North America* 178
Whaling 639
  history 641
*Who were the Fascists? social roots of
  European Fascism* 241

Whyte, A. 7
Wibley, C. 277-278
Wicken, O. 266
Wierenga, Evelyn Ostraat 340
Die Wikinger 191
Wild duck 732
Wilkins, S. 192
Williams, A. F. 49
Williams, J. Mickel 441
Williams, M. W. 202
Willis Dixon, C. 662
Willson, T. B. 410
Wilson, D. 163
Wilson, D. M. 170, 199-200, 203-204,
  758
Winge, S. 775
Winter War 263
Wisconsin 333, 348, 355
Wisconsin University 355
Wise, E. H. 841
Wisnes, A. H. 154, 392, 743
Wisti, F. 9, 315, 408, 453, 476, 481,
  485, 490, 499, 517, 521, 536, 550,
  579, 589, 592, 653, 667-668, 671,
  677, 860, 868
With Amundsen at the North Pole 746
Wollstonecraft, Mary 45
  travellers' accounts 32, 45
Women 455
  18th century peasants 458
  attitudes and values 452
  employment 456, 657
  feminism 453, 456-457
  feminist literature 694
  housewives 450, 452, 456
  in public life 451
  participation in politics 453
  participation in trade unions 453
  role in society 453-458
  role in Viking Age 191, 202
  status 450
Women in the modern world 454
*Women in Norway: their position in
  family life, employment and
  society* 456
Woodcuts 777
Woodwork 818, 823-824
Work Environment Act 654
World Court 556
World of Learning 910
World of the Norseman 132
World of the polar bear 119

Map of Norway

This map shows the more important towns and other features.

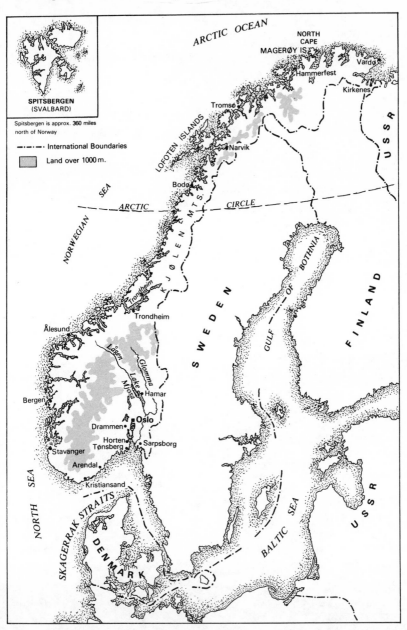

SPITSBERGEN
(SVALBARD)

Spitsbergen is approx. 360 miles
north of Norway

-·-·-·- International Boundaries

Land over 1000 m.

ARCTIC OCEAN

NORTH
CAPE

MAGERØY IS.

Vardø

Hammerfest

Kirkenes

Tromsø

LOFOTEN ISLANDS

Narvik

U.S.S.R.

Bodø

SEA

ARCTIC   CIRCLE

NORWEGIAN

KJØLEN MTS.

GULF OF BOTHNIA

FINLAND

Trondheim

Trondheim

SWEDEN

Ålesund

Lågen

Glomma

Lake Mjøsa

Bergen

Hamar

Drammen   Oslo

Horten   Sarpsborg
Tønsberg

Stavanger

Arendal

Kristiansand

NORTH SEA

SKAGERRAK STRAITS

BALTIC SEA

U.S.S.R.

DENMARK